RETIREMENT ISSUES, PLANS AND LIFESTYLES

SOCIAL SECURITY DISABILITY

BACKGROUND, BENEFITS AND PROGRAMS

RETIREMENT ISSUES, PLANS AND LIFESTYLES

Additional books and e-books in this series can be found on Nova's website under the Series tab.

RETIREMENT ISSUES, PLANS AND LIFESTYLES

SOCIAL SECURITY DISABILITY

BACKGROUND, BENEFITS AND PROGRAMS

MICHAEL DIMITRIADIS
EDITOR

snova
New York

Library of Congress Cataloging-in-Publication Data

ISBN: 978-1-53615-747-5

Published by Nova Science Publishers, Inc. † New York

CONTENTS

PREFACE

Social Security Disability Insurance (SSDI) provides benefits to nonelderly workers and their eligible dependents if the worker paid Social Security taxes for a certain number of years and is unable to perform substantial work due to a qualifying impairment. Chapter 1 provides an overview of the DI trust fund and its current financial outlook. Chapter 2 discusses the rules and processes used to determine eligibility for SSDI and SSI. It also explains how benefit amounts are computed, the types of non-cash benefits available to individuals who meet SSA's disability standards, and how each program is financed.

Chapter 3 analyzes the relative importance of factors affecting SSDI benefit receipts and terminations over the past 30 years. Chapter 4 examines what is known about how coverage and key features of SSDI and PDI compare, and the potential implications of three distinct proposals to expand employer-sponsored PDI on the Disability Insurance Trust Fund and various stakeholders. Chapter 5 examines trends in SSA's transfers and processing times of appealed cases over the past decade, SSA's monitoring of efforts to meet processing time goals through case transfers, and any challenges SSA faces in transferring cases between offices. Chapter 6 is the statement of Elizabeth Curda on SSA disabilty programs.

Chapter 1 - Social Security Disability Insurance (SSDI) provides benefits to nonelderly workers and their eligible dependents if the worker paid Social Security taxes for a certain number of years and is unable to perform substantial work due to a qualifying impairment. As in Old-Age and Survivors Insurance (OASI)—the retirement component of Social Security—benefits are based on a worker's past earnings in covered employment. In December 2014, SSDI provided disability insurance coverage to more than 151 million people and paid benefits to about 9 million disabled workers and 2 million of their spouses and children. Benefits and administrative costs for SSDI and OASI are financed primarily by dedicated payroll and self-employment taxes levied on the earnings of covered workers, which are deposited in the Federal Disability Insurance (DI) Trust Fund and the Federal Old-Age and Survivors Insurance (OASI) Trust Fund, respectively. The combined Social Security tax on earnings is 12.40%, which is split equally between workers and employers (6.20% each). Of that amount, 2.37% is allocated to the DI trust fund and 10.03% is allocated to the OASI trust fund. Each trust fund is a legally distinct account in the U.S. Treasury, and under current law, the two trust funds may not borrow from one another. Over the past few years, Congress has grown increasingly concerned with the financial outlook of the DI trust fund. Cost has exceeded total income since 2009, causing the balance of the DI trust fund to shrink. In their July 2015 report, the Social Security trustees projected that the DI trust fund would be depleted in the fourth quarter of calendar year 2016. Upon depletion of its asset reserves, the DI trust fund was projected to have enough ongoing revenues to pay only about 80% of scheduled benefits. The trustees projected that the OASI trust fund would be depleted in 2035. The Social Security Act provides no guidance on the payment of benefits once a trust fund's asset reserves have been depleted and current tax revenues are insufficient to meet current cost. Although individuals who meet Social Security's eligibility requirements are legally entitled to disability benefits, a provision in the Antideficiency Act prohibits a federal agency from spending in excess of available funds. Because the Social Security Act stipulates that SSDI benefit payments shall be made only from the DI trust fund, without a change in the law, monthly cash payments to beneficiaries could be delayed or reduced if the DI trust fund were depleted. The decreasing solvency of the DI trust fund is the result of an increasing imbalance between the fund's income and cost. Over the past 20 years, tax revenues to the DI trust fund have remained relatively flat as a percentage of taxable payroll, whereas cost as a share of taxable payroll has grown markedly. The increase in cost stems largely from the growth in the number of beneficiaries in the program. Between 1995 and 2014, the number of disabled workers and their dependents in receipt of SSDI grew 85%, from 5.9 million to 10.9 million. Because benefit payments account for nearly all program spending, the growth in the SSDI rolls has contributed heavily to the financial difficulties of the DI trust fund. On November 2, 2015, President Barack Obama signed into law the Bipartisan Budget Act of 2015 (H.R. 1314; P.L. 114-74). Among its many provisions, the act authorized a temporary reallocation of the Social Security payroll tax rate between the OASI and DI trust funds to provide DI with a larger share for 2016 through 2018. Specifically, the DI trust fund's share of the combined tax rate increased by 0.57 percentage point at the beginning of 2016, from 1.80% to 2.37%. Because the act did not change the combined payroll tax rate of 12.40%, the portion of the tax rate allocated to OASI *decreased* by a corresponding amount. This means that OASI's share of the combined tax rate declined by 0.57 percentage point at the start of 2016, from 10.60% to 10.03%. For 2019 and later, the shares allocated to the DI and OASI trust funds are scheduled to return to their 2015 levels (i.e., 1.80% to the DI trust fund and 10.60% to the OASI trust fund). The Social Security Administration's Office of the Chief Actuary (OACT) projects that the reallocation will extend the solvency of the DI trust fund from the fourth quarter of 2016 to the third quarter of 2022. Although the reallocation will reduce the solvency of the OASI trust fund slightly, OACT estimates that the *depletion year* for OASI will remain unchanged at 2035.

Chapter 2 - The Social Security Administration (SSA) is responsible for administering two federal entitlement programs established under the Social Security Act that provide income support to individuals with severe, longterm disabilities: Social Security Disability Insurance (SSDI) and Supplemental Security Income (SSI). SSDI is a workrelated social insurance program authorized under Title II of the act that provides monthly cash benefits to nonelderly disabled workers and their eligible dependents, provided the workers accrued a sufficient number of earnings credits during their careers in jobs subject to Social Security taxes. In contrast, SSI is a needbased public assistance program authorized under Title XVI of the act that provides monthly cash payments to aged, blind, or disabled individuals (including blind or disabled children) who have limited assets and little or no Social Security or other income. In 2017, SSDI and SSI combined paid an estimated $199 billion in federally administered benefits to 14.5 million qualified disabled individuals and 1.5 million non-disabled dependents of disabled workers. SSDI is part of the federal OldAge, Survivors, and Disability Insurance (OASDI) program, commonly known as Social Security. OASDI benefits are based on an insured worker's career average earnings in jobs covered by Social Security and designed to replace a portion of the income lost to a family due to the worker's retirement, disability, or death. Workers become insured against these events by acquiring a certain number of earnings credits during their careers in covered employment or self-employment. The SSDI component of the program provides benefits to disabled workers who are under Social Security's full retirement age and to their eligible spouses and children. The OldAge and Survivors Insurance (OASI) component also provides disability benefits to eligible disabled dependents of retired workers and to eligible disabled survivors of deceased beneficiaries and deceased insured workers. Although these individuals are not technically disability insurance beneficiaries, they are often included in the term *SSDI* because they receive Social Security benefits due to a qualifying impairment. SSDI and OASI disability benefits are paid from the Social Security trust funds, which are financed primarily by payroll and selfemployment taxes levied on the earnings of covered workers. SSI is a federal assistance program that provides needy aged, blind, or disabled individuals with a guaranteed minimum income to meet their basic living expenses. Although there are no work or contribution requirements to qualify for payments, the program is based on need and therefore is restricted to individuals with limited financial means. SSI is commonly known as a program of "last resort" because claimants must first apply for most other benefits for which they may be eligible; cash assistance is awarded only to those whose assets and other income (if any) are within prescribed limits. The basic federal SSI payment is the same for all recipients and is reduced by the amount of other income that an individual receives. Some states supplement the federal SSI payment with solely state funds. Unlike Social Security, SSI is financed by appropriations from general revenues. Most claimants are considered disabled for SSDI and SSI eligibility purposes if they are unable to engage in any substantial gainful activity (SGA) by reason of any medically determinable physical or mental impairment that is expected to last for at least 12 months or to result in death. In 2018, the SGA earnings limit is $1,180 per month for most individuals. Claimants generally qualify if they have an impairment (or combination of impairments) of such severity that they are unable to perform any kind of substantial work that exists in significant numbers in the national economy, taking into consideration their age, education, and work experience. If a claimant's application for benefits is denied at any point during the disability determination process, the claimant has the right to appeal the determination or decision.

Chapter 3 - The Social Security Disability Insurance (SSDI) program pays cash benefits to non-elderly workers and their dependents provided that the workers have paid into the Social Security system for a sufficient number of years and are determined to be unable to continue performing substantial work because of a qualifying disability. The total number of disabled-worker beneficiaries was approximately 2.7 million in 1985, peaked at approximately 9.0 million in 2014, and then declined over the last three years by nearly 0.3 million. In December 2017, 8.7 million disabled workers received SSDI benefits. Multiple factors have contributed to the growth in the SSDI enrollment between 1985 and 2014. Some of the main factors are (1) the increased eligibility and rising disability incidence among women, (2) the attainment of peak disability-claiming years (between age 50 and full retirement age) among baby boomers (people born between 1946 and 1964), (3) the increase in full retirement age (FRA) from 65 to 66, (4) fewer job opportunities during economic recessions, and (5) the legislative reform that expanded the eligibility standard in

SSDI. Some factors may have prolonged effects on SSDI benefit receipt. For example, the increase in the FRA from 65 to 66 has resulted in a larger proportion of SSDI beneficiaries who are ages 65 and older, and this proportion is likely to increase further as the FRA increases from 66 to 67 between 2020 and 2027. Another example is the consequence of the expansion in the eligibility criteria, which has resulted in more than half of the disabled-worker beneficiaries being enrolled into the program based on mental disorders or musculoskeletal disorders (typically back pain or arthritis). This trend is likely to persist in the future. However, some of the effects on the growth in SSDI enrollment are likely to diminish over time. For example, the rise in labor force participation among women resulted in more women becoming eligible for SSDI benefits during the 1980s and the 1990s, but its positive effect on SSDI rolls became smaller as the female labor force participation rate stabilized and the disability incidence rate of women approached that of men. In addition, some factors may have started to work in opposite directions. One example is the change in age distribution of the population. As the baby boomers reach their FRA (gradually increased from 65 to 66) between 2012 and 2031, there is expected to be a growing proportion of disabled workers who terminate disability benefits due to the attainment of FRA. About the same time, the lower-birth-rate cohorts (people born after 1964) started to enter peak disability-claiming years in 2015, which would likely reduce the size of the insured population between age 50 and the FRA and, consequently, result in a lower number of disability applications. Another example is the availability of more jobs during the post-Great Recession period. The increasing opportunity in employment may have made working more attractive than disability benefits for people who could qualify for SSDI, thus reducing the disability applications and awards after 2010. These factors are likely to contribute to a decline in the number of disabled-worker beneficiaries. In addition to the change in the population age distribution and the availability of jobs in the market, some other factors may also be acting to decrease SSDI rolls in the recent three years. These factors are likely to include the prevalence of the Affordable Care Act (ACA) and the decline in the allowance rate (i.e., the share of applicants who are awarded disability benefits). The nationwide effects of the ACA on disability benefit receipt and the cause of the decreasing allowance rate are as yet unclear.

Chapter 4 - SSDI, which is administered by SSA, provides financial and other assistance to qualifying individuals who are unable to work due to their disabilities. SSDI is primarily funded by employee and employer payroll taxes that are placed in the Disability Insurance Trust Fund, which is currently projected to not be able to pay full benefits starting in 2028. While there are a number of ways to address the fiscal condition of the Disability Insurance Trust Fund, some researchers have proposed expanding employer-provided PDI. GAO was asked to review whether expanding PDI could result in potential savings to the Disability Insurance Trust Fund. This chapter examines (1) what is known about how coverage and key features of SSDI and PDI compare, and (2) the potential implications of three distinct proposals to expand employer-sponsored PDI on the Disability Insurance Trust Fund and various stakeholders. GAO analyzed data on SSDI and PDI coverage from SSA and BLS for 2016 and 2017; reviewed relevant federal laws, regulations, and guidance; reviewed three PDI policies that three large insurers we selected described as typical for their companies; reviewed three distinct proposals to expand PDI identified through a literature review; and interviewed SSA and Department of Labor officials, authors, researchers, and representatives of insurance, employer, employee, and disability groups for a range of perspectives.

Chapter 5 - Individuals who do not agree with an initial decision on a claim for Social Security disability benefits can ultimately appeal by requesting a hearing before an administrative law judge. At the end of fiscal year 2017, more than 1 million claimants who had appealed were awaiting a decision, and they waited, on average, 605 days. To help reduce processing times of appeals, SSA transfers cases from backlogged offices to those with greater capacity. GAO was asked to review SSA's efforts to redistribute its appeals work. This chapter examines (1) trends in SSA's transfers and processing times of appealed cases over the past decade, (2) SSA's monitoring of efforts to meet processing time goals through case transfers, and (3) any challenges SSA faces in transferring cases between offices. GAO analyzed SSA case processing data from fiscal years 2008-2017; reviewed SSA policies and operational guidance; observed SSA's systems for case transfers; and interviewed SSA officials at the agency's headquarters and offices in 3 of its 10 regions, selected for the large number of cases transferred and proximity to national centers established to process transferred cases.

Chapter 6 - This is an edited, reformatted and augmented version of United States Government Accountability Office, Testimony Before the Subcommittee on Social Security, Committee on Ways and Means, House of Representatives, Publication No. GAO-18-677T, dated July 25, 2018.

In: Social Security Disability
Editor: Michael Dimitriadis
ISBN: 978-1-53615-747-5

Chapter 1

THE SOCIAL SECURITY DISABILITY INSURANCE (DI) TRUST FUND: BACKGROUND AND CURRENT STATUS*

William R. Morton

ABSTRACT

Social Security Disability Insurance (SSDI) provides benefits to nonelderly workers and their eligible dependents if the worker paid Social Security taxes for a certain number of years and is unable to perform substantial work due to a qualifying impairment. As in Old-Age and Survivors Insurance (OASI)—the retirement component of Social Security—benefits are based on a worker's past earnings in covered employment. In December 2014, SSDI provided disability insurance coverage to more than 151 million people and paid benefits to about 9 million disabled workers and 2 million of their spouses and children.

Benefits and administrative costs for SSDI and OASI are financed primarily by dedicated payroll and self-employment taxes levied on the earnings of covered workers, which are deposited in the Federal

* This is an edited, reformatted and augmented version of Congressional Research Service Publication No. R43318, dated January 19, 2016.

Disability Insurance (DI) Trust Fund and the Federal Old-Age and Survivors Insurance (OASI) Trust Fund, respectively. The combined Social Security tax on earnings is 12.40%, which is split equally between workers and employers (6.20% each). Of that amount, 2.37% is allocated to the DI trust fund and 10.03% is allocated to the OASI trust fund. Each trust fund is a legally distinct account in the U.S. Treasury, and under current law, the two trust funds may not borrow from one another.

Over the past few years, Congress has grown increasingly concerned with the financial outlook of the DI trust fund. Cost has exceeded total income since 2009, causing the balance of the DI trust fund to shrink. In their July 2015 report, the Social Security trustees projected that the DI trust fund would be depleted in the fourth quarter of calendar year 2016. Upon depletion of its asset reserves, the DI trust fund was projected to have enough ongoing revenues to pay only about 80% of scheduled benefits. The trustees projected that the OASI trust fund would be depleted in 2035.

The Social Security Act provides no guidance on the payment of benefits once a trust fund's asset reserves have been depleted and current tax revenues are insufficient to meet current cost. Although individuals who meet Social Security's eligibility requirements are legally entitled to disability benefits, a provision in the Antideficiency Act prohibits a federal agency from spending in excess of available funds. Because the Social Security Act stipulates that SSDI benefit payments shall be made only from the DI trust fund, without a change in the law, monthly cash payments to beneficiaries could be delayed or reduced if the DI trust fund were depleted.

The decreasing solvency of the DI trust fund is the result of an increasing imbalance between the fund's income and cost. Over the past 20 years, tax revenues to the DI trust fund have remained relatively flat as a percentage of taxable payroll, whereas cost as a share of taxable payroll has grown markedly. The increase in cost stems largely from the growth in the number of beneficiaries in the program. Between 1995 and 2014, the number of disabled workers and their dependents in receipt of SSDI grew 85%, from 5.9 million to 10.9 million. Because benefit payments account for nearly all program spending, the growth in the SSDI rolls has contributed heavily to the financial difficulties of the DI trust fund.

On November 2, 2015, President Barack Obama signed into law the Bipartisan Budget Act of 2015 (H.R. 1314; P.L. 114-74). Among its many provisions, the act authorized a temporary reallocation of the Social Security payroll tax rate between the OASI and DI trust funds to provide DI with a larger share for 2016 through 2018. Specifically, the DI trust fund's share of the combined tax rate increased by 0.57 percentage point at the beginning of 2016, from 1.80% to 2.37%. Because the act did not change the combined payroll tax rate of 12.40%, the portion of the tax rate allocated to OASI *decreased* by a corresponding amount. This means that OASI's share of the combined tax rate declined by 0.57 percentage point at the start of 2016, from 10.60% to

10.03%. For 2019 and later, the shares allocated to the DI and OASI trust funds are scheduled to return to their 2015 levels (i.e., 1.80% to the DI trust fund and 10.60% to the OASI trust fund).

The Social Security Administration's Office of the Chief Actuary (OACT) projects that the reallocation will extend the solvency of the DI trust fund from the fourth quarter of 2016 to the third quarter of 2022. Although the reallocation will reduce the solvency of the OASI trust fund slightly, OACT estimates that the *depletion year* for OASI will remain unchanged at 2035.

INTRODUCTION

Lawmakers and the public have expressed increasing concern over the solvency of the Disability Insurance (DI) trust fund, from which Social Security Disability Insurance (SSDI) benefits are paid.[1] Until recently, the DI trust fund was projected to be depleted in the fourth quarter of calendar year 2016, at which time ongoing revenues to the DI trust fund were projected to be sufficient to pay only about 80% of scheduled benefits.[2] In November 2015, the Bipartisan Budget Act of 2015 (H.R. 1314; P.L. 114-74) extended the projected solvency of the DI trust fund by authorizing a reallocation of the Social Security payroll tax rate between the DI and the Old-Age and Survivors Insurance (OASI) trust funds to provide DI with a

[1] For example, see U.S. Congress, House Committee on Ways and Means, Subcommittee on Social Security, *First in a Hearing Series on Securing the Future of the Social Security Disability Insurance Program*, 112th Cong., 1st sess., December 2, 2011, H.Hrg. 112-SS11 (Washington: GPO, 2012), pp. 4-5, http://www.gpo.gov/fdsys/pkg/CHRG112hhrg76319/pdf/CHRG-112hhrg76319.pdf. See also U.S. Congress, Senate Committee on Finance, *Social Security: A Fresh Look at Workers' Disability Insurance*, 113th Cong., 2nd sess., July 24, 2014, S.Hrg. 113-532 (Washington: GPO, 2015), p. 3, http://www.gpo.gov/fdsys/pkg/CHRG-113shrg92646/pdf/CHRG-113shrg92646.pdf. In addition, see U.S. Congress, Senate Committee on the Budget, *The Coming Crisis: Social Security Disability Trust Fund Insolvency*, 114th Cong., 1st sess., February 11, 2015, http://www.budget.senate.gov/republican/public/index.cfm/hearing-schedule?ID=ffb8d0f9-c572-47ee-9165-f5ae4317e82c.

[2] U.S. Congress, House Committee on Ways and Means, *The 2015 Annual Report of the Board of Trustees of the Federal Old-Age and Survivors Insurance and Federal Disability Insurance Trust Funds*, 114th Cong., 1st sess., July 22, 2015, H.Doc. 114-51 (Washington: GPO, 2015), http://www.ssa.gov/oact/tr/2015/index.html (hereinafter "2015 Social Security Trustees Report"). Projections based on the trustees' 2015 intermediate assumptions.

larger share. Although the reallocation averted a potential benefit cut in late 2016, without additional legislative action (i.e., revenue increases, cost reductions, or some combination thereof), the DI trust fund is projected to be unable to pay scheduled benefits in full and on a timely basis by the early 2020s.

This chapter provides an overview of the DI trust fund and its current financial outlook. It begins with background information on the SSDI program and the financing of the Social Security trust funds. Next, the report examines the financial status of the DI trust fund over the past 20 years and the causes of the DI trust fund's financial imbalance. It then discusses the projected status of the DI trust fund under prior law and under the Bipartisan Budget Act of 2015. Lastly, the report provides background information on the use of reallocations by Congress in the past, as well as on a House rules change in the 114th Congress concerning payroll tax reallocations. The appendix of the report provides a congressional rationale for the creation of a separate DI trust fund as part of the Social Security Amendments of 1956 (P.L. 84-880).

BACKGROUND ON SSDI

Enacted in 1956 under Title II of the Social Security Act, SSDI is part of the Old-Age, Survivors, and Disability Insurance (OASDI) program, more commonly known as Social Security. As in OASI—the retirement component of Social Security—SSDI is a form of social insurance that replaces a portion of a worker's income based on the individual's work history and career-average earnings in covered employment.[3] Specifically, SSDI provides benefits to nonelderly insured workers who meet the statutory definition of disability and to their eligible dependents. In November 2015, the Social Security Administration (SSA) paid benefits to

[3] For more information on Old-Age and Survivors Insurance (OASI), see CRS Report R42035, *Social Security Primer*, by Dawn Nuschler. For more information on the concept of *social insurance*, see Larry DeWitt, "The Development of Social Security in America," *Social Security Bulletin*, vol. 70, no. 3 (August 2010), http://www.ssa.gov/policy/docs/ssb/v70n3/v70n3p1.html.

more than 10.8 million SSDI recipients, including 8.9 million disabled workers, 142,000 spouses of disabled workers, and 1.8 million children of disabled workers.[4]

Eligibility

To qualify for SSDI, workers must be (1) under the full retirement age (FRA), (2) insured in the event of disability, and (3) statutorily disabled. The FRA is the age at which unreduced Social Security retirement benefits are first payable, which is currently 66.[5] To achieve insured status, individuals must have worked in covered employment for about a quarter of their adult lives before they became disabled and for at least 5 years of the 10 years immediately before the onset of disability.[6] However, younger workers may qualify with less work experience based on their age. In 2014, SSDI provided disability insurance coverage to more than 151 million nonelderly workers.[7]

To meet the statutory definition of disability, an insured worker must be unable to engage in any *substantial gainful activity* (SGA) by reason of any medically determinable physical or mental impairment that is expected to last for at least one year or result in death.[8] In 2016, the SGA earnings limit is $1,130 per month for most workers and $1,820 per month for statutorily blind workers.[9] Disability determinations are based on a five-step sequential evaluation process that takes into account a worker's medical records, age, education, and work experience. In general, workers must have a severe impairment (or combination of impairments) that

---

[4] Social Security Administration (SSA), "Monthly Statistical Snapshot, November 2015," December 2015, Table 2, http://www.ssa.gov/policy/docs/quickfacts/stat_snapshot/ (hereinafter "SSA Monthly Statistical Snapshot").

[5] See CRS Report R41962, *The Social Security Retirement Age: In Brief*, by Gary Sidor.

[6] For more information on Social Security Disability Insurance (SSDI), see CRS Report RL32279, *Primer on Disability Benefits: Social Security Disability Insurance (SSDI) and Supplemental Security Income (SSI)*, by William R. Morton.

[7] SSA, Office of the Chief Actuary (OACT), "Disabled Insured Workers," http://www.ssa.gov/ OACT/STATS/ table4c2DI.html.

[8] 42 U.S.C. §423(d)(1). See also 20 C.F.R. §§404.1504-1511.

[9] SSA, OACT, "Substantial Gainful Activity," http://www.ssa.gov/oact/cola/sga.html.

prevents them from performing any kind of substantial work that exists in the national economy in significant numbers.[10]

Benefits

Cash benefits begin five full months after a beneficiary's disability onset date.[11] Initial benefits are based on a worker's career-average earnings, indexed to reflect changes in national wage levels.[12] Benefits are subsequently adjusted to account for inflation through cost-of-living adjustments (COLAs), as measured by the Consumer Price Index for Urban Wage Earners and Clerical Workers (CPI-W).[13] Monthly benefits payable to the worker and family members are subject to a maximum family benefit amount.[14] Benefits may be offset if the disabled worker also receives workers' compensation or certain other public disability benefits.[15] In November 2015, the average monthly benefit was $1,166 for disabled workers, $318 for spouses of disabled workers, and $350 for children of disabled workers.[16]

In addition to cash benefits, disabled workers and certain dependents are eligible for health care coverage under Medicare after 24 months of entitlement to cash benefits (typically 29 months after the onset of

---

[10] An impairment (or combination of impairments) is considered *severe* if it significantly limits an individual's physical or mental ability to do basic work activities. For more information, see SSA, Program Operations Manual System (POMS), "DI 24505.001 Individual Must Have a Medically Determinable Severe Impairment," August 9, 2012, http://policy.ssa.gov/poms.nsf/lnx/0424505001.

[11] For additional information on the five-month waiting period, see CRS Report RS22220, *Social Security Disability Insurance (SSDI): The Five-Month Waiting Period for Benefits*, by William R. Morton.

[12] See CRS Report R43542, *How Social Security Benefits Are Computed: In Brief*, by Katelin P. Isaacs.

[13] See CRS Report 94-803, *Social Security: Cost-of-Living Adjustments*, by Gary Sidor.

[14] SSA, OACT, "Maximum Benefit for a Disabled-Worker Family," http://www.ssa.gov/oact/cola/dibfamilymax.html.

[15] For more information, see SSA, *How Workers' Compensation and Other Disability Payments May Affect Your Benefits*, No. 05-10018, June 2015, http://www.ssa.gov/pubs/EN-05-10018.pdf.

[16] SSA, Monthly Statistical Snapshot, Table 2.

disability).[17] In 2012, Medicare spending per disabled beneficiary averaged about $9,900.[18] Generally, disabled workers retain their benefits as long as they (1) are under the FRA, (2) exhibit no substantial medical improvement, and (3) have average monthly earnings at or below the SGA limit.

THE SOCIAL SECURITY TRUST FUNDS

Although Social Security is often viewed as a single program, its financing comes from two legally distinct sources known as trust funds. A *trust fund* is an accounting mechanism that "records the revenues, offsetting receipts, or offsetting collections earmarked for the purpose of the fund, as well as budget authority and outlays of the fund that are financed by those revenues or receipts."[19] The Federal Disability Insurance Trust Fund finances the benefits of disabled workers and their dependents, and the Federal Old-Age and Survivors Insurance Trust Fund pays for the benefits of retired workers and their dependents as well as survivors of deceased workers.[20] Administrative costs are also drawn from the trust

---

[17] For more information, see SSA, "Medicare Information," http://www.ssa.gov/disabilityresearch/wi/medicare.htm. See also CRS Report R40425, *Medicare Primer*, coordinated by Patricia A. Davis and Scott R. Talaga.

[18] U.S. Department of Health and Human Services (HHS), Centers for Medicare & Medicaid Services (CMS), *Medicare & Medicaid Statistical Supplement*, 2013 edition, Table 3.4, https://www.cms.gov/Research-Statistics-Dataand-Systems/Statistics-Trends-and-Reports/MedicareMedicaidStatSupp/Downloads/2013_Section3.pdf#Table3.4. Figure is per enrollee and includes disabled workers, disabled widow(er)s, disabled adult children, and individuals entitled to Medicare because of end-stage renal disease (ESRD) only.

[19] See U.S. Congressional Budget Office (CBO), *Glossary*, January 31, 2012, pp. 18-19, https://www.cbo.gov/ publication/42904. See also U.S. General Accounting Office (GAO; now the Government Accountability Office), *Federal Trust and Other Earmarked Funds: Answers to Frequently Asked Questions*, GAO-01-199SP, January 1, 2001, http://www.gao.gov/products/GAO-01-199SP.

[20] 42 U.S.C. §401. For more information on the Federal Disability Insurance (DI) Trust Fund, see SSA, OACT, "Disability Insurance Trust Fund," http://www.ssa.gov/oact/progdata/describedi.html. For more information on the Federal Old-Age and Survivors Insurance (OASI) Trust Fund, see SSA, OACT, "Old-Age & Survivors Insurance Trust Fund," http://www.ssa.gov/oact/ProgData/describeoasi.html.

funds. Each trust fund is a separate account in the U.S. Treasury, and under current law, the two trust funds may not borrow from one another. [21]

The OASI trust fund was created under the Social Security Amendments of 1939 (P.L. 76-379), and superseded the Old-Age Reserve Account established under the original Social Security Act in 1935 (P.L.74-271).[22] The DI trust fund was established as part of the Social Security

Amendments of 1956 (P.L. 84-880)—the same legislation that created SSDI.[23] The creation of a separate DI trust fund appears to have been a compromise to address concerns of some lawmakers at the time about SSDI's potential cost and potential negative impact on the OASI trust fund and its beneficiaries. For more information on the congressional rationale for the creation of a separate DI trust fund, see Appendix A.

Financing

SSDI and OASI are financed primarily by dedicated payroll and self-employment taxes levied on the earnings of covered workers under the Federal Insurance Contributions Act (FICA) [24] and the Self-Employment Contributions Act (SECA).[25] FICA taxes are split evenly between employees and employers, whereas SECA taxes are borne fully by self-

---

[21] See also SSA, OACT, "Trust Fund FAQs," http://www.ssa.gov/oact/ProgData/fundFAQ.html.

[22] The OASI trust fund became effective on January 1, 1940. For more information on the origins of the OASI trust fund and the Old-Age Reserve Account, see Board of Trustees of the Federal Old-Age and Survivors Insurance Trust Fund, *First Report of the Board of Trustees of the Federal Old-Age and Survivors Insurance Trust Fund*, January 3, 1941, https://www.ssa.gov/history/reports/trust/tf1941.html.

[23] The DI trust fund was established on August 1, 1956.

[24] Social Security payroll taxes on employees and employers were established under Title VIII of the Social Security Act in 1935 (P.L. 74-271). In 1939, the internal revenue laws of the United States were consolidated and codified under the Internal Revenue Code (IRC; P.L. 76-1). Title VI of the Social Security Amendments of 1939 (P.L. 76-379) amended Subchapter A of Chapter 9 of the IRC to read "Federal Insurance Contributions Act" (FICA). See 26 U.S.C. §3128.

[25] Section 208 of the Social Security Act Amendments of 1950 (P.L. 81-734) established Social Security payroll taxes on self-employed individuals under Subchapter E of Chapter 1 of the IRC. The 1950 amendments also coined the term "Self-Employment Contributions Act" (SECA). See 26 U.S.C. §1403.

employed individuals. As shown in Table 1, the Social Security FICA tax rate for employees and employers, *each* is 6.200%, with 1.185% allocated to the DI trust fund and 5.015% to the OASI trust fund. On a *combined basis*, the FICA tax rate is 12.400%, with 2.370% allocated to the DI trust fund and 10.030% to the OASI trust fund. The Social Security SECA tax rate is the same as the combined FICA tax rate. Social Security taxes are levied on covered earnings up to a maximum annual amount, which is $118,500 in 2016.[26]

Table 1. Social Security Payroll Tax Rates under Crrent Law (as a percentage of taxable earnings)

Trust Fund	FICA		SECA
	Employees and Employers, Each	Combined	Self Employed
OASI	5.015	10.030	10.030
DI	1.185	2.370	2.370
OASDI (Total)	6.200	12.400	12.400

Source: Congressional Research Service (CRS), based on Social Security Administration (SSA), Office of the Chief Actuary (OACT), "Social Security Tax Rates," https://www.ssa.gov/oact/progdata/oasdiRates.html.

Notes: The allocation of the Social Security payroll tax rate between the OASI and DI trust funds is scheduled to change in calendar year 2019. For more information, see the "Under the Bipartisan Budget Act of 2015" section of this chapter.

The FICA rates for employees and employers are prescribed in Sections 3101 and 3111 of the Internal Revenue Code (IRC), respectively; the SECA rate is specified in Section 1401 of the IRC.[27] The allocation of

---

[26] See SSA, OACT, "Contribution and Benefit Base," https://www.ssa.gov/oact/COLA/cbb.html. The taxable maximum is adjusted to reflect changes in average earnings levels in the United States for years in which a cost-ofliving adjustment (COLA) is payable. See 42 U.S.C. §430.

[27] 26 U.S.C. §§3101, 3111, and 1401. These sections of the IRC also prescribe the payroll tax rates for Medicare's Hospital Insurance (HI) trust fund. The total Medicare payroll tax rate, which applies to all covered earnings, is 2.90% (1.45% for employees and employers, each). The Patient Protection and Affordable Care Act (ACA; P.L. 111-148, as amended) imposes an additional 0.90% tax on high-income workers with wages and self-employment income over $200,000 for single filers and $250,000 for joint filers effective for taxable years beginning after December 31, 2012. The revenues from the 0.90% tax are credited to the HI trust fund. For more information, see CRS Report R43122, *Medicare Financial Status: In*

the tax rates between the OASI and DI trust funds, however, is set in Section 201(b) of the Social Security Act.[28] Section 201(b) specifies the *combined* share of the Social Security tax rate allocated to the DI trust fund for both wages (FICA) and self-employment income (SECA), which, as noted above, is 2.370% (1.185% for employees and employers, each). Section 201(a) states that the combined allocation to the OASI trust fund for both wages and self-employment income is the combined Social Security payroll tax rate set in the IRC *less* the combined share prescribed in Section 201(b).[29] Therefore, the combined allocation to the OASI trust fund is 12.400% *minus* 2.370%, which equals 10.030% (5.015% for employees and employers, each).

In addition to payroll taxes, the OASI and DI trust funds are credited with income from the taxation of some Social Security benefits.[30] The share of Social Security benefits that is taxable depends on whether the individual's provisional income exceeds certain thresholds.[31] *Provisional income* equals adjusted gross income *plus* otherwise tax-exempt interest income (i.e., interest from tax-exempt bonds), *plus* 50% of Social Security benefits. Income derived from the taxation of up to the first 50% of Social Security benefits is credited to the OASI and DI trust funds based on the source of the benefits taxed.[32] In other words, up to a certain rate, taxes paid on OASI benefits are deposited in the OASI trust fund and taxes paid on SSDI benefits are deposited in the DI trust fund.

Brief, by Patricia A. Davis. See also Internal Revenue Service (IRS), "Questions and Answers for the Additional Medicare Tax," http://www.irs.gov/Businesses/Small-Businesses-&-Self-Employed/ Questions-and-Answers-for-the-Additional-Medicare-Tax.

[28] 42 U.S.C. §401(b).

[29] 42 U.S.C. §401(a).

[30] 26 U.S.C. §86. For more information on the taxation of Social Security benefits, see CRS Report RL32552, *Social Security: Calculation and History of Taxing Benefits*, by Julie M. Whittaker and Katelin P. Isaacs.

[31] For more information on these thresholds, see U.S. Congress, Senate Committee on the Budget, *Tax Expenditures: Compendium of Background Material on Individual Provisions*, committee print, prepared by CRS, 113th Cong., 2nd sess., December 2014, S.Prt. 113-32 (Washington: GPO, 2014), pp. 989-990, http://www.gpo.gov/fdsys/pkg/CPRT-113SPRT91950/pdf/CPRT-113SPRT91950.pdf.

[32] The HI trust fund is credited with the remainder of income from the taxation of up to 85% of OASI and SSDI benefits.

Occasionally, the two trust funds receive reimbursements from the General Fund of the U.S. Treasury for various costs imposed on the Social Security program.[33] For example, the OASI and DI trust funds received reimbursements from the General Fund to compensate for the loss of revenues from a temporary payroll tax reduction in 2011 and 2012.

The final source of income to the trust funds is from the interest earned on investments held by the trust funds. When income exceeds cost in a given year, the *surplus* is credited to the trust funds in the form of special-issue (non-marketable) securities, which are backed by the full faith and credit of the U.S. government.[34] These securities earn interest, which the Department of the Treasury credits to the trust funds semiannually in the form of additional government securities. The accumulated securities held by a trust fund represent its balance.[35] A trust fund can use its balance, or *asset reserves*, to pay benefits whenever total program cost exceeds income.

FINANCIAL STATUS OF THE DI TRUST FUND

The Board of Trustees of the Federal Old-Age and Survivors Insurance and Federal Disability Insurance Trust Funds presents an annual report to Congress on the current and projected financial status of the Social Security trust funds.[36] The board is composed of six members: the Secretary of the Treasury, who is the Managing Trustee; the Secretary of

---

[33] The DI trust fund is reimbursed for the following costs: (1) the cost of noncontributory wage credits for military service before 1957; (2) the cost of payroll tax credits provided to employees in 1984 and self-employed persons in 1984-89 by P.L. 98-21; (3) the cost in 2009-17 of excluding certain self-employment earnings from SECA taxes under P.L. 110-246; and (4) payroll tax revenue forgone under the provisions of P.L. 111-147, P.L. 111-312, P.L. 112-78, and P.L. 112-96. See 2015 Social Security Trustees Report, Table IV.A2.

[34] In the past, the trust funds held publicly available securities. For more information on Social Security trust fund holdings, see CRS Report RS20607, *Social Security: Trust Fund Investment Practices*, by Dawn Nuschler.

[35] Although government securities held by the trust funds represent assets to Social Security, they are also liabilities to the rest of the federal government. For more information, see CBO, *The Budget and Economic Outlook: 2015 to 2025*, January 26, 2015, p. 145, https://www.cbo.gov/publication/49892.

[36] 42 U.S.C. §401(c).

Labor; the Secretary of Health and Human Services; the Commissioner of Social Security; and two public representatives, who are nominated by the President for a term of four years and subject to confirmation by the Senate.[37] The Board of Trustees (hereinafter "trustees") specifies the assumptions about future demographic and economic trends used in the projections; however, SSA's Office of the Chief Actuary advises the trustees on the assumptions as well as develops and runs the computer models that produce the forecasts. The trustees' latest report was released on July 22, 2015, and is available at http://www.ssa.gov/oact/tr/2015/index.html.[38]

DI Financial Operations in 2014

Table 2 shows the income, cost, and asset reserves of the DI trust fund in 2014. Of the $114.9 billion in total income credited to the DI trust fund, $109.7 billion (about 95%) came from net payroll tax contributions. The interest earned on the investments held by the DI trust fund amounted to $3.4 billion or 3% of total income.[39] Income from the taxation of SSDI benefits and reimbursements from the General Fund totaled $1.8 billion or 2% of total trust fund income.

Total cost for the year was $145.1 billion. About 98% of the DI trust fund's cost stemmed from benefit payments totaling $141.7 billion. Disbursements from the DI trust fund for administrative expenses and the financial interchange with the Railroad Retirement Board (RRB) amounted to $3.3 billion or 2% of total cost. According to the trustees, "the Railroad Retirement Act requires an annual financial interchange between the

[37] The Deputy Commissioner of SSA serves as the Secretary of the Board of Trustees. The two public representatives may not be from the same political party.

[38] For information about the trust funds on a combined basis, see CRS Report RL33028, *Social Security: The Trust Funds*, by Dawn Nuschler.

[39] In 2014, the asset reserves of the DI trust fund earned an effective annual interest rate of 4.5%. For more information, see SSA, OACT, "Effective Interest Rates," http://www.ssa.gov/OACT/ProgData/effectiveRates.html. For data on OASI and DI investment transactions, see SSA, OACT, "Investment Transactions," http://www.ssa.gov/OACT/ ProgData/transactions.html.

Railroad Retirement program and the OASDI program. The purpose of the interchange is to put the OASI and DI trust funds in the same financial position they would have been in had railroad employment always been covered directly by Social Security."[40]

To make up for the shortfall between total income and cost in 2014, the DI trust fund redeemed a net total of $30.2 billion in government bonds. Consequently, the asset reserves held by the DI trust fund decreased from $90.4 billion at the end of 2013 to $60.2 billion at the end of 2014.

Table 2. Summary of the Financial Operations of the DI Trust Fund in 2014 ($ in billions)

Item	DI Trust Fund
Asset reserves at the end of the 2013	$90.4
Total income in 2014	114.9
Net payroll tax contributions	109.7
Reimbursements from the General Fund of the Treasury	0.1
Taxation of SSDI benefits	1.7
Interest on asset reserves	3.4
Total expenditures in 2014	145.1
Benefit Payments	141.7
Railroad Retirement financial interchange	0.4
Administrative expenses	2.9
Net change in asset reserves in 2014	-30.2
Asset reserves at the end of 2014	60.2

Source: CRS, adapted from U.S. Congress, House Committee on Ways and Means, The 2015 Annual Report of the Board of Trustees of the Federal Old-Age and Survivors Insurance and Federal Disability Insurance Trust Funds, 114th Cong., 1st sess., July 22, 2015, H.Doc. 114-51 (Washington: GPO, 2015), Table II.B1, http://www.ssa.gov/oact/tr/2015/II_B_cyoper.html#96807 (hereinafter "2015 Social Security Trustees Report").

Note: Totals may not equal the sum of components due to rounding.

[40] 2015 Social Security Trustees Report, p. 30. For more information on the Railroad Retirement Board (RRB), see CRS Report RS22350, *Railroad Retirement Board: Retirement, Survivor, Disability, Unemployment, and Sickness Benefits*, by Scott D. Szymendera.

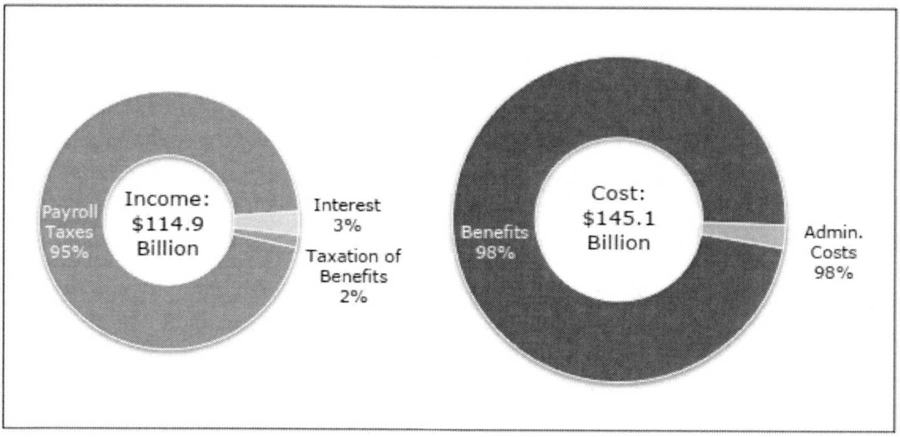

Source: CRS, based on data from the 2015 the Social Security Trustees Report, Table II.B1.

Notes: "Interest" refers to net interest earned on securities held by the DI trust fund. "Taxation of Benefits" includes reimbursements from the General Fund, which accounted for less than 0.1% of trust fund income. "Admin. Costs" include net expenses related to the administration of SSDI, as well as payments under the financial interchange with the Railroad Retirement Board (RRB), which accounted for less than 0.3% of trust fund cost.

Figure 1. DI Income and Cost in 2014, by Source.

Recent Experience of the DI Trust Fund

Between 1995 and 2004, non-interest income to the DI trust fund exceeded total cost, generating annual surpluses and increasing the fund's balance (Figure 2). *Non-interest income* includes net payroll tax contributions, revenues from the taxation of SSDI benefits, and General Fund reimbursements.

In 2005, total cost started to exceed non-interest income; however, because *total income*—tax revenues plus net interest on asset reserves—was greater than total cost, the balance of the DI trust fund continued to grow.

In 2009, total cost began to exceed total income, requiring the DI trust fund to use some of its asset reserves to cover benefit payments (Table 3).

As a result, the balance of the DI trust fund has been declining. At the end of November 2015, the amount of asset reserves held by the DI trust fund was $35.2 billion.[41]

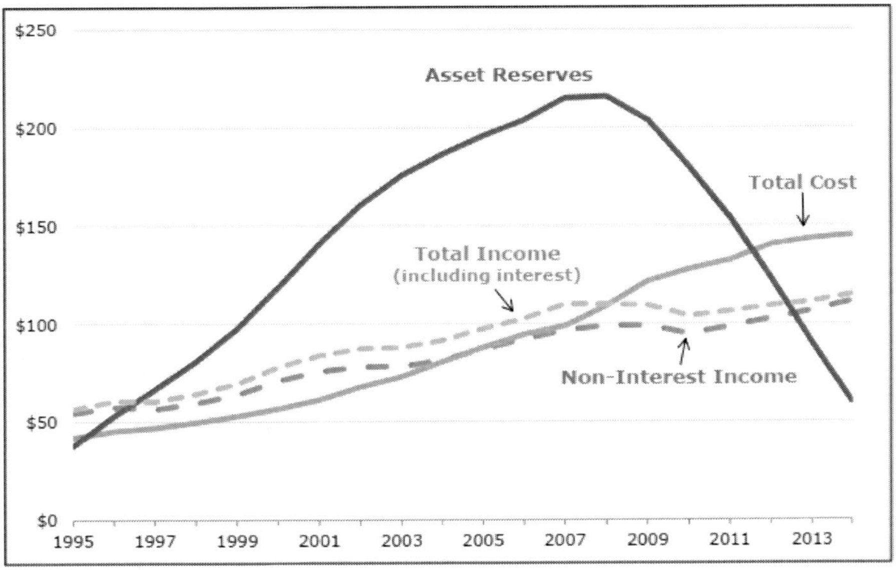

Source: CRS, based on data from the 2015 Social Security Trustees Report, Table VI.A2, at http://www.ssa.gov/ oact/tr/2015/VI_A_cyoper_hist.html#288797.

Notes: "Total Income" includes interest earned on the asset reserves held by the DI trust fund. The amount of asset reserves held by a trust fund represents its balance.

Figure 2. Operations of the DI Trust Fund, 1995-2014.

CAUSES OF THE DI TRUST FUND'S FINANCIAL IMBALANCE

The declining solvency of the DI trust fund is the result of an increasing imbalance between its income and cost. Figure 3 shows income and cost to the DI trust fund expressed as a percentage of taxable payroll.

---

41 See SSA, OACT, "Times Series For Selected Financial Items," https://www.ssa.gov/oact/ProgData/tsOps.html.

Table 3. Operations of the DI Trust Fund, 1995-2014 ($ in billions)

Year	Income			Cost				Asset Reserves	
	Total Income	Non Interest Income[a]	Net Interest[b]	Total Cost	Benefit Payments[c]	Administrative Expenses	RRB Interchange[d]	Change During the Year	Amount at the End of the Year
1995	$56.7	$54.5	$2.2	$42.1	$40.9	$1.1	$0.1	$14.6	$37.6
1996	60.7	57.7	3.0	45.4	44.2	1.2	e	15.4	52.9
1997	60.5	56.5	4.0	47.0	45.7	1.3	0.1	13.5	66.4
1998	64.4	59.6	4.8	49.9	48.2	1.6	0.2	14.4	80.8
1999	69.5	63.9	5.7	53.0	51.4	1.5	0.1	16.5	97.3
2000	77.9	71.0	6.9	56.8	55.0	1.6	0.2	21.1	118.5
2001	83.9	75.7	8.2	61.4	59.6	1.7	e	22.5	141.0
2002	87.4	78.2	9.2	67.9	65.7	2.0	0.2	19.5	160.5
2003	88.1	78.3	9.7	73.1	70.9	2.0	0.2	15.0	175.4
2004	91.4	81.4	10.0	80.6	78.2	2.2	0.2	10.8	186.2
2005	97.4	87.2	10.3	88.0	85.4	2.3	0.3	9.4	195.6
2006	102.6	92.0	10.6	94.5	91.7	2.3	0.4	8.2	203.8
2007	109.9	96.6	13.2	98.8	95.9	2.5	0.4	11.1	214.9
2008	109.8	98.9	11.0	109.0	106.0	2.5	0.4	0.9	215.8
2009	109.3	98.9	10.5	121.5	118.3	2.7	0.4	-12.2	203.5
2010	104.0	94.8	9.3	127.7	124.2	3.0	0.5	-23.6	179.9
2011	106.3	98.4	7.9	132.3	128.9	2.9	0.5	-26.1	153.9
2012	109.1	102.7	6.4	140.3	136.9	2.9	0.5	-31.2	122.7

Year	**Income**			**Cost**				**Asset Reserves**	
	Total Income	Non Interest Income[a]	Net Interest[b]	Total Cost	Benefit Payments[c]	Administrative Expenses	RRB Interchange[d]	Change During the Year	Amount at the End of the Year
2013	111.2	106.5	4.7	143.4	140.1	2.8	0.6	-32.2	90.4
2014	114.9	111.5	3.4	145.1	141.7	2.9	0.4	-30.2	60.2

Source: CRS, based on data from the 2015 Social Security Trustees Report, Table VI.A2, at http://www.ssa.gov/oact/tr/2015/VI_A_cyoper_hist.html#288797.

Notes: Totals may not equal the sum of components due to rounding.

a. "Non-Interest Income" includes net payroll tax contributions, General Fund reimbursements, and revenues from the taxation of benefits.

b. "Net Interest" includes (1) interests earned on the investments (asset reserves) held by the trust fund, (2) interest on adjustments in the allocation of administration expenses between the trust fund and the General Fund for the Supplemental Security Income (SSI) program, (3) interest arising from the revised allocation of administrative expenses among the trust funds, and (4) interest on certain reimbursements to the trust fund.

c. Includes payments for vocational rehabilitation services furnished to disabled beneficiaries and reimbursements from the General Fund for unnegotiated benefit checks.

d. "RRB Interchange" refers to the financial interchange with the Railroad Retirement Board (RRB). For more information, see CRS Report RS22350, *Railroad Retirement Board: Retirement, Survivor, Disability, Unemployment, and Sickness Benefits*, by Scott D. Szymendera.

e. Between -$50 million and $50 million.

Taxable payroll is the total amount of earnings in the economy that is subject to Social Security taxes (with some adjustments).[42] The ratio of non-interest income to taxable payroll for the year is known as the annual income rate; the ratio of cost to taxable payroll for the year is known as the annual cost rate. Over the past 20 years, the annual DI income rate has remained relatively flat at about 1.81% of taxable payroll, which is roughly the combined share of the tax rate allocated to the DI trust fund for that period plus a small amount of other income. At the same time, the annual DI cost rate has grown markedly, from 1.44% in 1995 to 2.36% in 2014.

The increase in the annual DI cost rate stems largely from the growth in the number of beneficiaries on SSDI. Between 1995 and 2014, the total number of disabled workers and their dependents in receipt of SSDI increased 85%, from 5.9 million to 10.9 million.[43] Because benefit payments account for nearly all spending, the increase in the number of SSDI beneficiaries drove the annual DI cost rate upward.

The rise in disability rolls can be attributed to a number of factors.[44] First, the overall growth in the working-age population increased the number of workers insured for disability.[45] Between 1995 and 2014, the insured-worker population increased 19%, from 127 million to 151 million.[46]

---

[42] 2015 Social Security Trustees Report, Table VI.G5. In 2014, taxable payroll was slightly more than one-third of gross domestic product (GDP).

[43] Ibid., pp. 55-56.

[44] Jeffrey B. Liebman, "Understanding the Increase in Disability Insurance Benefit Receipt in the United States," *Journal of Economic Perspective*, vol. 29, no. 2 (Spring 2015), https://www.aeaweb.org/jep/app/2902/ 29020123_corr.pdf. See also Mary C. Daly, Brian Lucking, and Jonathan A. Schwabish, *The Future of Social Security Disability Insurance*, Federal Reserve Bank of San Francisco, Economic Letter 2013-17, June 24, 2013, http://www.frbsf.org/economic-research/files/el2013-17.pdf.

[45] See David Pattison and Hilary Waldron, "Growth in New Disabled-Worker Entitlements, 1970–2008," *Social Security Bulletin*, vol. 73, no. 4 (November 2013), http://www.ssa.gov/policy/docs/ssb/v73n4/v73n4p25.html.

[46] SSA, OACT, "Disability Insured Workers," https://www.ssa.gov/oact/STATS/table4c2DI.html.

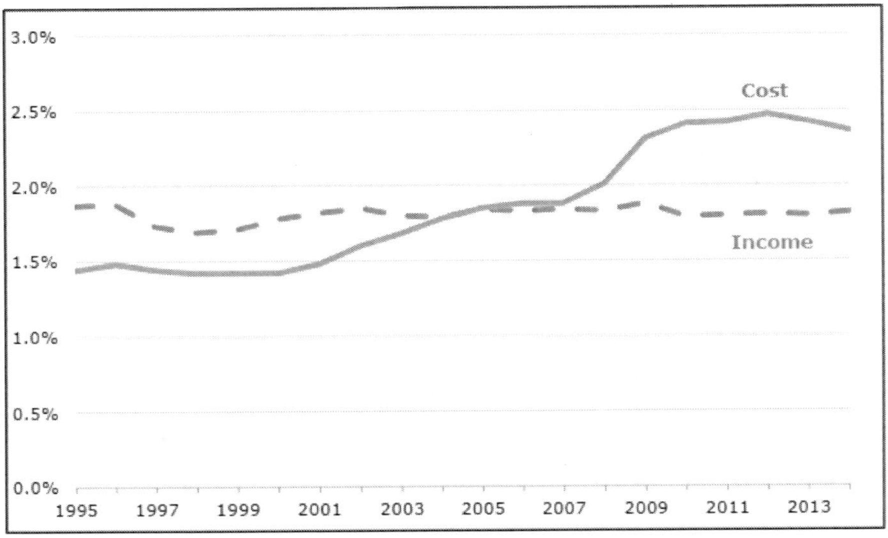

Source: CRS, based on data from the 2015 Social Security Trustees Report, Table IV.B1, Single-Year Tables, at http://www.ssa.gov/oact/tr/2015/lr4b1.html.

Notes: The "Income Rate" is the ratio of non-interest DI income to taxable payroll. Non-interest income includes payroll taxes, taxes paid on scheduled benefits, and reimbursements from the General Fund. The "Cost Rate" is the ratio of DI cost to taxable payroll. Cost includes scheduled benefits, administrative expenses, and the net interchange with the RRB. "Taxable payroll" is the total amount of earnings in the economy that is subject to Social Security taxes (with some adjustments).

Figure 3. Annual DI Income and Cost Rates, 1995-2014 (non-interest income and cost as a share of taxable payroll for the year).

Second, demographic changes in the composition of the insured-worker population contributed to the increase in the number of beneficiaries on SSDI.[47] Most importantly, the aging of the baby-boomer generation increased the number of older workers, who are more likely to become disabled than are younger workers. In addition, growth in the labor force participation rate of women in the latter half of the 20th century led to more women being insured for disability.[48] As the size of the female

---

[47] 2015 Social Security Trustees Report, pp. 137-140.

[48] See Kathy Ruffing, *How Much of the Growth in Disability Insurance Stems From Demographic Changes?*, Center on Budget and Policy Priorities (CBPP), January 27, 2014, Table 1, p. 5, http://www.cbpp.org/research/how-much-ofthe-growth-in-disability-insurance-stems-from-demographic-changes?fa=view&id=4080.

insured-worker population increased, the enrollment rate of women into the SSDI program grew to near parity with men.[49]

Third, changes in opportunities for work and compensation induced more individuals to apply for SSDI. For example, according to SSA's chief actuary, economic downturns are associated with a temporary increase in the enrollment rate of insured workers into the program.[50] During the last recession, the number of SSDI awards per 1,000 insured workers increased 25%, from 5.6 in 2007 to 7.0 in 2010.[51] In addition, the value of benefits has made applying for SSDI more desirable than work for some low-wage workers, because such individuals have experienced slower real earnings growth over the past three decades compared with medium- and high-wage workers.[52]

Fourth, various amendments to the Social Security program played a role in increasing the number of people on SSDI. For example, the Social Security Amendments of 1983 (P.L. 98-21) raised the full retirement age (FRA) for Social Security retirement benefits, thereby increasing both the number of insured workers in their older and more disability-prone years and the duration of benefit receipt for older SSDI beneficiaries close to the FRA. The increase in the FRA also raised the value of disability benefits relative to early retirement benefits, which likely impelled more individuals between the ages of 62 and FRA to apply for SSDI.

Furthermore, the Social Security Disability Benefits Reform Act of 1984 (P.L. 98-460), which changed the evaluative criteria used in making disability determinations, contributed to the growth in the number of SSDI

---

[49] Tim Zayatz, *Social Security Disability Insurance Program Work Experience*, SSA, OACT, Actuarial Study No. 123, Table 4, August 2015, p. 22, http://www.ssa.gov/oact/NOTES/pdf_studies/study123.pdf.

[50] Testimony of SSA Chief Actuary Stephen C. Goss, in U.S. Congress, House Committee on Ways and Means, Subcommittee on Social Security, *The Financing Challenges Facing the Social Security Disability Insurance Program*, 113th Cong., 1st sess., March 14, 2013, http://www.ssa.gov/legislation/testimony_031413a.html.

[51] SSA, *Annual Statistical Supplement, 2014*, April 2015, Table 6.C7, http://www.ssa.gov/policy/docs/statcomps/ supplement/2014/6c.html#table6.c7.

[52] See David H. Autor and Mark G. Duggan, "The Rise in the Disability Rolls and the Decline in Unemployment," *The Quarterly Journal of Economics* (February 2003), pp. 158-205, http://economics.mit.edu/files/579.

beneficiaries with mental and musculoskeletal disorders.[53] Because such disorders are less likely to result in death compared with other qualifying impairments, the growth in the share of beneficiaries with mental and musculoskeletal disorders likely increased the average duration of benefit receipt and thus SSDI caseloads.[54]

Although most researchers agree that changes in the demographic characteristics of the working-age population account for a large share of the growth in the number of beneficiaries on SSDI, there is considerable disagreement among researchers over how more "difficult to quantify factors"—such as changes in opportunities for work and compensation or changes to federal policy—have contributed to the growth in the program.[55]

The trustees project that the share of the insured population in receipt of SSDI will stabilize in the future, because some of the principal drivers of past growth—namely, the aging of the insured population and the increase in female enrollment rates—have come to pass and are not likely to occur again.[56] The 2015 Technical Panel on Assumptions and Methods—a panel of expert actuaries, economists, and demographers convened by the Social Security Advisory Board (SSAB) to review the assumptions and methods used by the trustees—recently concurred with this assessment.[57]

---

[53] David H. Autor, *The Unsustainable Rise of the Disability Rolls in the United States: Causes, Consequences, and Policy Options*, National Bureau of Economic Research, NBER Working Paper no. 17697, December 2011, p. 5, http://www.nber.org/papers/w17697. See also L. Scott Muller et al., *Trends in the Social Security and Supplemental Security Income Disability Programs*, SSA, August 2006, p. 44, http://www.ssa.gov/policy/docs/chartbooks/disability_trends/index.html.

[54] See Kalman Rupp and Charles G. Scott, "Trends in the Characteristics of DI and SSI Disability Awardees and Duration of Program Participation," *Social Security Bulletin*, vol. 59, no. 1 (January 1996), p. 3, http://www.ssa.gov/ policy/docs/ssb/v59n1/.

[55] Gina Livermore, David Wittenburg, and David Neumark, "Finding alternatives to disability benefit receipt," *IZA Journal of Labor Policy*, 2014, p. 2. http://www.izajolp.com/content/pdf/2193-9004-3-14.pdf.

[56] 2015 Social Security Trustees Report, p. 140.

[57] 2015 Technical Panel on Assumptions and Methods, *Report to the Social Security Advisory Board*, September 2015, p. 44, http://ssab.gov/Portals/0/Technical%20Panel/2015_TPAM_Final_Report.pdf?ver=2015-09-24-113145-693.

PROJECTED STATUS OF THE DI TRUST FUND

This section examines the financial outlook of the DI trust fund under prior law and under the Bipartisan Budget Act of 2015 (H.R. 1314; P.L. 114-74). Specifically, it discusses the projected depletion year of the DI trust fund, that is, the year in which the balance of the trust fund falls to zero. When a trust fund is *depleted*, it no longer has any asset reserves; however, it continues to receive income from payroll taxes and the taxation of benefits.

The Social Security Act provides no guidance on the payment of benefits once a trust fund's asset reserves have been depleted and current tax revenues are insufficient to meet current cost. Although individuals who meet Social Security's eligibility requirements are legally entitled to disability benefits,[58] a provision in the Antideficiency Act prohibits a federal agency from spending in excess of available funds.[59] Because the Social Security Act stipulates that SSDI benefit payments shall be made only from the DI trust fund, without a change in the law, monthly cash payments to beneficiaries could be delayed or reduced if the DI trust fund were depleted.[60]

Under Prior Law

The trustees estimate the future financial condition of the OASI and DI trust funds individually as well as on a theoretical combined basis (i.e., as if the two trust funds were a single fund). In their 2015 report, which was released *prior* to the enactment of the Bipartisan Budget Act of 2015, the trustees projected that the DI trust fund would be depleted in the fourth quarter of calendar year 2016. The trustees also projected that the OASI

---

[58] 42 U.S.C. §423.

[59] 31 U.S.C. §1341.

[60] 42 U.S.C. §401(h). See CRS Report RL33514, *Social Security: What Would Happen If the Trust Funds Ran Out?*, by Dawn Nuschler and William R. Morton, and CRS Report RL32822, *Social Security Reform: Legal Analysis of Social Security Benefit Entitlement Issues*, by Emily M. Lanza and Thomas J. Nicola.

trust fund would be depleted in 2035 and the theoretical combined OASDI trust funds would be depleted in 2034. Figure 4 shows the actual and projected trust fund ratios of the OASI, DI, and combined OASDI trust funds under prior law. A *trust fund ratio* is a measure of a trust fund's asset reserves at the beginning of a year expressed as a percentage of total cost for the year.[61]

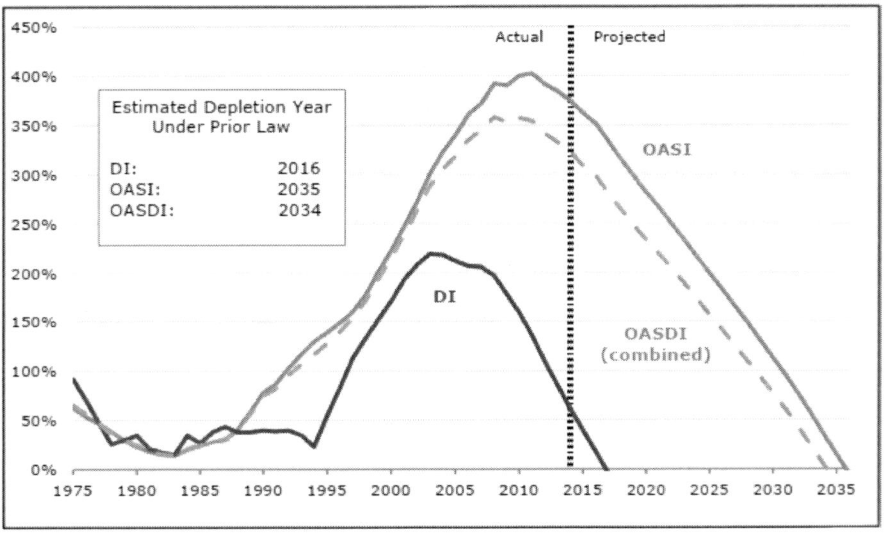

Source: CRS, based on data from the 2015 Social Security Trustees Report, Table IV.B4, Single-Year Tables, at https://www.ssa.gov/oact/tr/2015/lr4b4.html.

Note: Projections based on the intermediate assumptions of the 2015 trustees report.

Figure 4. Actual and Projected OASI, DI, and Combined OASDI Trust Fund Ratios Under Prior Law, 1975-2036 (asset reserves at the beginning of the year as a share of annual cost).

In its June 2015 long-term budget outlook, the Congressional Budget Office (CBO) estimated that the balance of the DI trust fund would be depleted sometime in FY2017.[62] CBO projected that the OASI trust fund would be depleted in calendar year 2031 and the theoretical combined OASDI trust funds would be depleted in calendar year 2029. The Social

[61] 2015 Social Security Trustees Report, p. 40.

[62] Congressional Budget Office (CBO), *The 2015 Long-Term Budget Outlook*, June 2015, p. 55, https://www.cbo.gov/ publication/50250.

Security trustees and CBO sometimes project different depletion dates because the two organizations base their forecasts on different demographic and economic assumptions.

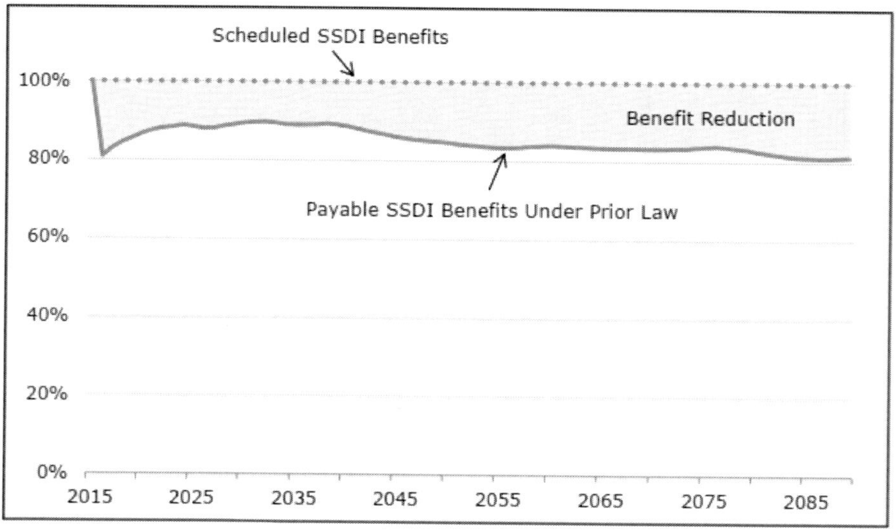

Source: CRS, based on data provided by SSA's OACT in Memorandum from Chris Chaplain, supervisory actuary, and Daniel Nickerson, actuary, to Alice H. Wade, deputy chief actuary, "Present-Law OASDI Payable.

Percentages: Present-Law Revenue as a Percent of the Cost of Providing Scheduled Benefits through Year 2089," August 27, 2015.

Note: Projections based on the intermediate assumptions of the 2015 trustees report.

Figure 5. Th Projected Share of SSDI Benefits Payable Under Prior Law, 2015-2089 (prior law DI income expressed as a share of the cost of providing scheduled benefits).

Upon depletion of its asset reserves in late 2016, the trustees projected that continuing tax revenues to the DI trust fund would have been sufficient to pay 81% of SSDI benefits.[63] That percentage was projected to rise to about 90% in the 2030s and then decline, returning to 81% in 2089 (Figure 5).[64] A recent SSA study examined the characteristics of disabled-

[63] 2015 Social Security Trustees Report, p.13.
[64] Ibid.

worker beneficiaries in 2013.[65] After accounting for SSDI benefits, the study's authors estimated that 18.5% of disabled workers had family income below the poverty threshold.[66] However, if only 81% of benefits had been payable that year, the authors estimated that the poverty rate for disabled-worker beneficiaries would have been 25.5%.

Under the Bipartisan Budget Act of 2015

On November 2, 2015, President Barack Obama signed into law the Bipartisan Budget Act of 2015 (H.R. 1314; P.L. 114-74). Among its many provisions, the act authorized a temporary reallocation of the Social Security payroll tax rate between the OASI and DI trust funds to provide DI with a larger share for 2016 through 2018. Specifically, the DI trust fund's share of the tax rate for employees and employers, each, increased by 0.285 percentage point at the beginning of 2016, from 0.900% to 1.185% (Table 4).

Table 4. Social Security Payroll Tax Rates under Prior Law and Under the Bipartisan Budget Act of 2015 (as a percentage of taxable earnings)

Year	Employees and Employers, Each (FICA)			Self-Employed (SECA		
	OASDI	OASI	DI	OASDI	OASI	DI
Rates Scheduled Under the Social Security Domestic Employment Reform Act of 1994 (P.L. 103-387)						
2015+	6.200	5.300	0.900	12.400	10.600	1.800
Rates Scheduled Under the Bipartisan Budget Act of 2015 (P.L. 114-74)						
2015	6.200	5.300	0.900	12.400	10.600	1.800
2016-2018	6.200	5.015	1.185	12.400	10.030	2.370
2019+	6.200	5.300	0.900	12.400	10.600	1.800

---

[65] Michelle Stegman Bailey and Jeffrey Hemmeter, "Characteristics of Noninstitutionalized DI and SSI Program Participants, 2013 Update," Research and Statistics Note no. 2015-2, September 2015, http://www.ssa.gov/policy/docs/ rsnotes/rsn2015-02.html.

[66] Ibid., Table 6B.

On a *combined basis*, DI's share of the tax rate increased by 0.570 percentage point, from 1.800% to 2.370%. The change in the SECA rate mirrors the change in the combined FICA rate.

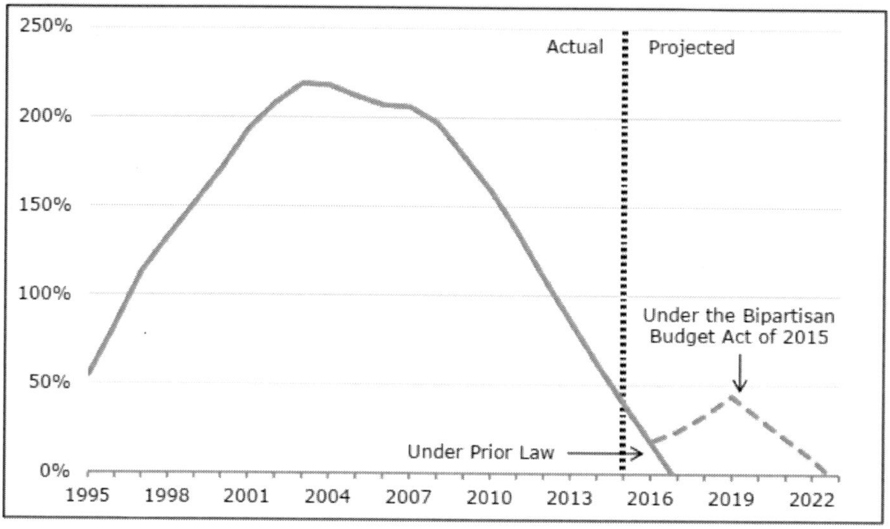

Source: CRS, based on the Social Security Advisory Board (SSAB), "Did You Know? The Bipartisan Budget Act of 2015 extended the expected date of the DI trust fund reserve depletion by 6 years to 2022 from 2016," Chart 1, http://www.ssab.gov/Facts-and-Figures/Did-You-Know-Charts/Disability-Trust-Fund-Solvency.

Note: Projections based on the intermediate assumptions of the 2015 trustees report.

Figure 6. Actual and Projected DI Trust Fund Ratios under Prior Law and Under the Bipartisan Budget Act of 2015, 1995-2023 (asset reserves at the beginning of the year as a share of annual cost).

Because the act did not change the Social Security payroll tax rate, the portion of the tax rate allocated to OASI *decreased* by a corresponding amount. This means that OASI's share of the 6.200% tax rate for employees and employers, each, declined by 0.285 percentage point at the start of 2016, from 5.300% to 5.015%. On a *combined basis*, OASI's share of the 12.400% tax rate declined by 0.570 percentage point, from 10.600% to 10.030%. Again, the change in the SECA rate mirrors the change in the combined FICA rate. For 2019 and later, the shares allocated to the DI and OASI trust funds are scheduled to return to their 2015 levels.

SSA's Office of the Chief Actuary (OACT) projects that the reallocation schedule in the Bipartisan Budget Act of 2015 will extend the solvency of the DI trust fund from the fourth quarter of 2016 to approximately the third quarter of 2022 (Figure 6).[67] Although the reallocation is projected to reduce the solvency of the OASI trust fund by a number of months, OACT estimates that the *depletion year* for OASI will remain unchanged at 2035.[68] Because the reallocation does not change the total amount of Social Security tax revenues, OACT projects that the depletion year for the theoretical combined OASDI trust funds will remain unchanged at 2034.

Table 5. Projected Depletion Years for the OASI, DI, and Combined OASDI Trust Funds under Prior Law and Under the Bipartisan Budget Act of 2015, by Agency

Depletion Year Projections—	**OACT**			**CBO**		
	OASDI	OASI	DI	OASDI	OASI	DI
Under Prior Law	2034	2035	2016	2029	2031	FY2017
Under the Bipartisan Budget Act of 2015[a]	2034	2035	2022	2029	2030	FY2021

Source: CRS, based on the following sources: the 2015 Social Security Trustees Report; Letter from Stephen C.

Goss, chief actuary, to the Honorable John Boehner, Speaker of the House of Representatives, October 27,

Notes: Unless otherwise stated, years presented in the table are calendar years. The "depletion year" is the year in which the balance of the trust fund falls to zero.

a. OACT's projections for the OASI trust fund and the theoretical combined OASDI trust funds account for the effects of several other provisions in the Bipartisan Budget Act of 2015 in addition to the temporary payroll tax reallocation. CBO's projections do not account for these effects.

---

67 Letter from Stephen C. Goss, chief actuary, to the Honorable John Boehner, Speaker of the House of Representatives, October 27, 2015, https://www.ssa.gov/oact/solvency/JBoehner_20151027.pdf (hereinafter "OACT Letter to Speaker Boehner, October 2015").

68 OACT's projections for the OASI trust fund and the theoretical combined OASDI trust funds account for the effects of several other provisions in the Bipartisan Budget Act of 2015 in addition to the payroll tax reallocation.

CBO projects that the reallocation will extend the solvency of the DI trust fund from FY2017 to FY2021.[69] The agency estimates that the reallocation will reduce the solvency of the OASI trust fund slightly, shifting the depletion year from calendar year 2031 to calendar year 2030. The depletion year for the theoretical combined OASDI trust funds is projected to remain unchanged at calendar year 2029 under CBO's extended baseline projections (see Table 5).

USE OF REALLOCATIONS BY CONGRESS IN THE PAST

As shown in Table 6, Congress has authorized the reallocation of the payroll tax rate multiple times in the past. For the purposes of this chapter, a *reallocation* occurs when (1) the overall tax rate remains the same but the shares allocated to the trust funds change proportionally or (2) the overall tax rate changes and the shares allocated to the trust funds change in opposite directions.[70] In other words, a reallocation increases tax revenues to one trust fund and decreases revenues to the other regardless of whether the overall Social Security tax rate increases, decreases, or stays the same.

Lawmakers have historically included payroll tax reallocations in major amendments to the Social Security Act in order to put the OASI and DI trust funds on a more or less equal financial footing.

---

[69] CBO, *CBO's 2015 Long-Term Projections for Social Security: Additional Information*, December 2015, p. 2, https://www.cbo.gov/publication/51047. 2015, https://www.ssa.gov/oact/solvency/JBoehner_20151027.pdf; U.S. Congressional Budget Office (CBO), *The 2015 Long-Term Budget Outlook*, June 2015, p. 55, https://www.cbo.gov/publication/50250; and CBO, *CBO's 2015 Long-Term Projections for Social Security: Additional Information*, December 2015, p. 2, https://www.cbo.gov/ publication/51047.

[70] See Kathy A. Ruffing and Paul N. Van de Water, *Congress Needs to Boost Disability Insurance Share of Payroll Tax by 2016: Traditional Step Would Avert Trust Fund Depletion, Benefit Cuts*, Center on Budget and Policy Priorities, July 31, 2014, http://www.cbpp.org//sites/default/files/atoms/files/7-16-14socsec.pdf. See also Virginia P. Reno, Elisa A. Walker, and Thomas N. Bethell, *Social Security Disability Insurance: Action Needed to Address Finances*, National Academy of Social Insurance, Brief no. 41, June 2013, https://www.nasi.org/sites/default/files/research/ SS_Brief_041.pdf.

Table 6. Legislation Reallocating the Social Security Payroll Tax Rate

Public Law Number	Name	Date of Enactment	Reallocation Direction	Reallocated the FICA Rate?[a]	Reallocated the SECA Rate?[a]
P.L. 90-248	Social Security Amendments of 1967	January 2, 1968	OASI to DI	Yes (once)	Yes (once)
P.L. 91-172	Tax Reform Act of 1969	December 30, 1969	OASI to DI	Yes (once)	Yes (once)
P.L. 92-603	Social Security Amendments of 1972[b]	October 30, 1972	DI to OASI	No	Yes (once)
P.L. 93-233	"Social Security Benefits Increase Act of 1973"[c]	December 31, 1973	OASI to DI	No	Yes (once)
P.L. 95-216	Social Security Amendments of 1977	December 20, 1977	Both Directions[d]	Yes (twice)	Yes (once)
P.L. 96-403	"Reallocation of Social Security Tax Receipts Act of 1980"[e]	October 9, 1980	Both Directions[f]	Yes (twice)	Yes (twice)
P.L. 98-21	Social Security Amendments of 1983	April 20, 1983	DI to OASI[g]	Yes (twice)	Yes (once)
P.L. 103-387	Social Security Domestic Employment Reform Act of 1994	October 22, 1994	Both Directions[h]	Yes (3 times)	Yes (3 times)

Table 6. (Continued)

Public Law Number	Name	Date of Enactment	Reallocation Direction	Reallocated the FICA Rate?[a]	Reallocated the SECA Rate?[a]
P.L. 114-74	Bipartisan Budget Act of 2015	November 2, 2015	Both Directions[i]	Yes (twice)	Yes (twice)

Source: Compiled by CRS from the following sources: SSA, OACT, "Social Security Tax Rates," https://www.ssa.gov/oact/progdata/oasdiRates.html; SSA, "Social Security History: Legislative Histories 1935-2004," Downey Books, https://www.ssa.gov/history/legislativehistory.html; and SSA, OACT, "Reports from the Board of Trustees," various years, https://www.ssa.gov/oact/tr/. (Continued …)

Notes: A reallocation occurs when (1) the overall tax rate remains the same but the shares allocated to the trust funds change proportionally or (2) the overall tax rate changes and the shares allocated to the trust funds change in opposite directions.

[a] This column refers to reallocations that were implemented (or are scheduled to be implemented) under each law specified in the table; it does not refer to reallocations that were scheduled and then superseded by subsequent law.

[b] P.L. 92-603 amended the rate schedule enacted earlier that year under P.L. 92-336, "An Act to provide for a four-month extension of the present temporary level in the public debt limitation, and for other purposes."

[c] P.L. 93-233 is titled "An Act to provide a 7-percent increase in social security benefits beginning with March 1974 and an additional 4-percent increase beginning with June 1974, to provide increases in supplemental security income benefits, and for other purposes."

[d] The 1977 amendments reallocated the FICA and SECA rates to improve the balance of the DI trust fund in 1978 and reallocated the FICA rate to improve the balance of the OASI trust fund in 1979.

[e] P.L. 96-403 is titled "An Act to amend title II of the Social Security Act to make necessary adjustments in the allocation of social security tax receipts between the Federal Old-Age and Survivors Insurance Trust Fund and the Federal Disability Insurance Trust Fund."

[f] The 1980 amendments provided for a temporary reallocation of the total tax rate to improve the balance of the OASI trust fund in 1980. In 1982, the change in the tax rates expired and more revenues were directed back to the DI trust fund.

[g] The 1983 amendments reallocated the FICA and SECA rates to improve the balance of the OASI trust fund in 1983. In 1984, the total tax rate increased and the FICA rate was reallocated again to give additional revenues to the OASI trust fund.

[h] The 1994 reallocation, which was enacted to improve the balance of the DI trust fund, occurred in three stages. The first and third stages reallocated the payroll tax rate from the OASI trust fund to the DI trust fund, while the second stage reallocated the tax rate from the DI trust fund to the OASI trust fund.

[i] In 2016, the share of the payroll tax rate allocated to the DI trust fund increased and the share allocated to the OASI trust fund decreased. In 2019, the share allocated to the OASI trust fund is scheduled to increase and the share allocated to the DI trust fund is scheduled to decrease.

However, reallocations have been used at times to extend the solvency of nearly depleted trust funds. Payroll tax reallocations have sometimes benefited the DI trust fund and at other times have favored the OASI trust fund. Reallocation legislation may contain a rate schedule that changes the allocation between the trust funds multiple times and in different directions. With respect to the "number of times" the payroll tax rate has been reallocated, some people tally pieces of legislation authorizing either a single reallocation or a reallocation schedule, whereas others count each instance in which a reallocation occurred. Because FICA taxes account for nearly all payroll tax revenues to the Social Security trust funds, people generally count reallocations affecting the FICA rate.[71]

House Rules Change in the 114th Congress Concerning Reallocations Between the Social Security Trust Funds

At the start of the 114th Congress, the House adopted a rule sponsored by Representative Sam Johnson intended to engender structural changes to SSDI.[72] Known as the "Johnson Rule," Section 3(q) of H.Res. 5 allows a point of order to be raised against legislation that would reduce the actuarial balance of the OASI trust fund by at least 0.01% of the present value of projected future taxable payroll over the 75-year period used in the most recent Social Security trustees report.[73] However, the point of

---

[71] In 2014, FICA taxes accounted for 94% of all payroll tax revenues to the Social Security trust funds on a combined basis. See SSA, OACT, "Social Security & Medicare Tax Data," https://www.ssa.gov/oact/ProgData/taxquery.html.

[72] Office of Rep. Sam Johnson, "House Passes Johnson Measure to Protect Social Security," press release, January 6, 2015, http://samjohnson.house.gov/news/document single.aspx?DocumentID=397616. The House rule was also included in the FY2016 budget resolution (see Section 3301 of S.Con.Res. 11).

[73] For general information on points of order, see CRS Report 98-307, *Points of Order, Rulings, and Appeals in the House of Representatives*, by Valerie Heitshusen. *Actuarial balance* is the difference between a trust fund's summarized income and cost rates. The *summarized income rate* is the sum of the present value of non-interest income and the balance of the trust fund at the beginning of the 75-year period, expressed as a share of the present value of taxable payroll for the period. The *summarized cost rate* is the sum of the present value of

order would not apply if the legislation, as a whole, were projected to improve the long-term actuarial balance of the OASI and DI trust funds on a combined basis. Therefore, a short-term financing measure (such as a reallocation) could be considered if it also included revenue increases, cost reductions, or both, even if those changes were projected to have very small positive effects on the theoretical combined OASDI trust funds.

In their 2015 report, the trustees project that the present value of future taxable payroll from 2015 through 2089 will be nearly $421 trillion.[74] The current threshold, therefore, is $42.1 billion (0.01% of $421 trillion).[75] CBO projects that the reallocation schedule enacted in the Bipartisan Budget Act of 2015 (H.R. 1314; P.L. 114-74) will increase income from payroll taxes to the DI trust fund by $117 billion and reduce income from payroll taxes to the OASI trust fund by the same amount.[76]

If the reallocation provision in the Bipartisan Budget Act of 2015 had been proposed as a standalone piece of legislation, it could have been vulnerable to a point of order under the new rule because it would have reduced the actuarial balance of the OASI trust fund by more than $42.1 billion. However, because the budget agreement also contained several provisions that are projected to improve the long-term actuarial balance of

---

cost over the 75-year period and the present value of the cost of reaching a trust fund ratio of 100% at the end of the period, expressed as a percentage of the present value of taxable payroll for the same period. *Present value* is "a single number that expresses a flow of past and future income (in taxes) or payments (in benefits) in terms of an equivalent lump sum received or paid at a specific time. The value depends on the rate of interest, known as the discount rate, used to translate past and future cash flows into current dollars at that time." See CBO, *Social Security Policy Options, 2015*, December 2015, p. 91, https://www.cbo.gov/publication/51011.

[74] 2015 Social Security Trustees Report, Table IV.B6.

[75] SSA's Chief Actuary, Stephen C. Goss, told *Politico* in January 2015 that the threshold under H.Res. 5 was $38.6 billion. That threshold was based on the present value of projected future taxable payroll in the *2014 trustees report* (0.01% of $386.884 trillion is $38.6884 billion). See David Rogers, "Republicans target Social Security disability," *Politico*, January 20, 2015, http://www.politico.com/story/2015/01/republicans-target-social-security-114382. See also U.S. Congress, House Committee on Ways and Means, *The 2014 Annual Report of the Board of Trustees of the Federal Old-Age and Survivors Insurance and Federal Disability Insurance Trust Funds*, 113th Cong., 2nd sess., July 28, 2014, H.Doc. 113-139 (Washington: GPO, 2015), Table IV.B5, https://www.ssa.gov/oact/tr/2014/IV_B_LRest.html#493472.

[76] CBO, *Estimate of the Budgetary Effects of H.R. 1314, the Bipartisan Budget Act of 2015, as reported by the House Committee on Rules on October 27, 2015*, p. 5, footnote 2, https://www.cbo.gov/publication/50938.

the theoretical combined OASDI trust funds by 0.04% of taxable payroll, the point of order under Section 3(q) of H.Res. 5 was not applicable during House consideration of the Bipartisan Budget Act of 2015.[77]

LONG-TERM POLICY OPTIONS

To improve the financial outlook of the DI trust fund over the long term, Congress could consider a variety of legislative changes to increase tax revenues, reduce program cost (i.e., alter benefit levels or program eligibility requirements), or some combination of those approaches. The last major congressional effort to address the financial condition of one of the Social Security trust funds occurred in the early 1980s with the passage of the Social Security Amendments of 1983 (P.L. 98-21). Under the 1983 amendments, Congress used a combination of revenue increases and cost reductions to stabilize and eventually improve the solvency of the OASI trust fund.[78] Congress could enact similar legislation to improve the long-term solvency of either the DI trust fund only or both trust funds.

APPENDIX A. CONGRESSIONAL RATIONALE FOR THE CREATION OF A SEPARATE DI TRUST FUND

The creation of a separate DI trust fund came about during the debate over the establishment of SSDI as part of the Social Security Amendments of 1956 (P.L. 84-880).[79] Since the late 1930s, policymakers had discussed proposals to amend the Social Security Act to provide covered workers

---

[77] For more information on the effects of other provisions in the Bipartisan Budget Act of 2015 on the solvency of the Social Security trust funds, see OACT Letter to Speaker Boehner, October 2015.

[78] See John A. Svahn and Mary Ross, "Social Security Amendments of 1983: Legislative History and Summary of Provisions," *Social Security Bulletin*, vol. 46, no. 7 (July 1983), https://socialsecurity.gov/policy/docs/ssb/v46n7/ v46n7p3.pdf.

[79] See Charles I. Schottland, "Social Security Amendments of 1956: A Summary and Legislative History," *Social Security Bulletin*, vol. 19, no. 9 (September 1956), https://www.ssa.gov/policy/docs/ssb/v19n9/.

with disability insurance.[80] However, persistent disagreements among policymakers over how to implement a disability insurance program or whether such a program should be enacted at all derailed most proposals early in the deliberative process.[81] Nevertheless, by the 1950s, there was enough support for the creation of a federal disability insurance program for Congress to consider the matter.[82]

Origins of Social Security (OASDI)

1935 (Old-Age Insurance): The Social Security Act (P.L. 74-271) created a national old-age benefits program, covering nearly all workers in commerce and industry and providing monthly pensions at age 65 for insured workers.
1939 (Survivors Insurance): The Social Security Amendments of 1939 (P.L. 76-379) amended Title II of the Social Security Act to provide monthly benefits to eligible dependents and survivors of insured workers. The 1939 amendments also established the OASI trust fund.[83]
1956 (Disability Insurance): The Social Security Amendments of 1956 (P.L. 84-880) amended Title II to provide monthly benefits to insured workers aged 50 to 64 with qualifying impairments. The 1956 amendments also created the DI trust fund.

On July 11, 1955, Representative Jere Cooper (D-TN), the chair of the House Committee on Ways and Means, introduced a bill to amend Title II of the Social Security Act to provide monthly benefits to insured workers

---

80 Edward D. Berkowitz, *Disabled Policy: American's Programs for the Handicapped* (New York: Cambridge University Press, 1987), pp. 41-78 (hereinafter "Berkowitz 1987").

81 Ibid. See also U.S. Congress, House Committee on Ways and Means, *Committee Staff Report on the Disability Insurance Program*, prepared by the Staff of the Committee of on Ways and Means, 93rd Cong., 2nd sess., July 1974 (Washington: GPO, 1974), pp. 107-113, http://www.ssa.gov/history/reports/dibhistory.html.

82 Ibid. See also John R. Kearney, "Social Security and the 'D' in OASDI: The History of a Federal Program Insuring Earners Against Disability," *Social Security Bulletin*, vol. 66, no. 3 (August 2006), https://www.ssa.gov/policy/docs/ ssb/v66n3/v66n3p1.html.

83 The OASI trust fund superseded the Old-Age Reserve Account created under the Social Security Act in 1935 (P.L.74-271). The OASI trust fund became effective on January 1, 1940. For more information on the origins of the OASI trust fund and Old-Age Reserve Account, see Board of Trustees of the Federal Old-Age and Survivors Insurance Trust Fund, *First Report of the Board of Trustees of the Federal Old-Age and Survivors Insurance Trust Fund*, January 3, 1941, https://www.ssa.gov/history/reports/ trust/tf1941.html.

aged 50 to 64 with qualifying impairments, among other provisions (H.R. 7225). Under the bill, disability benefits would have been paid from the OASI trust fund and payroll tax rates would have been increased to cover the associated costs. The House report accompanying H.R. 7225 did not discuss the creation of a separate trust fund for the proposed disability insurance program.[84] The House passed H.R. 7225, with amendments, by a vote of 372 (169-R, 203-D) to 31 (23-R, 8-D) on July 18, 1955 (R = Republican, D = Democrat).[85]

Although H.R. 7225 passed overwhelmingly in the House, the bill faced marked opposition in the Senate. One of the main concerns among Members who opposed the bill was the uncertainty over its potential cost. Some lawmakers worried that economic downturns would impel unemployed workers to apply to the disability insurance program, affecting the solvency of the OASI trust fund. Given these concerns, the Senate Committee on Finance removed the disability insurance provisions from H.R. 7225. The Senate report accompanying the 1956 amendments stated,

> Difficulties in determining eligibility, and other factors, lead to uncertainty as to the future costs of a cash disability program. Cost estimates in the field of disability benefits, as pointed out by the Chief Actuary of the Social Security Administration, are subject to a wider range of variation than are estimates for other types of benefits. The basic cost estimates which have been presented to the committee were based on high employment conditions; under low employment conditions, the cost would be significantly higher. The old-age and survivors insurance system is on a sound financial basis; your committee strongly believes that it must be kept so and should not be altered by adding a benefit

---

[84] U.S. Congress, House Committee on Ways and Means, *Social Security Amendments of 1955*, report to accompany H.R. 7225, 84th Cong., 1st sess., July 14, 1955, H.Rept. 1189.

[85] "Social Security Amendments of 1955," *Congressional Record*, vol. 101, part 8 (July 18, 1955), Roll call no. 119, not voting 29, pp. 10798-10799. See also SSA, "Vote Tallies: 1956 Social Security Amendments," https://www.ssa.gov/history/tally56.html. CRS was unable to find any discussion of a separate DI trust fund during the House floor debate on H.R. 7225.

> feature that could involve substantially higher costs than can be estimated.[86]

During Senate floor debate on H.R. 7225, Senator Walter F. George (D-GA) offered an amendment reinstating the disability insurance program along with the tax increase to finance it. To address concerns that a disability insurance program would pose a risk to the solvency of the OASI trust fund, the George amendment provided for a separate trust fund from which disability benefits would be paid. Supporters of the George amendment argued that a separate DI trust fund would isolate the OASI trust fund from any cost increases stemming from the new disability insurance program. For instance, during floor debate, Senator Thomas C. Hennings, Jr. (D-MO) remarked,

> The pending proposal, which the senior Senator from Georgia has submitted for himself ... proposes to set aside a separate trust fund for disability, and consequently does not go so far as to include it within the social-security framework. I believe this to be an extremely workable compromise—one which will eliminate any fear that the old-age and survivors insurance fund will be endangered, although I for one never shared this concern.[87]

Opponents of the George amendment argued that the creation of a separate DI trust fund would not sufficiently address their concerns about the potential cost of the program. Senator Wallace F. Bennett (R-UT) noted,

> The supporters of this amendment tell us that by setting up a separate trust fund they are not going to jeopardize the actuarial balance of the program of social security. I think it is rather obvious that once this amendment is enacted, there is small chance that the program would be

---

[86] U.S. Congress, Senate Committee on Finance, *Social Security Amendments of 1956*, 84th Cong., 2nd sess., June 5, 1956, S.Rept. 2133, p. 4, http://www.finance.senate.gov/imo/media/doc/Rpt84-2133.pdf.

[87] Sen. Thomas C. Hennings, Jr., "Social Security Amendments of 1956," Senate debate, *Congressional Record*, vol. 102, part 10 (July 17, 1956), p. 13043.

> discontinued because of lack of funds. The pressure to provide the necessary funds, either through direct Government grant or through increased taxes on the social security taxpayers, would demand the employment of one of those alternatives.[88]

The Senate narrowly passed the George amendment by a vote of 47 (6-R, 41-D) to 45 (38-R, 7- D).[89] The Senate went on to pass its version of H.R. 7225 by a vote of 90 (45-R, 45-D) to 0 on July 17, 1956.[90]

In conference, the House adopted the Senate provision establishing a separate DI trust fund.[91] The conference report on H.R. 7225 was cleared, without amendments, by voice votes in the House on July 26, 1956,[92] and in the Senate on July 27, 1956.[93] Following consideration of the conference report, Senator George stated in support of his amendment:

> Another feature of our proposal is that the funds for disability payments are earmarked in a wholly separate fund. These moneys will not be commingled in any way with the funds for old age insurance or for widows and orphans. The contribution income and the disbursements for disability payments will be kept completely distinct and separate. In this way the cost of disability benefits always will be definitely known and the costs always will be shown separately.
>
> The disability program is limited to a total of one-quarter of 1 percent of payroll from employers, one-quarter of 1 percent from employees' and three-eighths of 1 percent from the self-employed and disbursements cannot exceed the amount available for this purpose. Thus,

---

88 Sen. Wallace F. Bennett, "Social Security Amendments of 1956," Senate debate, *Congressional Record*, vol. 102, part 10 (July 17, 1956), p. 13035.

89 "Social Security Amendments of 1956," *Congressional Record*, vol. 102, part 10 (July 17, 1956), not voting 4, p. 13056. For background information on the George amendment, see SSA, "Legislative History: 1993 Disability Forum," https://www.ssa.gov/history/dibforum93.html. See also Berkowitz 1987, pp. 73-77.

90 "Social Security Amendments of 1956," *Congressional Record*, vol. 102, part 10 (July 17, 1956), p. 13103.

91 U.S. Congress, Conference Committee, *Social Security Amendments Act of 1956*, report to accompany H.R. 7225, 84th Cong., 2nd sess., July 26, 1956, H.Rept. 2936, pp. 25-26, http://www.finance.senate.gov/imo/media/doc/ ConfRpt84-2936.pdf.

92 "Amending Title II of Social Security Act," House, *Congressional Record*, vol. 102, part 11 (July 26, 1956), p. 14828.

93 "Social Security Act Amendments of 1956—Conference Report," *Congressional Record*, vol. 102, part 11 (July 27, 1956), p. 15107.

> the argument that has been made against the original proposal as considered by the Finance Committee, namely, that the cost of the proposal cannot be determined, is met by our amendment. Moreover, another argument that was made against the original proposal that the program eventually may cost more than originally estimated and may thus divert some of the funds from old-age or survivors insurance is also met by our proposal. Senators who have had any doubts about the financial aspects of the proposal can vote for the amendment with complete assurance as to its financial soundness.[94]

The DI trust fund was established on August 1, 1956—the day President Dwight D. Eisenhower signed into law the Social Security Amendments of 1956 (P.L. 84-880).[95]

APPENDIX B. KEY DATES PROJECTED FOR THE SOCIAL SECURITY TRUST FUNDS

Table B-1. Key Dates Projected for the Social Security Trust Funds as Shown Under the Intermediate Assumptions in Trustees Reports from 1983 to 2015

Year of Report	Year of Projected Depletion			Year That Cost First Exceeds Non-Interest Income			Year That Cost First Exceeds Total Income		
	OASI	DI	OASDI	OASI	DI	OASDI	OASI	DI	OASDI
Intermediate II-B Projections[a]									
1983	[b]	[b]	[b]	[c]	[c]	2021	[c]	[c]	2047
1984	[b]	2050	[b]	2021	2012	2021	2045	2038	2044
1985	2050	2034	2049	2019	2010	2019	2032	2020	2032
1986	2054	2026	2051	2020	2009	2019	2035	2017	2033
1987	2055	2023	2051	2020	2008	2019	2036	2013	2033
1988	2050	2027	2048	2019	2009	2019	2033	2016	2032

[94] Sen. Walter F. George, "Social Security Act Amendments of 1956—Conference Report," remarks in the Senate, *Congressional Record*, vol. 102, part 11 (July 27, 1956), p. 15108.

[95] U.S. Department of Health, Education, and Welfare, SSA, *Social Security Amendments of 1956 Volume 1*, 84th Congress, Downey Books, https://www.ssa.gov/history/legislative history.html.

Year of Report	**Year of Projected Depletion**			**Year That Cost First Exceeds Non-Interest Income**			**Year That Cost First Exceeds Total Income**		
	OASI	DI	OASDI	OASI	DI	OASDI	OASI	DI	OASDI
1989	2049	2025	2046	2019	2009	2018	2032	2014	2030
1990	2046	2020	2043	2019	2008	2017	2030	2011	2028
Intermediate Projections									
1991	2045	2015	2041	2018	1998	2017	2030	2011	2028
1992	2042	1997	2036	2018	1992	2016	2028	1992	2024
1993	2044	1995	2036	2019	1993	2017	2030	1993	2025
1994	2036	1995	2029	2016	1994	2013	2024	1994	2019
1995	2031	2016	2030	2014	2003	2013	2021	2007	2020
1996	2031	2015	2029	2014	2003	2012	2021	2007	2019
1997	2031	2015	2029	2014	2004	2012	2021	2007	2019
1998	2034	2019	2032	2015	2006	2013	2023	2009	2021
1999	2036	2020	2034	2015	2006	2014	2024	2009	2022
2000	2039	2023	2037	2016	2007	2015	2026	2012	2025
2001	2040	2026	2038	2016	2008	2016	2027	2015	2027
2002	2043	2028	2041	2018	2009	2017	2028	2018	2027
2003	2044	2028	2042	2018	2008	2018	2030	2018	2028
2004	2044	2029	2042	2018	2008	2018	2029	2017	2028
2005	2043	2027	2041	2018	2005	2017	2028	2014	2027
2006	2042	2025	2040	2018	2005	2017	2028	2013	2027
2007	2042	2026	2041	2018	2005	2017	2028	2013	2027
2008	2042	2025	2041	2018	2005	2017	2028	2012	2027

Source: CRS, based on data from the 1983 to 2015 Social Security trustees reports and information provided by SSA.

[a] From 1983 to 1990, two intermediate forecasts were prepared (II-A and II-B). The intermediate II-B forecast corresponds more closely to the intermediate forecast in subsequent years.

[b] Trust fund expected to remain solvent throughout the long-range projection period.

[c] Not available.

[d] The depletion dates in the 2015 trustees report were projected before the enactment of the Bipartisan Budget Act of 2015 (P.L. 114-74).

In: Social Security Disability
Editor: Michael Dimitriadis
ISBN: 978-1-53615-747-5

Chapter 2

SOCIAL SECURITY DISABILITY INSURANCE (SSDI) AND SUPPLEMENTAL SECURITY INCOME (SSI): ELIGIBILITY, BENEFITS, AND FINANCING*

William R. Morton

ABSTRACT

The Social Security Administration (SSA) is responsible for administering two federal entitlement programs established under the Social Security Act that provide income support to individuals with severe, longterm disabilities: Social Security Disability Insurance (SSDI) and Supplemental Security Income (SSI). SSDI is a workrelated social insurance program authorized under Title II of the act that provides monthly cash benefits to nonelderly disabled workers and their eligible dependents, provided the workers accrued a sufficient number of earnings credits during their careers in jobs subject to Social Security taxes. In contrast, SSI is a needbased public assistance program authorized under

* This is an edited, reformatted and augmented version of Congressional Research Service, Publication No. R44948, dated May 16, 2018.

Title XVI of the act that provides monthly cash payments to aged, blind, or disabled individuals (including blind or disabled children) who have limited assets and little or no Social Security or other income. In 2017, SSDI and SSI combined paid an estimated $199 billion in federally administered benefits to 14.5 million qualified disabled individuals and 1.5 million non-disabled dependents of disabled workers.

SSDI is part of the federal OldAge, Survivors, and Disability Insurance (OASDI) program, commonly known as Social Security. OASDI benefits are based on an insured worker's career average earnings in jobs covered by Social Security and designed to replace a portion of the income lost to a family due to the worker's retirement, disability, or death. Workers become insured against these events by acquiring a certain number of earnings credits during their careers in covered employment or self-employment. The SSDI component of the program provides benefits to disabled workers who are under Social Security's full retirement age and to their eligible spouses and children. The OldAge and Survivors Insurance (OASI) component also provides disability benefits to eligible disabled dependents of retired workers and to eligible disabled survivors of deceased beneficiaries and deceased insured workers. Although these individuals are not technically disability insurance beneficiaries, they are often included in the term *SSDI* because they receive Social Security benefits due to a qualifying impairment. SSDI and OASI disability benefits are paid from the Social Security trust funds, which are financed primarily by payroll and selfemployment taxes levied on the earnings of covered workers.

SSI is a federal assistance program that provides needy aged, blind, or disabled individuals with a guaranteed minimum income to meet their basic living expenses. Although there are no work or contribution requirements to qualify for payments, the program is based on need and therefore is restricted to individuals with limited financial means. SSI is commonly known as a program of "last resort" because claimants must first apply for most other benefits for which they may be eligible; cash assistance is awarded only to those whose assets and other income (if any) are within prescribed limits. The basic federal SSI payment is the same for all recipients and is reduced by the amount of other income that an individual receives. Some states supplement the federal SSI payment with solely state funds. Unlike Social Security, SSI is financed by appropriations from general revenues.

Most claimants are considered disabled for SSDI and SSI eligibility purposes if they are unable to engage in any substantial gainful activity (SGA) by reason of any medically determinable physical or mental impairment that is expected to last for at least 12 months or to result in death. In 2018, the SGA earnings limit is $1,180 per month for most individuals. Claimants generally qualify if they have an impairment (or combination of impairments) of such severity that they are unable to perform any kind of substantial work that exists in significant numbers in the national economy, taking into consideration their age, education, and work experience. If a claimant's application for benefits is denied at any point during the disability determination process, the claimant has the right to appeal the determination or decision.

INTRODUCTION

The Social Security Administration (SSA) is responsible for administering two federal entitlement programs that provide income support to individuals with severe, long-term disabilities: Social Security Disability Insurance (SSDI) and Supplemental Security Income (SSI).[1] SSDI is a workrelated social insurance program that provides monthly cash benefits to nonelderly disabled workers and their eligible dependents, provided the workers accrued a sufficient number of earnings credits during their careers in jobs subject to Social Security taxes. In contrast, SSI is a needbased public assistance program that provides monthly cash payments to aged, blind, or disabled individuals (including blind or disabled children) who have limited assets and little or no Social Security or other income. Both programs use the same basic definition of disability to determine eligibility; however, by virtue of design, each program serves a somewhat different population. In 2017, SSDI and SSI combined paid an estimated $199 billion in federally administered benefits to 14.5 million qualified disabled individuals and 1.5 million nondisabled dependents of disabled workers.[2]

This chapter discusses the rules and processes used to determine eligibility for SSDI and SSI. It also explains how benefit amounts are

---

[1] See 2 U.S.C. §622 for the definition of *entitlement authority*.

[2] Estimates calculated by the Congressional Research Service (CRS) based on a variety of data sources available on the Social Security Administration's (SSA) website. For purposes of these estimates, the term *Social Security Disability Insurance (SSDI)* includes Social Security disability beneficiaries whose benefits are paid from the Old-Age and Survivors Insurance (OASI) trust fund. In addition, the term *qualified disabled individuals* excludes SSI-only recipients aged 65 or older. Congressional clients may contact the author for the specific methodology used in the calculations.

computed, the types of non-cash benefits available to individuals who meet SSA's disability standards, and how each program is financed.

Social Security Disability Insurance

Old-Age, Survivors, and Disability Insurance (OASDI), commonly known as Social Security, is a federal social insurance program established under Title II of the Social Security Act that provides workers and their families with a measure of protection against the loss of income due to the worker's retirement, disability, or death.[3] Workers obtain insurance protection by working for a sufficient number of years in jobs where their earnings are subject to Social Security taxes and therefore are creditable for program purposes. Social Security is financed largely on a payas you-go basis, which means that payroll and self-employment tax contributions from current workers, their employers, and self-employed individuals are used to make monthly benefit payments to today's beneficiaries. In 2017, an estimated 173 million people (or about 94% of all workers) worked in paid employment or selfemployment covered by Social Security, and the program paid monthly benefits to approximately 62 million beneficiaries (Figure 1).[4]

The SSDI component of the program, which was enacted in 1956 and implemented in 1957, provides monthly benefits to statutorily disabled workers who are under Social Security's full retirement age (FRA) and to their eligible spouses, divorced spouses, minor children, student children, and disabled adult children. The Old-Age and Survivors Insurance (OASI) component of Social Security also provides benefits to eligible disabled dependents of retired workers and to eligible survivors of deceased beneficiaries and deceased insured workers. Although these individuals are not technically disability insurance beneficiaries, they are often included in

---

[3] 42 U.S.C. §§401 et seq. See CRS Report R42035, *Social Security Primer*.

[4] SSA, Office of Legislation and Congressional Affairs (OLCA), *2018 Social Security/SSI/Medicare Information*, February 15, 2018, https://www.ssa.gov/legislation/2018%20Fact%20Sheet.pdf.

the term *SSDI*, because they receive Social Security benefits due to a qualifying impairment. In December 2017, the SSDI component of Social Security paid benefits to 10.4 million individuals, including 8.7 million disabled workers and 1.7 million of their dependents.[5] That same month, the OASI component paid benefits to 1.2 million OASI disability beneficiaries.[6]

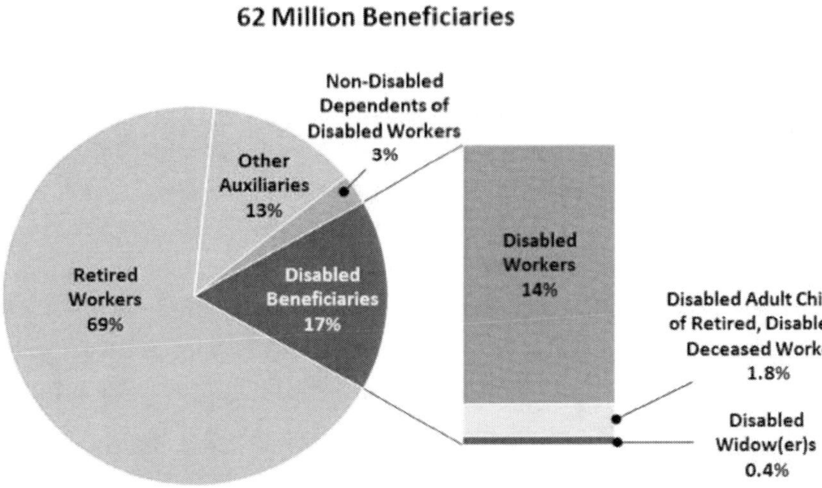

Source: Congressional Research Service (CRS), based on Social Security Administration (SSA), Office of the Chief Actuary (OCACT), "Benefits Paid by Type of Beneficiary," https://www.ssa.gov/oact/ProgData/icp.html.

Notes: Subtotals may not sum to totals due to rounding. The term *other auxiliaries* refers to non-disabled dependents and survivors under the Old-Age and Survivors Insurance (OASI) component of the program.

Figure 1. Social Security Beneficiaries, by Type, December 2017.

Eligibility Requirements for Disabled Workers

To qualify for SSDI, disabled workers must (1) be insured in the event of disability, (2) be under Social Security's FRA, (3) have a qualifying

[5] SSA, Office of the Chief Actuary (OCACT), "Benefits Paid by Type of Beneficiary," https://www.ssa.gov/oact/ProgData/icp.html.

[6] Ibid.

impairment (see the "Definition of Disability" section of this chapter), and (4) have filed an application for benefits.[7]

Disability-Insured Status

Workers become insured for Social Security by acquiring a certain number of *quarters of coverage* (QCs) during their careers in paid employment or self-employment covered by Social Security. A worker's job is considered *covered* if the services performed in that job or net earnings derived by the individual result in wages or net earnings from selfemployment income that are taxable and creditable for insured status and benefit computation purposes. In 2018, workers receive one QC for each $1,320 in covered earnings, up to the maximum of four QCs per year, regardless of when the money is earned.[8] Thus, if a worker earns $5,280 in covered wages or net earnings from selfemployment income during the first week of January 2018, then he or she would be credited with the maximum number of QCs for the calendar year. The amount of earnings needed for one QC is adjusted annually for average earnings growth in the national economy, as measured by SSA's Average Wage Index (AWI).[9] Requiring individuals to have earned a certain number of QCs to qualify for cash benefits ensures that such individuals contribute a minimum amount to the insurance system via payroll and self-employment taxes on each QC's worth of covered earnings.

To be insured in the event of disability, known as *disability insured*, covered workers must be both fully insured for Social Security and meet a recencyofwork requirement. To be*fully insured* for SSDI, covered workers must have at least one QC for each calendar year after they turned 21 years old and before the year they became disabled.[10] The minimum number of QCs for fully insured status is six for the youngest workers (or 1.5 years of covered work); the minimum number of QCs needed for workers aged 62 or older is 40 (or 10 years of covered work). In effect, individuals must

[7] Section 223(a) of the Social Security Act; 42 U.S.C. §423(a).
[8] SSA, OCACT, "Quarter of Coverage," https://www.ssa.gov/oact/cola/QC.html.
[9] SSA, OCACT, "National Average Wage Index," https://www.ssa.gov/oact/cola/AWI.html.
[10] Section 214(a) of the Social Security Act; 42 U.S.C. §414(a). See also 20 C.F.R. §404.110.

have worked in covered employment or self-employment for about a quarter of their adult lives to be fully insured.

To meet the *recency-of-work requirement*, disabled workers generally need 20 QCs during the 40- quarter period immediately before the onset of the disability.[11] In other words, individuals must have worked in covered employment or selfemployment for five of the 10 years before becoming disabled. However, workers under 31 years old may meet the recencyofwork requirement with fewer QCs based on their age.[12] In 2017, SSDI provided disability insurance coverage to 154 million workers, with about 89% of covered workers aged 2164 insured for SSDI.[13]

Under the Full Retirement Age

An insured worker must also be under Social Security's FRA to be entitled to SSDI, which for workers born from 1943 through 1954 is age 66.[14] FRA is the age at which unreduced Social Security retired-worker benefits are first payable. Upon attaining FRA, disabled workers are automatically transitioned from disabledworker benefits (or SSDI) to retiredworker benefits (or OASI); however, this change generally does not affect the amount of Social Security benefits paid to them or their dependents. Under current law, Social Security's FRA increases in two-month increments for workers born from 1955 through 1959 until reaching the age of 67 for workers born in 1960 or later. SSDI is not available to workers who have already attained FRA.

---

[11] Section 223(c)(1) of the Social Security Act; 42 U.S.C. §423(c)(1). See also 20 C.F.R. §404.130.

[12] Workers aged 24-30 need quarters of coverage (QCs) in at least one-half of the quarters in the period beginning with the quarter after the quarter they attained the age of 21 and ending in the quarter in which their disability began. Workers under 24 years old need at least six QCs in the 12-quarter period ending with the quarter in which they became disabled. Blind workers are exempt from the recency-of-work requirement. Special rules apply to individuals who become disabled again at age 31 or older after having had a prior period of disability established which began before age 31. See SSA, *How You Earn Credits*, January 2018, https://www.ssa.gov/pubs/EN-05-10072.pdf.

[13] SSA, OCACT, "Disability Insured Workers," https://www.ssa.gov/OACT/STATS/table4c2DI.html, See also SSA, OCACT, "Social Security Program Fact Sheet," March 1, 2018, https://www.ssa.gov/oact/FACTS/.

[14] Section 216(l) of the Social Security Act; 42 U.S.C. §416(l).

Eligibility Requirements for Dependents and Survivors

In addition to the disabled worker's own benefit, SSDI provides benefits to certain family members of the worker. Social Security pays benefits to family members because workers with one or more dependents are presumed to have greater financial need when they retire, become disabled, or die than similarly situated workers who are single. The OASI component also provides benefits to eligible disabled dependents of retired workers and to eligible survivors of deceased insured workers. The term *deceased insured workers* includes deceased individuals who received Social Security retired or disabled-worker benefits and non-beneficiary workers who were insured for Social Security at the time of their deaths.

SSDI Spouses

Validly married spouses of disabled workers qualify for benefits if they (1) are aged 62 or older or are any age and have an eligible child in their care who is under the age of 16 or disabled, (2) are not entitled to a retired or disabled-worker benefit equal to or larger than the spousal benefit, and (3) have filed an application for benefits.[15] Spouses also must have been married to the worker for at least one continuous year immediately before the day on which the claimant's application is filed.[16] This provision is known as a *duration-of-marriage requirement*.

Divorced spouses of disabled workers may qualify if they (1) are aged 62 or older, (2) are unmarried, (3) are not entitled to a retired or disabledworker benefit equal to or larger than the spousal benefit, and (4) have filed an application for benefits.[17] Divorced spouses must have been

---

[15] Section 202(b) and 202(c) of the Social Security Act; 42 U.S.C. §402(b) and 402(c). See also 20 C.F.R. §404.330.

[16] Section 216(b)(2) and 216(f)(2) of the Social Security Act; 42 U.S.C. §416(b)(2) and 416(f)(2). See also 20 C.F.R. §404.330(a)(1). To determine the *validity* of the marriage, SSA looks to the laws of the state (as interpreted by the courts of that state) in which the insured worker is domiciled at the time of application. Alternatively, the relationship requirement is met if, under state intestate law, the applicant would be able to inherit a wife's or husband's share of the insured worker's personal property if the insured worker were to die without leaving a will.

[17] Section 202(b) and 202(c) of the Social Security Act; 42 U.S.C. §402(b) and 402(c). See also 20 C.F.R. §404.331.

married to the worker for at least 10 years immediately before the date the divorce became final.[18]

SSDI Minor Children

Eligible minor children of disabled workers qualify for benefits if they (1) are unmarried, (2) are under the age of 18, and (3) have filed an application for benefits.[19] An *eligible child* is the natural (i.e., biological) child, adopted child, stepchild, equitably adopted child, grandchild, or step grandchild of the insured worker on whose earnings record the claim is based.[20] For certain child claims, such as those involving stepchildren, an explicit dependency requirement must be met, which generally involves the insured worker providing evidence that the child is living with the worker or is receiving at least onehalf of his or her support from the worker.[21] Otherwise, the child is presumed to be dependent on the insured worker for his or her support. For more information on the rules governing a child's status for purposes of SSDI entitlement, see "GN 00306.001 Determining Status as Child," in SSA's policy manual, the Program Operations Manual System (POMS).[22]

SSDI Student Children

Eligible student children of disabled workers qualify for benefits if they (1) are unmarried, (2) are aged 18-19, (3) are a full-time student at an elementary or secondary school, and (4) have filed an application for benefits.[23] To be considered a full-time student, the child's scheduled

---

[18] Section 216(d) of the Social Security Act; 42 U.S.C. §416 (d). See also 20 C.F.R. §404.331.

[19] Section 202(d)(1)(B)(i) of the Social Security Act; 42 U.S.C. §402(d)(1)(B)(i). See also 20 C.F.R. §404.350.

[20] Section 216(e) and 216(h) of the Social Security Act; 42 U.S.C. §416(e) and 416(h). See also 20 C.F.R. §§404.354- 404.359. In determining a child's relationship to an insured worker, SSA looks to the laws of the state (as interpreted by the courts of that state) in which the parent is domiciled at the time of application. A child may qualify as an insured worker's child for purposes of entitlement to child's insurance benefits if he or she would inherit the parent's personal property under state intestate law.

[21] 20 C.F.R. §§404.360-404.366.

[22] SSA, Program Operations Manual System (POMS), "GN 00306.001 Determining Status as Child," August 30, 2016, https://secure.ssa.gov/poms.nsf/lnx/0200306001.

[23] Section 202(d)(1)(B)(i) of the Social Security Act; 42 U.S.C. §402(d)(1)(B)(i). See also 20 C.F.R. §404.350.

attendance must generally be at the rate of at least 20 hours per week (certain exceptions apply).[24] Benefits usually continue until the child graduates or until two months after the child attains the age of 19, whichever occurs first. (Social Security benefits for students aged 18-21 enrolled in post-secondary education [i.e., college] were phased out during the 1980s).

SSDI Disabled Adult Children

Eligible disabled adult children of disabled workers qualify for benefits if they (1) are unmarried, (2) are aged 18 or older, (3) have a qualifying impairment that began before they attained the age of 22, and (4) have filed an application for benefits.[25] Disabled adult children (DACs) are also called Childhood Disability Beneficiaries (CDB) by SSA. DAC beneficiaries must meet same the disability standard as disabled workers (discussed later in this chapter). Although DAC beneficiaries must generally be unmarried to be entitled to benefits, the law provides that they may marry other DAC beneficiaries, along with most other types of Social Security beneficiaries.[26] This exception does not apply if the marriage was to a minor or student Social Security beneficiary or to a SSI only recipient.

OASI Disabled Widow(er)s

Disabled surviving spouses of deceased insured workers qualify for benefits if they (1) are at least 50 years of age but not yet 60 years of age, (2) are unmarried unless the remarriage occurred after attainment of age 50 and the claimant was disabled at the time of the remarriage, (3) are not entitled to a retired-worker benefit equal to or larger than the divorced spousal benefit, (4) have a qualifying impairment that began within seven

---

[24] 20 C.F.R. §404.367.

[25] Section 202(d)(1)(B)(ii) of the Social Security Act; 42 U.S.C. §402(d) (1)(B)(ii). See also 20 C.F.R. §404.350.

[26] Section 202(d)(5) of the Social Security Act; 42 U.S.C. §402(d)(5). See also 20 C.F.R. §404.352(b)(4).

years of the insured worker's death or within seven years of a previous entitlement to such benefits, and (5) have filed an application for benefits.[27]

The disabled surviving spouse must also have married to the worker for at least nine months. The duration of marriage requirement may be waived, however, if the worker was reasonably expected to live for nine months at the time of the marriage and (1) the worker's death was accidental, (2) the worker's death was in the line of duty while he or she was a member of a military serving on active duty, or (3) the claimant was married to the worker for at least nine months as a result of a previous marriage.[28] Disabled divorced surviving spouses may qualify if they were married to the deceased insured worker for at least 10 years immediately before the date the divorce became final.[29] As with disabled adult children, disabled widow(er)s must meet same the disability standard as disabled workers.

OASI Disabled Adult Children

Eligible disabled adult children of retired or deceased insured workers qualify for benefits if they (1) are unmarried, (2) are aged 18 or older, (3) have a qualifying impairment that began before they attained the age of 22, and (4) have filed an application for benefits.[30] (The same provisions governing SSDI DAC beneficiaries also govern OASI DAC beneficiaries.) Unlike most types of Social Security beneficiaries, there is no maximum age limit for disabled adult children. In December 2016, there were 11,260 DAC beneficiaries aged 80 or older, all of whom were dependents or survivors of retired or deceased insured workers.[31]

---

[27] Section 202(e) and 202(f) of the Social Security Act; 42 U.S.C. §402(e) and 402(f). See also 20 C.F.R. §§404.335- 404.336.

[28] Section 216(k) of the Social Security Act; 42 U.S.C. §416(k). See also 20 C.F.R. §404.335(a).

[29] Section 216(d)(2) and 216(d)(5) of the Social Security Act; 42 U.S.C. §416(d)(2) and 416(d)(5). See also 20 C.F.R. §404.336(a)(2).

[30] Section 202(d)(1)(B)(ii) of the Social Security Act; 42 U.S.C. §402(d) (1)(B)(ii). See also 20 C.F.R. §404.350.

[31] SSA, Office of Research, Evaluation, and Statistics (ORES), *Annual Statistical Supplement, 2017*, March 2018, Table 5.A1.4, https://www.ssa.gov/policy/docs/statcomps/supplement/ (hereinafter "2017 Annual Statistical Supplement").

Termination Events

Table 1. Number and Share of Disabled Workers Terminated from SSDI and the Annual Termination Rate, by Reason for Termination, 2016

Reason for Termination	Terminations		Termination Rate
	Number	Share	
Total	820,372	100.0%	9.3%
Attainment of Full Retirement Age (FRA)	470,320	57.3	5.3
Death of Beneficiary	251,492	30.7	2.8
Return to Work	47,887	5.8	0.5
Medical Improvement	37,623	4.6	0.4
Other	13,050	1.6	0.1

Source: Congressional Research Service (CRS), based on the following data sources: Social Security Administration (SSA), Office of Research, Evaluation, and Statistics (ORES), *Annual Statistical Report on the Social Security Disability Insurance Program, 2016,* October 2017, Table 50, https://www.ssa.gov/policy/docs/statcomps/di_asr/2016/sect03f.html#table50; and SSA, Office of the Chief Actuary (OCACT), "Benefits Paid by Type of Beneficiary," https://www.ssa.gov/oact/ProgData/icp.html.

Notes: The term *termination rate* is the ratio of the number of terminations to the average number of disabled-worker beneficiaries during the year. In 2016, the average number of disabled-worker beneficiaries was 8,862,068. The term *return to work* means that the disabled worker's termination was due to monthly earnings above the substantial gainful activity (SGA) threshold, which in 2016 was $1,130 per month for most workers.

In general, disabled workers continue to receive SSDI benefits until they (1) die, (2) attain FRA, (3) no longer meet the statutory definition of disability (i.e., medically improve), or (4) return to work (i.e., have monthly earnings that exceed certain thresholds discussed later in this chapter). In 2016, the SSDI *termination rate* the ratio of disabled-worker terminations to the average number of disabled worker beneficiaries during the year was 9.3% (Table 1). The majority of disabled worker terminations in 2016 were due to attainment of FRA.

With the exception of certain divorced spouses, receipt of SSDI dependents' benefits is linked to the disabled worker's entitlement to Social Security. If a disabled worker's benefits are terminated, benefits payable on his or her earnings record are also generally terminated.

Dependents and survivors who no longer meet the relevant entitlement factors are terminated from the rolls as well.[32]

Cash Benefits

Social Security Benefit Formula

Initial monthly Social Security benefits are based on an insured worker's creditable, career average earnings in Social Security covered employment or self employment. The Social Security benefit formula is progressive, replacing a greater share of career-average earnings for low wage or intermittent workers than for high wage workers. In computing the initial benefit amount, a worker's annual taxable earnings are indexed (i.e., adjusted) to reflect changes in national earnings levels over his or her career, up to the second calendar year before the *year of eligibility* (i.e., the year a worker attains age 62, becomes disabled, or dies).[33] Next, years with the highest earnings in the applicable computation period are summed and then divided over the number of months in that period to produce the worker's *average indexed monthly earnings* (AIME).[34] A formula is then applied to the worker's AIME to compute the *primary insurance amount* (PIA), which is the worker's basic benefit before any adjustments are made. In 2018, the PIA is determined using the following formula:

- 90% of the first $895 of AIME, *plus*
- 32% of AIME over $985 and through $5,397 (if any), *plus*
- 15% of AIME over $5,397 (if any).[35]

---

[32] For termination data on SSDI dependents and OASI disability beneficiaries, SSA, ORES, *Annual Statistical Report on the Social Security Disability Insurance Program, 2016,* October 2017, Table 50, https://www.ssa.gov/policy/docs/statcomps/di_asr/2015/index.html (hereinafter "2016 SSDI Annual Report").

[33] CRS Report R43542, *How Social Security Benefits Are Computed: In Brief.* Earnings in years after the indexing year are counted at their actual value.

[34] Up to five of the worker's lowest-earning years are dropped from the computation.

[35] SSA, OCACT, "Benefit Formula Bend Points," https://www.ssa.gov/oact/cola/bendpoints.html.

The dollar amounts used in this formula are adjusted annually for average earnings growth in the national economy, as measured by the AWI. The worker's PIA is subsequently adjusted to account for inflation through cost of living adjustments (COLAs), as measured by the Consumer Price Index for Urban Wage Earners and Clerical Workers (CPI-W).[36]

Spouses and dependent children of disabled workers each receive up to 50% of the worker's basic benefit amount (i.e., the PIA). These supplementary benefits effectively increase the worker's overall *replacement rate*—the ratio of benefits received to the worker's previous earnings—to account for additional expenses associated with each dependent. Benefits for dependents are less than the worker's own benefit because a family is assumed to have economics of scale.

Disabled widow(er)s receive up to 71.5% of a deceased worker's PIA. Disabled adult children of retired workers receive up to 50% of the worker's PIA, and disabled adult children of deceased insured workers receive up to 75% of the worker's basic benefit. Initial benefits for survivors are higher than benefits for dependents because a family of a deceased worker experiences a complete loss of that worker's earnings, whereas a family of a retired or disabled worker is compensated partially through the worker's own Social Security benefit.

Maximum Family Benefit Limits

Monthly benefits for retired or disabled workers and their eligible family members and for survivors of deceased insured workers are subject to family maximum provisions, which limit the total amount of benefits that can be paid on a worker's earnings record. Therefore, a dependent's or survivor's *payable benefit amount* may be less than the maximum share of the worker's PIA for that type of benefit. The family maximum for a disabled worker is the smaller of (1) 85% of the worker's AIME (or 100%

[36] CRS Report 94-803, *Social Security: Cost-of-Living Adjustments*. Pursuant to the Department of the Treasury's 2010 rule (75 *Federal Register* 80315), all federal benefit payments must be made via electronic funds transfer (ETF), unless the individual can demonstrate hardship due to age, mental impairment, or geographic location. Social Security beneficiaries receive their payments by direct deposit, either to a bank account or to a Direct Express® card account.

of the PIA if larger) or (2) 150% of the PIA.[37] If the total amount of all family benefits exceeds the maximum amount, then the benefit of each family member (other than the worker) is reduced proportionately. In December 2016, 27% of all disabled-worker families were receiving maximum family benefits.[38] A different family maximum formula applies to OASI disability beneficiaries.[39]

Workers' Compensation and Public Disability Benefit Offset

Disabled workers who also receive workers' compensation (WC) or certain other public disability benefits (PDB) may have their SSDI benefits reduced.[40] The Social Security Act contains a provision that reduces the SSDI benefits of disabled workers whose combined disability benefits from SSDI and WC/PDB exceed 80% of their average earnings prior to the onset of disability.[41] PDBs *do not* include disability compensation or pension benefits administered by the Department of Veterans Affairs (VA), disability benefits based on need (e.g., SSI, state or local general assistance [GA]), disability payments made to public employees based on employment covered by Social Security (except for WC), or wholly private pensions or private disability insurance benefits.[42] The purpose of this provision is to reduce the attractiveness of SSDI benefits for concurrently eligible individuals who could otherwise remain in the labor force. The WC/PDB offset no longer applies once the disabled worker attains FRA and converts to retired worker benefits.[43] In 17 states and the Commonwealth of Puerto

---

[37] Section 203(a)(6) of the Social Security Act; 42 U.S.C. §403(a)(6). See also 20 C.F.R. §404.403d-1.

[38] 2016 SSDI Annual Report, Table 30.

[39] Section 203(a)(1) of the Social Security Act; 42 U.S.C. §403(a)(1). See also 20 C.F.R. §404.403(d) and SSA, OCACT, "Formula for Family Maximum Benefit," https://www.ssa.gov/oact/cola/familymax.html.

[40] CRS Report R44580, *Workers' Compensation: Overview and Issues*.

[41] Section 224 of the Social Security Act; 42 U.S.C. §424a. See also 20 C.F.R. §404.408 and *SSA, How Workers' Compensation and Other Disability Payments May Affect Your Benefits*, https://www.ssa.gov/pubs/EN-05-10018.pdf.

[42] Section 224(a)(2)(B) of the Social Security Act; 42 U.S.C. §424a(A)(2)(B). See also 20 C.F.R. §404.408(b).

[43] Section 201 of the Stephen Beck, Jr., Achieving a Better Life Experience Act of 2014 (ABLE Act; Division B of P.L. 113-295) increased the age at which the offset no longer applies from 65 years old to full retirement age (FRA).

Rico, the direction of the offset is reversed, resulting in a reduction in the WC or PDB payment instead of the SSDI benefit.[44] In December 2016, approximately 5.2% of disabled workers were eligible for WC or PDB payments, and about 1.2% of disabled workers were subject to the WC/PDB offset.[45]

Average and Total Monthly Benefit Levels

Table 2. Average and Total Monthly Benefit Amounts of SSDI and OASI Disability Beneficiaries, by Type of Beneficiary, December 2017

Type of Beneficiary	Number of Beneficiaries	Average Monthly Benefit	Estimated Total Monthly Benefits (in thousands)
Social Security Disability Insurance (SSDI)			
Disabled Workers	8,695,475	$1,197	$10,407,353
Spouses of Disabled Workers	126,154	335	42,315
Minor Children of Disabled Workers	1,418,446	351	497,761
Student Children of Disabled Workers	47,920	499	23,898
Disabled Adult Children of Disabled Workers	123,257	493	60,782
Total	10,411,252	$1,060	$11,032,075
Old-Age and Survivors Insurance (OASI)			
Disabled Widow(er)s	258,286	729	188,404
Disabled Adult Children of Retired Workers	319,162	696	222,255
Disabled Adult Children of Deceased Workers	662,986	877	581,419
Total	1,240,416	$800	$992,063

Source: CRS, based on SSA, OCACT, "Benefits Paid by Type of Beneficiary," https://www.ssa.gov/oact/ProgData/icp.html.

Notes: Average and total monthly benefit amounts are rounded to the nearest whole dollar. Total monthly benefits are derived by multiplying the number of beneficiaries by the unrounded average benefit amount. These estimates are nearly identical to the rounded total monthly benefit data reported in Table 2 of SSA's "Monthly Statistical Snapshot." Estimated data are used because the snapshot does not provide data for the same beneficiary categories used in this chapter.

---

[44] SSA, POMS, "DI 52105.001 Reverse Offset Plans," February 12, 2018, http://policy.ssa.gov/poms.nsf/lnx/0452105001. The reverse offset also applies to railroad sickness pensions administered by the Railroad Retirement Board (RRB).

[45] 2016 SSDI Annual Report, Tables 1 and 31.

In December 2017, the average monthly SSDI benefit was $1,197 for disabled workers, which on an annualized basis was $14,364 (Table 2).[46] The average monthly benefit for SSDI dependents ranged from $335 to $499. That month, SSDI paid out over $11 billion in benefits. For OASI disability beneficiaries, the average benefit that month was $800, and total monthly benefits were $992 million.

When SSDI Benefits Start (The Five-Month Waiting Period)

For disabled workers[47] and disabled widow(er)s,[48] entitlement to cash benefits begins five full consecutive calendar months after their disability onset date. This requirement is known as the *five-month waiting period.* The *onset date* is the first day that a claimant meets the definition of disability under Title II of the Social Security Act in addition to all relevant entitlement factors. If SSA establishes an onset date after the first day of the month, the five-month waiting period starts on the first day of the following month. For example, if a claimant's onset date were April 11, the waiting period would begin on May 1 and would end on September 30. Benefits would first be payable for the month of October, which is the sixth full month after the disability onset date. Because SSA pays Social Security benefits in the month *following* the month for which they are due, the individual would receive October's payment on one of several possible payment dates in November (i.e., the seventh month after the onset of disability).[49]

Exceptions to the Five-Month Waiting Period for Cash Benefits

Disabled adult children are not subject to the five month waiting period; their entitlement to benefits begins the month after their disability

---

[46] SSA, OCACT, "Benefits Paid by Type of Beneficiary," https://www.ssa.gov/oact/ProgData/icp.html.

[47] Section 223(a)(1) and 223(c)(2) of the Social Security Act; 42 U.S.C. §423(a)(1) and 423(c)(2).

[48] Section 202(e)(1)(F)(i), 202(e)(5)(A), 202(f)(1)(F)(i), and 202(f)(5)(A) of the Social Security Act; 42 U.S.C. §402(e)(1)(F)(i), 402(e)(5)(A), 402(f)(1)(F)(i), and 402(f)(5)(A).

[49] See 20 C.F.R. §404.1807 and SSA, "Schedule of Social Security Payments," https://www.ssa.gov/pubs/calendar.htm.

onset date, provided they meet all other entitlement factors.[50] In addition, former disabled workers do not have to serve a new waiting period if they become disabled again within 60 months (or five years) after their previous entitlement to cash benefits or period of disability ended.[51] A similar provision applies to disabled widow(er)s who become disabled again before age 60, and the new period of disability began within 84 months (or seven years) of the month they were last entitled to disabled-widow(er) benefits.[52] Furthermore, disabled widow(er)s may count months of eligibility for SSI or federally administered state supplementary payments (discussed later in this chapter) toward the five-month waiting period.[53] Under current law, there are no exceptions to the five-month waiting period for claimants with specific medical conditions, even those considered terminal.

Retroactive Benefits

SSDI provides retroactive benefits for up to 12 months immediately *before* the month the disabled worker files an application, provided the worker met all other entitlement factors prior to the filing date. Because of the five-month waiting period for cash benefits, the earliest effective date for a SSDI application can be no more than 17 months before the month in which the application is filed.[54] The retroactivity provision was established because an early study of the program found that a large share of claimants did not file for benefits in the first month for which they were eligible.

---

[50] There is no statutory exception to the five-month waiting period for disabled adult children. Section 202(d) of the Social Security Act (42 U.S.C. §402[d]) simply does not require claimants to serve a waiting period to be entitled to child's insurance benefits due to a disability. In the case of disabled adult child of a disabled worker, the disabled adult child's benefits start only after the disabled worker has satisfied the five-month waiting period requirement and is entitled to disabled-worker benefits.

[51] Section 223(a)(1) of the Social Security Act; 42 U.S.C. §423(a)(1). See also 20 C.F.R. §404.315(a)(4).

[52] Sections 202(e)(4)(C), 202(e)(5)(A)(ii)(II), 202(f)(4)(C), and 202(f)(5)(A)(ii)(II) of the Social Security Act; 42 U.S.C. §§402(e)(4)(C), 402(e)(5)(A)(ii)(II), 402(f)(4)(C), and 402(f)(5)(A)(ii)(II). See also 20 C.F.R. §§404.335(c)(2) and 404.336(c)(2).

[53] Section 202(e)(5)(B) and 202(f)(5)(B) of the Social Security Act; 42 U.S.C. §402(e)(5)(B) and 402(f)(5)(B). See also 20 C.F.R. §§404.335(c)(3) and 404.336(c)(3).

[54] Sections 202(e)(5)(A), 202(f)(5)(A), and 223(c)(2) of the Social Security Act; 42 U.S.C. §§402(e)(5)(A), 402(f)(5)(A), and 423(c)(2). See also 20 C.F.R. §§404.315(a)(4), 404.335(c)(2), and 404.336(c)(2).

Retroactive benefits should not be confused with *past-due benefits*, which include both retroactive benefits and benefits owed to claimants for months in which they met all relevant entitlement factors *in or after* the month of application.

Medicare

In addition to cash benefits, Social Security disability beneficiaries (i.e., disabled workers, disabled widow[er]s, and disabled adult children) qualify for health coverage under Medicare.[55] Established under Title XVIII of the Social Security Act, Medicare is a federal social insurance program that pays for covered health care services for most individuals aged 65 or older, the majority of Social Security disability beneficiaries and railroad disability annuitants under 65 years old, and certain other individuals who have qualifying impairments.[56] (Medicare is not provided to nondisabled dependents under 65 years old.) As with Social Security, workers earn Medicare coverage by working and paying taxes for a sufficient number of years in covered employment or self-employment. For most individuals, entitlement to Medicare is linked to entitlement to Social Security benefits. Social Security disability beneficiaries under 65 years old are provided Medicare because they generally have medical conditions that require significant health care resources. However, many beneficiaries are often unable to work enough to gain health insurance through an employer or to pay for such insurance on their own. In 2013, annual Medicare spending per disabled beneficiary under 65 years old was about $12,776.[57]

---

[55] See SSA, "Medicare Information," https://www.ssa.gov/disabilityresearch/wi/medicare.htm.

[56] 42 U.S.C. §§1395 et seq. For more information on Medicare, see CRS Report R40425, *Medicare Primer*.

[57] Medicare Payment Advisory Commission (MEDPAC), *A Data Book: Health Care Spending and the Medicare Program,* June 2017, p. 21, http://www.medpac.gov/docs/default-source/data-book/jun17_databookentirereport_sec.pdf. Estimate excludes spending on individuals under 65 years old who are entitled to Medicare on the basis of end-stage renal disease (ESRD).

24-Month Waiting Period

Social Security disability beneficiaries under the age of 65 are entitled to Medicare after 24 months of entitlement to cash benefits.[58] This requirement is known as the *24-month waiting period.* After factoring in the five-month waiting period for cash benefits, disabled workers and disabled widow(er)s typically become entitled to Medicare 29full calendar months after their disability onset date (i.e., the first day of the 30th full month following disablement). For example, if a claimant's onset date were January 11, 2016, the five-month waiting period for cash benefits would be February 2016 through June 2016, with entitlement to cash benefits beginning July 2016. The claimant would become entitled to Medicare on July 1, 2018, which is the first day of the 25th month of disability benefit entitlement. Disabled adult children are not subject to the five-month waiting period for cash benefits and therefore generally become entitled to Medicare 24 full calendar months after the onset of disability. Due in part to the 24month waiting period, only 68% of all disabled beneficiaries under 65 years old reported entitlement to Medicare in 2016.[59]

Exceptions to the 24-Month Waiting Period

General

Social Security disability beneficiaries may count months in which they were previously entitled (or deemed entitled) to cash benefits toward the current Medicare waiting period if their previous entitlement ended within 60 months (or five years) before the month of current onset for disabled workers or 84 months (or seven years) before the month of current onset for disabled widow(er)s and disabled adult children.[60] Disability beneficiaries who meet the criteria above and were previously entitled to

---

[58] Section 226(b)(2)(A) of the Social Security Act; 42 U.S.C. §426(b)(2)(A). See also 42 C.F.R. §406.12.

[59] CRS analysis of the 2017 Current Population Survey Annual Social and Economic Supplement (CPS ASEC).

[60] Section 226(f) of the Social Security Act; 42 U.S.C. §426(f). See also 42 C.F.R. §406.12(b)(1) and 406.12(b)(2).

Medicare do not have to serve a *second waiting period* for Medicare, because they received cash benefits for at least 24 months during their previous period of disability benefit entitlement and therefore have a sufficient number of months to credit toward the new waiting period. Individuals who become disabled again *after* the prescribed period may still be able to count months of previous disability benefit entitlement toward the Medicare waiting period if their current impairment is the same, or directly related to, the impairment that served as the basis for disability during a previous period of entitlement.[61]

In addition, disabled widow(er)s may count months of eligibility for SSI or federally administered state supplementary payments (discussed later in this chapter) toward the Medicare waiting period.[62] It is worth noting that Social Security disability beneficiaries aged 65 or older are entitled to Medicare on the basis of age and thus are not subject to the 24month waiting period.[63]

Impairment Related

The Social Security Act specifically excludes disability beneficiaries with amyotrophic lateral sclerosis (ALS; also known as Lou Gehrig's Disease) from having to satisfy the 24month waiting period requirement.[64] Most disability beneficiaries with ALS become entitled to Medicare the first day of the month that entitlement to cash benefits begins, which for disabled workers and disabled widow(er)s is five full calendar months after the onset of disability.

The Social Security Act also contains separate Medicare entitlement provisions for individuals with end-stage renal disease (ESRD)[65] or certain medical conditions caused by exposure to qualifying environmental health

---

[61] Section 226(f) of the Social Security Act; 42 U.S.C. §426(f). See also 42 C.F.R. § 406.12(b)(3).

[62] Section 226(e)(1)(B) of the Social Security Act; 42 U.S.C. §426(e)(1)(B).

[63] Based on information provided to CRS by SSA on August 10, 2017.

[64] Section 226(h) of the Social Security Act; 42 U.S.C. §426(h).

[65] Section 226A of the Social Security Act; 42 U.S.C. § 426-1. ESRD is a stage of kidney impairment that appears to be irreversible and permanent, requiring a regular course of dialysis treatments or a kidney transplantation to maintain life.

hazards,[66] meaning that individuals who meet the relevant entitlement factors may enroll in Medicare without having to be entitled (or deemed to be entitled) to Social Security benefits. Neither of these entitlement provisions requires eligible individuals to satisfy a 24month waiting period requirement, although individuals with ESRD may have to satisfy a three month waiting period requirement if they are on dialysis and do not self-dialyze on a regular basis.[67] Social Security disability beneficiaries who meet the requirements specific to these separate entitlement provisions generally receive Medicare coverage in the month they become entitled to cash benefits.

Financing

Social Security's receipts and outlays are accounted for through two legally distinct trust funds: the Federal Disability Insurance (DI) Trust Fund and the Federal Old Age and Survivors Insurance (OASI) Trust Fund. In the federal accounting structure, a *trust fund* is an accounting mechanism used by the Department of the Treasury to track and report receipts dedicated for spending on specific purposes, as well as expenditures made to its beneficiaries that are financed by those receipts, in accordance with the terms of a statute that designates the fund as a trust fund. The DI trust fund records receipts and outlays associated with disabled workers and their dependents, and the OASI trust fund records receipts and outlays associated with retired workers and their dependents as well as survivors of deceased insured workers. Administrative costs are also drawn from the trust funds. Each trust fund is a separate account in the U.S. Treasury, and the two funds may not borrow from one another under current law.

Social Security is financed primarily by dedicated payroll and self employment taxes levied on the earnings of workers in jobs covered by

---

[66] Section 1881A of the Social Security Act; 42 U.S.C. §1395rr-1. See SSA, "Libby," https://www.ssa.gov/libby/.

[67] 42 U.S.C. §426-1(b) and 42 C.F.R. §406.13(e).

Social Security. Federal Insurance Contributions Act (FICA) taxes are split evenly between employees and employers, while Self-Employment Contributions Act (SECA) taxes are borne fully by self employed individuals.[68] The overall Social Security payroll tax rate is 12.4% of a worker's earnings (6.2% for employees and employers, each), up to a maximum annual amount, which in 2018 is $128,400.[69] Of the 12.4%, 2.37% is allocated to the DI trust fund and 10.03% is allocated to the OASI trust fund.[70] The two trust funds are also credited with income from the taxation of a portion of some Social Security benefits[71] and from interest earned on special-issue U.S. securities held by the trust funds for years when receipts exceeded outlays.[72]

In 2017, total receipts to the Social Security trust funds were $997 billion, with $171 billion (or 17%) credited to the DI trust fund (**Table 3**). That same year, total outlays from the trust funds were $952 billion, with $146 billion (or 15%) coming from the DI trust fund. The trust funds held a combined balance of $2.9 trillion in U.S. securities at the end of 2017, with $71 billion (or 2%) credited to the DI trust fund. In 2017, 98% of the DI trust fund's outlays were for benefit payments, with 1.9% for administrative expenses, and 0.1% for certain transfers.

In their 2017 report and under current law, the Social Security trustees project that the trust funds on a hypothetical combined basis will be able to pay benefits in full and on time until 2034.[73] However, as noted earlier, the two trust funds are legally distinct entities. Individually, the trustees project that the DI trust fund will be depleted in 2028 and the OASI trust fund will be depleted in 2035. Upon depletion, the trustees project that continuing

---

[68] 26 U.S.C. §§3101, 3111, 1401, respectively.

[69] SSA, OCACT, "Contribution and Benefit Base," https://www.ssa.gov/oact/cola/cbb.html.

[70] Section 201(a) and 201(b) of the Social Security Act; 42 U.S.C. §401(a) and 401(b). The allocation of the tax rate between the OASI and Disability Insurance (DI) trust funds is scheduled to change in 2019. See SSA, OCACT, "Social Security Taxes Rates," https://www.ssa.gov/oact/progdata/oasdiRates.html.

[71] Section 121(e) of the Social Security Amendments of 1983 (P.L. 98-21); 42 U.S.C. §401 note.

[72] Section 201(f) of the Social Security Act; 42 U.S.C. §401(f).

[73] U.S. Congress, House Committee on Ways and Means, *The 2017 Annual Report of the Board of Trustees of the Federal Old-Age and Survivors Insurance and Federal Disability Insurance Trust Funds*, 115th Cong., 1st sess., July 18, 2016, H.Doc. 115-54 (Washington: GPO, 2017), p. 3, https://www.ssa.gov/oact/tr/2017/index.html.

revenues to the DI trust fund would be sufficient to pay about 93% of benefits scheduled under law, declining to 82% by 2091.

Table 3. Operations of the Social Security Trust Funds, 2017 (in millions of dollars)

Category	Old-Age and Survivors Insurance (OASI) Trust Fund	Disability Insurance (DI) Trust Fund	Hypothetical Combined OASDI Trust Funds
Receipts			
Payroll Taxes	$706,505	$167,087	$873,592
Income from Taxation of Benefits	35,877	1,973	37,850
Interest	83,231	1,888	85,119
Other Income	17	3	20
Total Receipts	$825,630	$170,951	$996,581
Outlays			
Benefit Payments	798,692	142,806	941,499
Administrative Expenses	3,661	2,796	6,457
Transfers	4,316	207	4,522
Total Outlays	$806,669	$145,809	$952,478
Asset Reserves at End of the Year	$2,820,309	$71,480	$2,891,789

Source: CRS, based on SSA, OCACT, "Financial Data for a Selected Time Period," https://www.ssa.gov/oact/ProgData/allOps.html.

Under its June 2017 baseline and under current law, the Congressional Budget Office (CBO) projected that the trust funds on a hypothetical combined basis would be depleted in calendar year (CY) 2030, with the DI trust fund depleted in FY2023 and the OASI trust fund in CY2031.[74] Under its April 2018 baseline, CBO now projects that the DI trust fund will be depleted in early FY2025.[75] Upon depletion, CBO projects that continuing

[74] See CBO, *Old-Age, Survivors, and Disability Insurance Trust Funds—CBO's June 2017 Baseline*, June 2017, https://www.cbo.gov/sites/default/files/recurringdata/51309-2017-06-trustfund.pdf.

[75] CBO, *The Budget and Economic Outlook: 2018 to 2028*, April 9, 2018, p. 134, https://www.cbo.gov/publication/ 53651. Newer projections for the OASI and hypothetical combined trust funds have not been released by CBO as of the date of this chapter.

revenues to the DI trust fund would be sufficient to pay about 88% of benefits scheduled under law.

SUPPLEMENTAL SECURITY INCOME

Established under Title XVI of the Social Security Act in 1972 and implemented in 1974, SSI is a means tested federal assistance program that provides monthly cash payments to the needy individuals and couples who are aged, blind, or disabled.[76] The program is intended to provide a guaranteed minimum income to adults who have difficulty covering their basic living expenses due to age or disability and who have little or no Social Security or other income. It is also designed to supplement the support and maintenance of needy children who have severe disabilities. SSI is commonly known as a program of "last resort" because claimants must first apply for most other benefits for which they may be eligible; cash assistance is awarded only to those whose assets and other income (if any) are within prescribed limits. The basic federal SSI payment is the same for all recipients and is reduced by most other income that an individual receives. Some states supplement the federal payment using state funds. In December 2017, SSA issued federally administered payments to 8.2 million SSI recipients, including 1.2 million children under 18 years old, 4.8 million adults aged 1864, and 2.2 million seniors aged 65 or older.[77]

As shown in Figure 2, the vast majority of SSI recipients enter the program through the disability pathway. In other words, most individuals become eligible for SSI due to a qualifying impairment other than blindness. Blind or disabled SSI recipients who attain age 65 continue to be classified by SSA as blind or disabled, even though they meet the categorical requirements to be classified as aged. To avoid confusion, this

---

[76] 42 U.S.C. §§1381 et seq.

[77] SSA, ORES, "SSI Monthly Statistics, 2017," January 2018, Table 2, https://www.ssa.gov/policy/docs/statcomps/ ssi_monthly/2017/index.html.

chapter focuses primarily on blind or disabled SSI recipients under 65 years old.

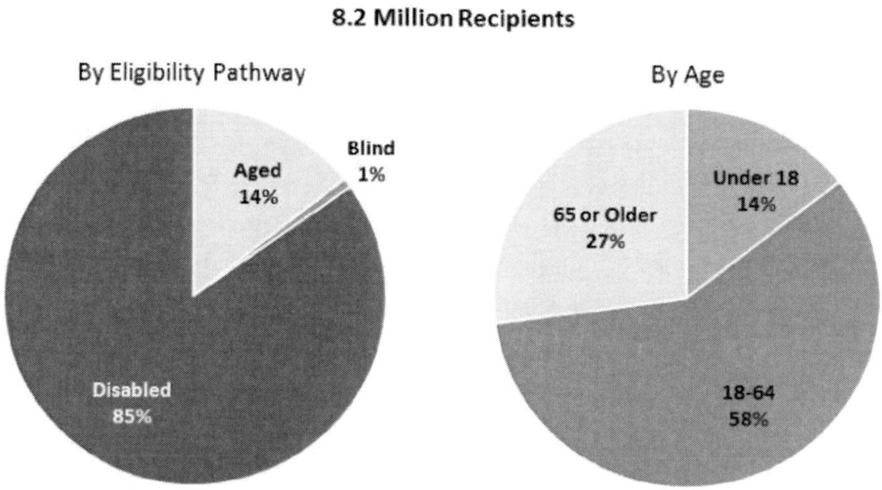

Source: CRS, based on SSA, "SSI Monthly Statistics, 2017," January 2018, Table 2, https://www.ssa.gov/policy/ docs/statcomps/ssi_monthly/2017/index.html.

Notes: The share of blind SSI recipients is estimated based on 2016 administrative data. See SSA, Office of Research, Evaluation, and Statistics (ORES), *SSI Annual Statistical Report, 2016*, Table 5, https://www.ssa.gov/ policy/docs/statcomps/ ssi_asr/.

Figure 2. SSI Recipients, by Eligibility Pathway and Age Group, December 2017.

Eligibility Requirements

To qualify for SSI, a person must (1) be aged, blind, or disabled as defined in the Social Security Act, (2) have limited income and resources, (3) meet certain other requirements, and (4) have filed an application for payments.[78]

---

[78] 20 C.F.R. §416.202.

Categorical Requirements

Public assistance programs usually limit eligibility to certain groups or *categories* of people who often have difficulty providing for themselves. Under the SSI program, an individual or couple must be aged, blind, or disabled to qualify for payments.[79] *Aged* refers to individuals who are aged 65 or older.[80] *Blind* refers to individuals of any age who have central visual acuity of 20/200 or less in the better eye with the use of a correcting lens or a limitation in the fields of vision so that the widest diameter of the visual field subtends an angle of 20 degrees or less (i.e., tunnel vision).[81] Individuals are considered *disabled* if they meet SSI's agespecific definition of disability (see the "Definition of Disability" section of this chapter).

Financial Requirements

In addition to meeting one of the aforementioned categories, an individual or couple must have limited income and other financial resources. *Income* is defined as anything one receives in cash or in kind that can be used to meet one's needs for food and shelter.[82] *Resources* are cash or other liquid assets or any real or personal property that an individual (or spouse, if any) owns and could convert to cash to be used for his or her support and maintenance.[83] Under SSI, a person's *countable* income and resources must be within the program's statutory limits. Because certain income and resources are disregarded (i.e., not counted), a person may have *gross* income or resources above the countable limits and still be eligible for the program. In addition to the person's own income and resources, the income and resources of certain ineligible family members (such as a spouse or parent) may be deemed available to meet the needs of the person, and as such, may be included in his or her countable income and resources.

---

[79] Section 1602 of the Social Security Act; 42 U.S.C. §1381a.

[80] Section 1614(a)(1) of the Social Security Act; 42 U.S.C. §1382c(a)(1). See also 20 C.F.R. §416.202(a)(1).

[81] Section 1614(a)(2) of the Social Security Act; 42 U.S.C. §1382c(a)(2). See also 20 C.F.R. §§416.202(a)(2) and 416.981.

[82] 20 C.F.R. §416.1102.

[83] 20 C.F.R. §416.1201(a).

Countable Income Limits

The limit for countable income – gross income *minus* all applicable exclusions – is equal to the federal benefit rate (FBR), which is the maximum monthly SSI payment available to qualified individuals and couples who have no other income.[84] In 2018, the FBR is $750 per month for an individual living in his or her own household and $1,125 per month for a couple living in their own household if both members are SSI eligible.[85] The FBR is adjusted annually for inflation by the same COLA applied to Social Security benefits.[86] Countable income is subtracted from the FBR in determining eligibility for SSI and the amount of the cash payment. In general, individuals and couples are eligible for SSI if their countable income is less than or equal to the FBR.[87] In states that have an agreement with SSA for the agency to administer their state supplementation program (primarily California, Nevada, New Jersey, and Vermont), a person is considered eligible for SSI if his or her countable income is less than the FBR *plus* the amount of the applicable federally administered state supplementary payment.

Income That Is Counted

Under the SSI program, all income is counted unless excluded under federal law or, if provided in statute, at the discretion of the Commissioner of Social Security through agency regulations or subregulatory guidance. SSI classifies income as either earned or unearned. *Earned income* includes wages, net earnings from self-employment, payments for services performed in a sheltered workshop (now known as a Community Rehabilitation Program [CRP]), and certain royalties and honoraria.[88] *Unearned income* refers to all income that is not earned income (i.e.,

---

[84] Section 1611(a)(1)(A), 1611(a)(2)(A), and 1611(b) of the Social Security Act; 42 U.S.C. §1382(a)(1)(A), §1382(a)(2)(A), and §1382(b).

[85] SSA, OCACT, "SSI Federal Payment Amounts," https://www.ssa.gov/oact/cola/SSIamts.html.

[86] Section 1617 of the Social Security Act; 42 U.S.C. §1382f. See also 20 C.F.R. §416.405.

[87] SSA, POMS, "SI 02301.215 Summary of Posteligibility (PE) Suspension, Stop Payment and Termination Events by Payment Status Code (PSC)," February 18, 2016, http://policy.ssa.gov/poms.nsf/lnx/0502301215.

[88] Section 1612(a)(1) of the Social Security Act; 42 U.S.C. §1382a(a)(1). See also 20 C.F.R. §416.1110.

income not derived from current work), such as Social Security, benefits administered by the VA, unemployment insurance (UI),[89] benefits administered by the Railroad Retirement Board (RRB),[90] the individual's share of the Temporary Assistance for Needy Families (TANF) grant,[91] workers' compensation, public or private pensions, interest income, cash from family or friends, and in-kind support and maintenance (i.e., the value of non-cash benefits such as food or shelter).[92]

Income That Is Not Counted

Certain income is disregarded in determining eligibility for and the amount of assistance provided by SSI.[93] For example, the program excludes the following:

- the first $20 per month of any income (earned or unearned), other than unearned income based on need that is totally or partially funded by the federal government or by a non-governmental agency (e.g., TANF);[94]
- the first $65 per month of earned income plus one half of any earnings above $65;[95]
- the first $30 per calendar quarter of infrequent or irregular earned income;[96]
- the first $60 per calendar quarter of infrequent or irregular unearned income;[97]

---

[89] CRS Report RL33362, *Unemployment Insurance: Programs and Benefits*.

[90] CRS Report RS22350, *Railroad Retirement Board: Retirement, Survivor, Disability, Unemployment, and Sickness Benefits*.

[91] CRS In Focus IF10036, *The Temporary Assistance for Needy Families (TANF) Block Grant*.

[92] Section 1612(a)(2) of the Social Security Act; 42 U.S.C. §1382a(a)(2). See also 20 C.F.R. §416.1120.

[93] Section 1612(b) of the Social Security Act; 42 U.S.C. §1382a(b). See also 20 C.F.R. §§416.1112, 416.1124, and the Appendix to Subpart K.

[94] Section 1612(b)(2)(A) of the Social Security Act; 42 U.S.C. §1382a(b)(2)(A). See also 20 C.F.R. §§416.1112(c)(4) and 416.1124(c)(12).

[95] Section 1612(b)(4)(A)(i), 1612(b)(4)(B)(i), 1612(b)(4)(B)(iii), and 1612(b)(4)(C) of the Social Security Act; 42 U.S.C. §1382a(b)(4)(A)(i), 1382a(b)(4)(B)(i), 1382a(b)(4)(B)(iii), and1382a(b)(4)(C). See also 20 C.F.R. §416.1112(c)(5) and 416.1112(c)(7).

[96] Section 1612(b)(3)(B) of the Social Security Act; 42 U.S.C. §1382a(b)(3)(B). See also 20 C.F.R. §416.1112(c)(5).

- food assistance provided under the Supplemental Nutrition Assistance Program (SNAP) and the Special Supplemental Nutrition Program for Women, Infants, and Children (WIC) program;[98]
- energy assistance provided under the Low Income Home Energy Assistance Program (LIHEAP);[99]
- housing assistance provided by most federally funded housing programs;[100]
- federal tax refunds and advanced tax credits, including the Earned Income Tax Credit (EITC) and the child tax credit (CTC);[101]
- assistance based on need that is funded wholly by a state or local entity;[102]
- the first $2,000 received during a calendar year as compensation for participation in a clinical trial involving research and testing of treatments for a rare disease or condition;[103]
- impairment related work expenses (IRWEs) for disabled recipients and blind work expenses (BWEs) for blind recipients;[104] and
- any income used to fulfill a plan to achieving self-support (PASS).[105]

---

[97] Section 1612(b)(3)(A) of the Social Security Act; 42 U.S.C. §1382a(b)(3)(A). See also 20 C.F.R. §416.1124(c)(6).

[98] 7 U.S.C. §2017(b) and 42 U.S.C. 1780(b). See also CRS Report R42505, *Supplemental Nutrition Assistance Program (SNAP): A Primer on Eligibility and Benefits*, and CRS Report R44115, *A Primer on WIC: The Special Supplemental Nutrition Program for Women, Infants, and Children*.

[99] Section 1612(b)(13) of the Social Security Act; 42 U.S.C. §1382a(b)(13). See also 42 U.S.C. §8624(f) and 20 C.F.R. §§416.1124(c)(2) and 416.1157. Moreover, see CRS Report RL31865, *LIHEAP: Program and Funding*.

[100] Section 1612(b)(14) of the Social Security Act; 42 U.S.C. §1382a(b)(14). See also 20 C.F.R. §416.1124(c)(14) and 42 U.S.C. §1382 note. Moreover, see CRS Report RL34591, *Overview of Federal Housing Assistance Programs and Policy*.

[101] 26 U.S.C. §§24 note and 6409. See also 20 C.F.R. §§416.1103(d). Moreover, see CRS Report R43805, *The Earned Income Tax Credit (EITC): An Overview*, and CRS Report R41873, *The Child Tax Credit: Current Law*.

[102] Section 1612(b)(13) of the Social Security Act; 42 U.S.C. §1382a(b)(13). See also 20 C.F.R. §416.1124(c)(2).

[103] Section 1612(b)(26) of the Social Security Act; 42 U.S.C. §1382a(b)(26).

[104] Section 1612(b)(4)(A)(ii) and 1612(b)(4)(B)(ii) of the Social Security Act; 42 U.S.C. §1382a(b)(4)(A)(ii) and 1382a(b)(4)(B)(ii). See also 20 C.F.R. §416.1112(c)(6) and 416.1112(c)(8).

For a more detailed list of unearned income exclusions, see "SI 00830.099 Guide to Unearned Income Exclusions" in POMS.[106]

The $20 per month general income exclusion and the $65 per month earned income exclusion are not indexed to inflation and have remained at their current levels since the SSI program was enacted in 1972.

Treatment of In-Kind Support and Maintenance

SSA defines in kind support and maintenance (ISM) as food or shelter that a person receives from someone else who pays for it.[107] *Shelter* includes room, rent, mortgage payments, real property taxes, heating fuel, gas, electricity, water, sewerage, and garbage collection services.[108] ISM is treated as unearned income subject to special rules based on a person's living arrangement. If a person lives throughout a month in another's household and receives *both* food and shelter from others living in the household, the FBR is reduced by one third. This reduction is known as the *value of the one-third reduction* (VTR) and is not rebuttable.[109] In 2018, the VTR is $250 per month for an individual ($750 x 1/3) and $375 per month for a couple ($1,125 x 1/3).[110] The $20 per month general income exclusion does not apply to ISM reduced under the VTR.

However, if a person receives ISM but does not receive both food and shelter from the household in which the individual lives (either his or her own household or the household of another), then the FBR is reduced by the *presumed maximum value* (PMV) rule.[111] The PMV is a regulatory cap on ISM designed to address situations in which an individual receives ISM but is not subject to the statutory VTR. The reduction under the PMV is

---

105 Section 1612(b)(4)(A)(iii) and 1612(b)(4)(B)(iv) of the Social Security Act; 42 U.S.C. §1382a(b)(4)(A)(iii) and 1382a(b)(4)(B)(iv). See also 20 C.F.R. §§416.1112(c)(9) and 416.1124(c)(13).

106 SSA, POMS, "SI 00830.099 Guide to Unearned Income Exclusions," April 23, 2013, https://secure.ssa.gov/apps10/ poms.nsf/lnx/0500830099.

107 SSA no longer includes clothing in the definition of in-kind support and maintenance (ISM).

108 20 C.F.R. §416.1130(b).

109 Section 1612(a)(2)(A) of the Social Security Act; 42 U.S.C. §1382a(a)(2)(A). See also 20 C.F.R. §416.1131.

110 SSA, POMS, "SI 00835.901 Values for In-Kind Support and Maintenance for 2006 and Later," January 24, 2018, http://policy.ssa.gov/poms.nsf/lnx/0500835901.

111 20 C.F.R. §416.1140.

equal to one-third of the FBR *plus* $20, which in 2018 is $270 per month for an individual ($750 x 1/3 + $20) and $395 per month for a couple ($1,125 x 1/3 + $20). Unlike the VTR, the PMV is rebuttable. If the SSI recipient can show that the value of food or shelter received is less than the PMV reduction, then SSA reduces the FBR by the actual value of food or shelter received. Some ISM is disregarded, such as federal housing assistance.[112] According to SSA, only about 9% of SSI recipients have ISM reductions.[113]

Countable Resource (Asset) Limits

The limit for countable resources gross resources *minus* all applicable exclusions is $2,000 for an individual and $3,000 for a couple.[114] Individuals and couples are eligible for SSI if their countable resources are less than or equal to the applicable statutory limit at any given time.[115] Claimants and recipients who transfer (i.e., sell or give away) resources at less than fair market value (FMV) may become ineligible SSI for up to 36 months.[116] The *look-back period* for determining if a transfer was made at less than FMV is also 36 months. Unlike the FBR, the countable resource limits are not adjusted for inflation and have remained at their current levels since 1989.

Resources That Are Counted

As with income, all resources are counted under the SSI program unless excluded federal law or, if provided in statute, at the discretion of the Commissioner of Social Security through agency regulations or

---

[112] See CRS Report RL34591, *Overview of Federal Housing Assistance Programs and Policy*.

[113] Ken Brown, *In-kind Support & Maintenance in the Supplemental Security Income Program*, July 12, 2016, slide 4, http://www.ssab.gov/Portals/0/2016%20SSI%20Forum/Presentations/Ken%20Brown%20-%20ISM%20Presentation.pdf?ver=2016-07-09-131547-763.

[114] Section 1611(a)(3) of the Social Security Act; 42 U.S.C. §1382(a)(3). See also 20 C.F.R. §416.1205.

[115] Under certain circumstances, individuals who have excess countable resources but who meet all other eligibility requirements may receive SSI benefits for a limited period, provided they dispose of their excess resources at current market value (CMV). See Section 1613(b) of the Social Security Act; 42 U.S.C. §1382b(b). See also 20 C.F.R. §§416.1240-416.1245.

[116] Section 1613(c) of the Social Security Act; 42 U.S.C. §1382b(c).

subregulatory guidance. The person must have the right, authority, or power to liquidate the property (or his or her share of the property) for the asset to be considered a resource. Countable resources include the following:

- cash retained as of the first moment of the month following the month of receipt;
- bank savings or checking accounts;
- stocks, bonds, mutual funds, and certificates of deposit;
- tractors, boats, machinery, livestock, buildings, and land;
- individual retirement accounts (IRAs) and 401(k) plans under certain conditions;
- unrestricted health savings accounts (HSAs); and
- most types of trusts established with the assets of an individual on or after January 1, 2000.[117]

Resources That Are Not Counted

Certain resources are excluded in determining SSI eligibility.[118] For example, the program excludes the following:

- the person's primary residence;[119]
- household goods and personal effects;[120]
- one automobile used for transportation;[121]
- property essential to self-support (PESS);[122]
- health flexible spending arrangements (FSAs);[123]

---

[117] Section 1613(e) of the Social Security Act; 42 U.S.C. §1382b(e).

[118] Section 1613(a) of the Social Security Act; 42 U.S.C. §1382b(a). See also 20 C.F.R. §§416.1210-416.1266. Not all resource exclusions are specified in Title XVI or in SSA regulations.

[119] Section 1613(a)(1) of the Social Security Act; 42 U.S.C. §1382b(a)(1). See also 20 C.F.R. §§416.1210(a) and 416.1212.

[120] Section 1613(a)(2)(A) of the Social Security Act; 42 U.S.C. §1382b(a)(2)(A). See also 20 C.F.R. §§416.1210(b) and 416.1216.

[121] Section 1613(a)(2)(A) of the Social Security Act; 42 U.S.C. §1382b(a)(2)(A). See also 20 C.F.R. §§416.1210(c) and 416.1218.

[122] Section 1613(a)(3) of the Social Security Act; 42 U.S.C. §1382b(a)(3). See also 20 C.F.R. §§416.1210(e) and 416.1224.

- resources needed to fulfill a PASS;[124]
- federal tax refunds and advanced tax credits for a 12month period;[125]
- all life insurance policies on a person up to a combined face value of $1,500;[126]
- up to $1,500 in burial funds set aside for burial expenses of the individual or the individual's spouse;[127]
- special needs trusts (SNTs) or pooled trusts (PTs) that meet the requirements of Medicaid law;[128] and
- the first $100,000 in an Achieving a Better Life Experience (ABLE) account.[129]

For a more detailed list of resource exclusions, see "SI 01130.050 Guide to Resources Exclusions" in POMS.[130]

Deeming of Income and Resources from Certain Close Family Members

As a program of "last resort," SSI expects close family members to provide support to low-income aged, blind, and disabled individuals in determining their level of need. Specifically, the income and resources of certain ineligible family members are deemed to be available to meet the

---

[123] SSA, POMS, "SI 01120.230 Health Flexible Spending Arrangements (FSAs)," November 13, 2013, https://secure.ssa.gov/poms.nsf/lnx/0501120230.

[124] Section 1613(a)(4) of the Social Security Act; 42 U.S.C. §1382b(a)(4). See also 20 C.F.R. §§416.1210(f) and 416.1226.

[125] 26 U.S.C. §§24 note and 6409. See also 20 C.F.R. §§416.1210(o) and 416.1235. Moreover, see SSA, POMS, "SI 01130.676 Federal Tax Refunds and Advanced Tax Credits for SSI Resources," August 11, 2014, https://secure.ssa.gov/poms.nsf/lnx/0501130676.

[126] Section 1613(a)(16) of the Social Security Act; 42 U.S.C. §1382b(a)(16). See also 20 C.F.R. §§416.1210(h) and 416.1230.

[127] Section 1613(d) of the Social Security Act; 42 U.S.C. §1382b(d). See also 20 C.F.R. §§416.1210(l) and 416.1231.

[128] Sections 1613(c)(1)(C)(ii), 1613(e)(5), 1917(d)(4)(A), and 1917(d)(4)(C) of the Social Security Act; 42 U.S.C. §§1382b(c)(1)(C)(ii), 1382b(e)(5), 1396p(d)(4)(A), and 1396p(d)(4)(C).

[129] 26 U.S.C. §529A note. CRS In Focus IF10363, *Achieving a Better Life Experience (ABLE) Programs*.

[130] SSA, POMS, "SI 01130.050 Guide to Resources Exclusions," August 16, 2017, https://secure.ssa.gov/apps10/poms.nsf/lnx/0501130050.

basic needs of eligible individuals, and as such, may be included in the individual's countable income or resources for purposes of determining SSI eligibility and the amount of assistance.

This process, known as *deeming*, is used instead of determining the amount of ISM provided by a *deemor* (i.e., the ineligible family member whose income and resources are subject to deeming) under the VTR or PMV rule. The Social Security Act specifies that deeming applies to the following types of relationships.

- Spouse-to-Spouse. An eligible individual resides in the same household with his or her ineligible spouse.
- Parent-to-Child. An eligible child under 18 years old resides in the same household with his or her ineligible natural (i.e., biological) or adoptive parent(s) or with his or her ineligible natural parent and the spouse of a parent (i.e., a stepparent).
- Sponsor-to-Alien. An eligible alien has a sponsor (usually a relative) who assumes financial responsibility for him of her for purposes of the alien being lawfully admitted to the United States.[131]

In determining the amount of the deemor's income and resources available to the eligible individual, SSA first applies the basic income and resource exclusions mentioned previously. Next, the agency deducts from the income of the ineligible family member an allocation for his or her living expenses, as well as an allocation for each ineligible child under 18 years old (or under 22 years old and a student) living in the household. This allocation does not apply, however, if the ineligible family member receives public income maintenance payments, such as TANF or VA pensions based on need.[132] Finally, SSA charges the remaining countable

---

[131] Section 1614(f) of the Social Security Act; 42 U.S.C. §1382c(f). See also 20 C.F.R. §§416.1160-416.1169 and 416.1202-416.1204a.

[132] The allocation for an ineligible spouse is the difference between the federal benefit rate (FBR) for a couple and the FBR for an individual (20 C.F.R. §416.1163[d]). (Although SSA effectively deducts an allocation equal to this amount from the ineligible spouse's income, the agency does not call it an allocation because the calculation process used for ineligible

income of the deemor (if any) to the eligible individual's unearned income and then applies the normal income counting rules to determine SSI eligibility and the amount of the payment. Under deeming, the countable resource limits are $3,000 for an eligible individual with an ineligible spouse, $4,000 for an eligible child with one ineligible parent, and $5,000 for an eligible child with two ineligible parents.[133] For more information on deeming, see Virginia Commonwealth University's National Training and Data Center's page titled, "Understanding the Supplemental Security Income (SSI) Program."[134]

Residency Requirements

To qualify for SSI, individuals or couples must reside in United States, which the program defines as the 50 states, the District of Columbia, and the Commonwealth of the Northern Mariana Islands.[135] People residing in Puerto Rico, Guam, the U.S. Virgin Islands, American Samoa, or any other territory or possession of the United State (other than the Northern Mariana Islands) are considered to be residing outside of the United States and thus are ineligible for SSI. However, residents of these territories may become eligible for SSI if they move to one of the 50 states, the District of

---

spouses is different from the process used for other ineligible family members.) The allocation for each ineligible child is the difference between the FBR for a couple and the FBR for an individual (20 C.F.R. §§416.1163[b][1] and 416.1165[b]). In the case of an eligible child, the parental allocation is equal to the FBR for an individual for one ineligible parent or the FBR for a couple for two ineligible parents (20 C.F.R. §416.1165[d][3]).

[133] The countable resource limit for an eligible individual with an ineligible spouse is the amount applicable to an eligible couple. The countable resource limit for an eligible child is equal to his or her own $2,000 limit *plus* the amount applicable to an eligible individual in the case of one ineligible parent or the amount application to an eligible couple in the case of two ineligible parents (20 C.F.R. §416.1202[b]).

[134] Virginia Commonwealth University (VCU) National Training and Data Center (NTDC), "Understanding the Supplemental Security Income (SSI) Program," https://vcu-ntdc.org/resources/resourceDetail.cfm?id=1.

[135] Section 1614(a)(1)(B)(i) and 1614(e) of the Social Security Act; 42 U.S.C. §1382c(a)(1)(B)(i) and 1382c(e). See also 20 C.F.R. §§416.202(b) and 416.1603(c). Although 1614(e) of the Social Security Act specifies that the term "United States" includes only the 50 states and the District of Columbia, the Northern Mariana Islands territorial covenant specifies that "[t]he following laws of the United States in existence on the effective date of this Section and subsequent amendments to such laws will apply to the Northern Mariana Islands ... Title XVI of the Social Security Act as it applies to the several States." See Section 503(a) of P.L. 94-241; 48 U.S.C. §1801 note.

Columbia, or the Northern Mariana Islands, establish residency there, and meet the physical presence requirement.

Cash Assistance for the Aged, Blind, and Disabled in the Territories

The Supplemental Security Income (SSI) program is not available in Puerto Rico, Guam, and the U.S. Virgin Islands. Instead, these territories continue to operate the joint federal-state programs for the aged, blind, and disabled, which SSI replaced in the 50 states and the District of Columbia in 1974. These programs offer federal funds (up to a specified amount) to the territories in the form of capped categorical matching grants to help pay for the costs of providing cash assistance to needy aged, blind, or disabled adults aged 18 or older. Guam and the U.S. Virgin Islands operate separate programs of Old-Age Assistance (OAA), Aid to the Blind (AB), and Aid to the Permanently and Totally Disabled (APTD) under Titles I, X, and XIV of the Social Security Act, respectively.[136] Puerto Rico operates the consolidated program of Aid to the Aged, Blind, or Disabled (AABD) under Title XVI as it existed prior to reenactment by P.L. 92-603.[137] The Administration for Children and Families (ACF) within the Department of Health and Human Services (HHS) oversees the matching-grant programs at the federal level. Neither SSI nor the matching-grant programs are available in American Samoa. SSI was extended to the Commonwealth of the Northern Mariana Islands as part of its 1976 covenant (P.L. 94-241), effective January 1978.

Individuals or couples are generally ineligible for SSI for months in which they are not physically present in the United States (as defined above). A person who leaves the United States for 30 consecutive days or more is treated as remaining outside the United States until he or she has returned to and remained in the United States for a period of 30 consecutive days.[138] The physical presence requirement does not apply to blind or disabled children of military personnel assigned to permanent duty

---

[136] 42 U.S.C. §§301-306, 1201-1206, and 1351-1355, respectively.

[137] 42 U.S.C. §§1381 note-1385 note.

[138] Section 1611(f) of the Social Security Act; 42 U.S.C. §1382(f). See also 20 C.F.R. §§416.215 and 416.1327.

ashore outside the United States[139] or to certain students who are temporarily abroad.[140]

Citizenship Requirements

In addition to the residency requirement, a person must be a citizen or national of the United States or an eligible noncitizen.[141] For the purposes of this chapter, an *eligible noncitizen* is an alien who (1) has been granted a qualifying legal status by the federal government (i.e., is a *qualified alien*) and (2) meets certain other requirements.[142] As a result of changes made to federal law under the Personal Responsibility and Work Opportunity Reconciliation Act of 1996 (PRWORA; P.L. 104-193) as well as legislation enacted shortly thereafter,[143] SSI eligibility for noncitizens is limited largely to lawful permanent residents (LPRs, also known as *green card holders*) with significant past work history in jobs covered by Social Security, "grandfathered aliens" who received SSI when PRWORA was enacted, certain aliens who are exempted by law from PRWORA's requirements, and refugees and asylees.[144] Eligible noncitizens *do not* include aliens who are not authorized to be present in the United States (i.e., "illegal aliens"), nor do they include aliens with certain types of legal (or quasi-legal) status.[145] For example, SSI is not available to aliens lawfully admitted to the United States on tourist visas or to beneficiaries of the Deferred Action for Childhood Arrivals (DACA) policy.

---

[139] Sections 1611(f)(1) and 1614(a)(1)(B)(ii) of the Social Security Act; 42 U.S.C. §§1382(f)(1) and 1382c(a)(1)(B)(ii). See also 20 C.F.R. §416.216.

[140] Section 1611(f)(2) of the Social Security Act; 42 U.S.C. §1382(f)(2). See also SSA, POMS, "SI 00501.411 SSI Eligibility for Students Temporarily AbroadOverview," September 13, 2012, https://secure.ssa.gov/poms.nsf/lnx/ 0500501411.

[141] Section 1614(a)(1)(B)(i) of the Social Security Act; 42 U.S.C. §1382c(a)(1)(B)(i). See also 20 C.F.R. §416.202(b) and 416.1610-416.1619.

[142] For a discussion of qualified and non-qualified aliens, see Appendix C of CRS Report RL33809, *Noncitizen Eligibility for Federal Public Assistance: Policy Overview*.

[143] Title V of the Illegal Immigration Reform and Immigrant Responsibility Act of 1996 (Division C of the Omnibus Consolidated Appropriations Act, 1997 [P.L. 104-208]), Title V of the Balanced Budget Act of 1997 (P.L. 105-33), and the Noncitizen Benefit Clarification and Other Technical Amendments Act of 1998 (P.L. 105-306).

[144] CRS Report RL33809, *Noncitizen Eligibility for Federal Public Assistance: Policy Overview*.

[145] CRS Report R45020, *A Primer on U.S. Immigration Policy*.

Eligible noncitizens are often classified into two groups: (1) those without a time limit and (2) those subject to a seven-year limit. Eligible noncitizens without a time limit include, but are not limited to, the following categories:

- LPRs who (1) have satisfied a five-year waiting period requirement from the date of entry and (2) have 40 qualifying quarters of coverage from earnings based on Social Security-covered work (or can be credited with such qualifying quarters from a parent or spouse);
- qualified aliens who are (1) active duty military members, (2) honorably discharged veterans, or (3) the dependents of active duty military members or honorably discharged veterans;
- qualified aliens who are lawfully residing in the United States and were receiving SSI on August 22, 1996;
- qualified aliens who were lawfully residing in the United States on August 22, 1996, and who meet SSI's blindness or disability standard, regardless of the onset date;
- American Indians born in Canada who are admitted to the United States under certain conditions; and
- American Indians who are members of federallyrecognized tribes and who meet certain conditions.[146]

Eligible noncitizens subject to a seven-year limit from the date their status was acquired include, but are not limited to, the following categories:

- refugees and asylees who meet certain conditions;
- Cuban/Haitian entrants and Amerasian immigrants who meet certain conditions;[147]

[146] 8 U.S.C. §§1612(a)(2), 1613, and 1641(b).
[147] CRS Report R44714, *U.S. Policy on Cuban Migrants: In Brief.*

- quailed aliens whose deportation is being withheld or whose removal has been withheld (subject to certain conditions);
- Iraqi or Afghan nationals who are admitted to the United States under special immigrant visa (SIV) programs;[148] and
- aliens who are deemed to be victims of severe forms of human trafficking and who meet certain other conditions.[149]

In December 2016, eligible noncitizens made up 6.1% of the total SSI recipient population.[150] About 11% of all noncitizen recipients received time limited payments.[151] The average federally administered payment made to all noncitizen recipients that month was $510.[152] Roughly 71% of all noncitizen SSI recipients were aged 65 or older, and about 58% of all noncitizen recipients resided in the United States for at least 10 years before applying for SSI.[153] Since the enactment of PRWORA, both the number and share of noncitizen SSI recipients has fallen.

Other Requirements

Residents of public institutions (such as a jail, prison, or other facility operated directly or indirectly by a governmental entity) are ineligible for SSI for any month throughout which they reside in such institution.[154] In other words, a person is ineligible to receive SSI for any full calendar month in which they are in residence. This requirement does not apply to publicly operated community residences that serve 16 or fewer residents.[155] It also does not apply to medical treatment facilities in which more than 50% of the cost of care is paid for by Medicaid or, in the case of a child

---

[148] CRS Report R43725, *Iraqi and Afghan Special Immigrant Visa Programs.*

[149] 8 U.S.C. §§1612(a)(2), 1613, and 1641(b).

[150] SSA, ORES, *SSI Annual Statistical Report, 2016*, Table 29, https://www.ssa.gov/policy/docs/statcomps/ssi_asr/ (hereinafter "2016 SSI Annual Statistical Report").

[151] SSA, OCACT, *Annual Report of the Supplemental Security Income Program, 2017*, September 1, 2017, p. 21, https://www.ssa.gov/oact/ssir/SSI17/ssi2017.pdf (hereinafter "2017 Annual Report of the SSI Program").

[152] 2016 SSI Annual Statistical Report, Table 6.

[153] Ibid., Tables 30 and 33.

[154] Section 1611(e)(1)(A) of the Social Security Act; 42 U.S.C. §1382(e)(1)(A). See also 20 C.F.R. §416.211.

[155] Section 1611(e)(1)(C) of the Social Security Act; 42 U.S.C. §1382(e)(1)(C). See also 20 C.F.R. §416.211(c).

under 18 years old, by any combination of Medicaid and private health insurance.[156] In addition, a person is required to file for all other applicable benefits for which he or she may be eligible.[157] Furthermore, a person must not be fleeing to avoid (1) prosecution for certain felonies, (2) custody or confinement after conviction for certain felonies, or (3) recapture because of escape from custody.[158] Finally, a person must allow SSA to contact his or her financial institutions for purposes of determining or redetermining eligibility.[159]

Termination Events

In general, SSI payments are suspended for any month during which a recipient fails to meet the aforementioned eligibility requirements. After 12 consecutive months of payment suspension, most recipients are terminated from the SSI rolls and must file a new application.[160] In 2016, the SSI termination rate the ratio of the number of terminations to the average number of SSI recipients during the year for a given age group was 7.7% for children and 10.0% for working age adults (Table 4). In 2016, the majority of SSI terminations for children were due to excess income or no longer meeting the applicable definition of disability. For working-age adults that year, most terminations were due to excess income or death.

---

156 Section 1611(e)(1)(B) of the Social Security Act; 42 U.S.C. §1382(e)(1)(B). See also 20 C.F.R. §§416.212 and 416.414.

157 Section 1611(e)(2) of the Social Security Act; 42 U.S.C. §1382(e)(2). See also 20 C.F.R. §416.210.

158 Section 1611(e)(4)(A) of the Social Security Act; 42 U.S.C. §1382(e)(4)(A). See also 20 C.F.R. §§416.202(f) and 416.1339.

159 Section 1631(e)(1)(B)(ii) of the Social Security Act; 42 U.S.C. §1383(e)(1)(B)(ii). See also 20 C.F.R. §416.207.

160 Section 1631(j)(1) of the Social Security Act; 42 U.S.C. §1383(j)(1). Blind or disabled children of military personnel stationed overseas and military-related individuals who become ineligible for SSI because their spouse or parent(s) is called to active duty have 24-consecutive months after the suspension to have eligibility reinstated without having to file a new application. See 20 C.F.R. §416.216.

Table 4. Number and Share of Nonelderly Blind or Disabled SSI Recipients Terminated and the Annual Termination Rate, by Age Group and Reason for Termination, 2016

	Under 18 Years Old			**Aged 18-64**		
Reason for Termination	Terminations		Termination Rate	Terminations		Termination Rate
	Number	Share		Number	Share	
Total	93,078	100.0%	7.7%	481,280	100.0%	10.0%
Excess Income	25,074	26.9	2.1	247,278	51.4	5.1
Death	4,274	4.6	0.4	117,685	24.5	2.4
Whereabouts Unknown	3,976	4.3	0.3	6,501	1.4	0.1
Excess Resources	8,163	8.8	0.7	17,111	3.6	0.4
In Public Institution	798	0.9	0.1	27,021	5.6	0.6
Failed to Furnish Report	7,364	7.9	0.6	10,394	2.2	0.2
Outside United States	375	0.4	0.0	2,170	0.5	0.0
No Longer Disabled	40,779	43.8	3.4	47,636	9.9	1.0
Other	2,275	2.4	0.2	5,288	1.1	0.1

Source: CRS, based on the following sources: SSA, ORES, *SSI Annual Statistical Report, 2016*, November 2017, Table 77, https://www.ssa.gov/policy/docs/statcomps/ssi_asr/2016/sect11.html#table77; and SSA, "SSI Monthly Statistics, December 2017," January 2018, Table 2.

Notes: The *termination rate* is the ratio of the number of terminations to the average number of SSI recipients during the year for a given age group. In 2016, the average number of SSI recipients under 18 years old was 1,201,455, and the average number of SSI recipients aged 18-64 was 4,833,829.

Cash Payments

Federal Benefit Rate

In 2018, the federal benefit rate (FBR) is $750 per month for an individual living in his or her own household and $1,125 per month for a couple living in their own household.[161] On an annualized basis, the FBR in 2018 is $9,000 for an individual and $13,500 for a couple. Individuals and couples with no countable income receive the maximum SSI payment; those with countable income below the applicable FBR have their SSI payment reduced so that their own income plus the reduced SSI payment

[161] Section 1611(b) of the Social Security Act; 42 U.S.C. §1382(b). See also 20 C.F.R. §§416.410-416.415.

equals at least the FBR.[162] In this way, the FBR acts as an income floor, providing a minimum level of support in 2018 equal to at least 74% of the federal poverty level (FPL) for an individual and 82% of FPL for a couple.[163] As noted earlier, the FBR is adjusted annually for inflation by the same COLA applied to Social Security benefits.[164] The COLA effective for SSI payments at the start of 2018 was 2.0%, which raised the FBR for an individual from $733 to $750 per month and the FBR for a couple from $1,103 to $1,125 per month.[165]

State Supplementary Payments

Some states complement federal SSI payments with state supplementary payments (SSPs) that are made solely with state funds.[166] SSPs are intended to help individuals whose basic needs are not met fully by the FBR. States may provide SSPs to all SSI recipients, or they may limit payments to certain recipients, such as blind individuals or residents of domiciliary care homes. Currently, 43 states and the District of Columbia have *optional state supplementation programs*.[167] Most states are required to continue to operate *mandatory minimum supplementation*

---

[162] Pursuant to the Department of the Treasury's 2010 rule (75 *Federal Register* 80315), all federal benefit payments must be made via EFT, unless the individual can demonstrate hardship due to age, mental impairment, or geographic location. SSI recipients receive their payments by direct deposit, either to a bank account or to a Direct Express® card account.

[163] The term *federal poverty level (FPL)* used in this chapter refers to the Department of Health and Human Services' (HHS) 2018 federal poverty guidelines for the 48 contiguous states and the District of Columbia. See HHS, Office of the Assistant Secretary for Planning and Evaluation (ASPE), "Poverty Guidelines," https://aspe.hhs.gov/povertyguidelines. See also 42 U.S.C. §9902(2).

[164] Section 1617 of the Social Security Act; 42 U.S.C. §1382f. See also 20 C.F.R. §416.405.

[165] SSA, OCACT, "SSI Federal Payment Amounts," https://www.ssa.gov/oact/cola/SSIamts.html.

[166] Section 1616(a) of the Social Security Act; 42 U.S.C. §1382e(a). See also 20 C.F.R. §§416.2001-416.2075.

[167] 2017 Annual Report of the SSI Program, Table III.H1, p. 25. The 2017 Annual Report of the SSI program states "[c]urrently, 44 States and the District of Columbia have optional State supplementation programs" (p. 21). Although Table III.H1 counts 44 states (including Kansas) and D.C. as having optional state supplementation programs, a footnote to Kansas states "[m]andatory minimum State supplementation program is federally administered. No optional program." Based on the documentation in the footnotes to Table III.H1, the following areas do not operate optional state supplementation programs: Arizona, Arkansas, Kansas, Mississippi, North Dakota, the Northern Mariana Islands, Tennessee, and West Virginia.

programs for certain individuals who were converted to SSI in 1974 from the former federal state cash assistance programs for the aged, blind, and disabled.[168] North Dakota, the Northern Mariana Islands, and West Virginia do not operate any supplementation programs.[169]

States may self administer their supplementation programs or contract with SSA for the agency to issue SSPs to eligible recipients on the states' behalf.[170] In states that contract with SSA to administer their supplementation programs, SSI recipients receive a single payment composed of the federal SSI payment and the SSP. In states that self-administer their supplementation programs, SSI recipients receive separate payments for SSI and SSP. States that elect federal administration of their supplementation program reimburse SSA for the cost of the SSPs that the agency makes to eligible recipients on behalf of the state.[171] Since FY1994, SSA has charged participating states for the cost of administering their program by assessing a user fee on each SSP made by the agency based on a fee schedule prescribed in federal law.[172]

SSA administers optional SSPs for all (or nearly all) SSI recipients in California, New Jersey, Nevada, and Vermont. The agency also administers optional SSPs for a small number of SSI recipients in special living arrangements (e.g., domiciliary care homes, medical treatment facilities) in the following areas: Delaware, the District of Columbia,

---

[168] Section 212(a) of P.L. 93-66. See also 20 C.F.R. §§416.2050-416.2075. Texas never operated a mandatory minimum supplementation program because it has a state constitutional barrier against such a requirement. The Commonwealth of the Northern Mariana Islands was not required to operate a mandatory minimum supplementation program because the former federal-state programs of cash assistance for the aged, blind, and disabled were never available in the territory. In addition, SSI was not extended to the Northern Mariana Islands until 1978.

[169] North Dakota and West Virginia are required to operate mandatory minimum supplementation programs; however, they currently have no recipients.

[170] Section 1616(b) of the Social Security Act; 42 U.S.C. §1382e(b). See also 20 C.F.R. §416.2005.

[171] Section 1616(d) of the Social Security Act; 42 U.S.C. §1382e(d). See also 20 C.F.R. §416.2010.

[172] The user fee per state supplementary payment (SSP) for FY2018 is $11.87. See SSA, OCACT, "Fee for Administration of State Supplementary Payments," https://www.ssa.gov/oact/cola/statesuppfee.html.

Hawaii, Iowa, Michigan, Montana, Pennsylvania, and Rhode Island.[173] In December 2017, almost 1.5 million individuals received a federally administered SSP from SSA, approximately 84% of whom lived in California.[174] All other SSI recipients live in states that (1) self administer SSPs for their living arrangement, (2) do not provide SSPs for their living arrangement, or (3) do not operate an optional supplementation program at all. SSA stopped publishing data on SSI recipients who receive state administered SSPs in 2011.[175] Of the 44 areas that operated optional supplementation programs in 2017, only 22 provided SSPs to SSI recipients living in their own household, which is the most frequent type of living arrangement for SSI recipients.[176]

Basic Payment Calculation Example

As noted earlier, certain income is disregarded in determining SSI eligibility and the amount of assistance. For example, the program excludes the first $20 per month of any income (earned or unearned) and the first $65 per month of earned income plus onehalf of any earnings above $65.[177] After the application of the $20 general income exclusion, the offset for unearned income is $1 for $1; in other words, the SSI payment is reduced by one dollar for each dollar of unearned income. For earned income above $65 (or $85 if the individual has no unearned income), the offset is $1 for $2; that is, the SSI payment is reduced by one

---

173 See SSA, *A Guide to Supplemental Security Income (SSI) for Groups and Organizations*, January 2018, Publication No. 05-11015, p. 5, https://www.ssa.gov/pubs/EN-05-11015.pdf.

174 SSA, ORES "SSI Monthly Statistics, 2017," https://www.ssa.gov/policy/docs/ statcomps/ssi_monthly/2017/ index.html; and SSA, ORES, *Congressional Statistics, 2017*, April 2018, Table 2 for California, https://www.ssa.gov/ policy/docs/factsheets/cong_stats/ index.html (hereinafter "2017 Congressional Statistics").

175 SSA, ORES, *State Assistance Programs for SSI Recipients, January 2011*, November 2011, https://www.ssa.gov/ policy/docs/progdesc/ssi_st_asst/.

176 See SSA, POMS, "SI 02302.200 Charted Threshold Amounts," January 25, 2017, https://secure.ssa.gov/poms.nsf/ lnx/0502302200.

177 Section 1612(b)(2) and 1612(b)(4) of the Social Security Act; 42 U.S.C. §1382a(b)(2) and 1382a(b)(4). See also 20 C.F.R. §§416.1112(c)(5) and 416.1124(c)(12).

dollar for every two dollars of earned income.[178] Income used for certain expenses is also excludable.

Table 5. Calculating a SSI Payment

	Step	Amount	Description
(1)	Countable Unearned Income	$361	SSDI Benefit
		-20	General Income Exclusion
		$341	Countable Unearned Income
(2)	Countable Earned Income	$289	Earnings
		-65	Earned Income Exclusion
		$224	
		-112	½ of Remaining Earnings
		$112	Countable Earned Income
(3)	Total Countable Income	$341	Countable Unearned Income
		+112	Countable Earned Income
		$453	Total Countable Income
(4)	SSI Payment	$750	2018 Federal Benefit Rate (FBR) for an Individual
		-453	Total Countable Income
		$297	Monthly SSI Payment

Source: CRS.

Notes: The example is of an individual who (1) lives in his or her own household, (2) is not eligible for a SSP, and (3) uses no other income exclusions other than those shown.

Table 5 shows an example of how a SSI payment is calculated for an individual living in his or her own household who receives a $361 monthly SSDI benefit and has earnings of $289 each month. The $20 general income exclusion is first applied to unearned income, meaning that only $341 of the SSDI benefit is countable. Next, the $65 earned income exclusion is applied to the $289 in earnings; the remaining $224 in earnings is counted on a 50% basis (i.e., a $1 for $2 offset). Finally, earned and unearned countable income are summed and then subtracted from the $750 FBR, which results in a monthly SSI payment of $297.

[178] Any portion of the $20 general income exclusion that has not been used to disregard unearned income in a given month can be applied to earned income for that month. See 20 C.F.R. §416.1112(c)(4).

Gross Income Breakeven Points

Individuals are ineligible for a monthly SSI *payment* if their countable income reduces the FBR to $0.[179] The amount of gross income a person can have so that countable income equals the applicable FBR is known as the *income breakeven point*. The dollar amount of the breakeven point in 2018 depends on the type of other income that an individual or couple receives. If a person has only unearned income, the *unearned income breakeven point* is $770 per month for an individual and $1,145 for a couple (i.e., the applicable FBR *plus* the $20 general income exclusion). However, if the person has only earned income, the *earned income breakeven point* is $1,585 per month for an individual and $2,335 for a couple (i.e., 2 x the applicable FBR *plus* the combined $85 earned income exclusion).[180] Depending on the composition of other income, a person who receives both earned and unearned income in 2018 faces a breakeven point somewhere between $770 and $1,585 per month for an individual and between $1,145 and $2,335 per month for a couple.[181] However, most people who receive SSI have no other income, and of those recipients who do, only about 3% have any earnings from work in a given month.[182]

Reduced SSI Payment for Residents of Certain Medical Facilities

Residents of public institutions are generally ineligible for SSI payments, because the institution provides for their basic needs. However, residents of medical treatment facilities in which more than 50% of the cost of their care is paid for by Medicaid (or in the case of a child under 18 years old, by any combination of Medicaid and private health insurance)

---

[179] A person is eligible for the SSI *program* if his or her monthly countable income is (1) equal to or less than the FBR or (2) less than the FBR *plus* the amount of applicable federally administered SSP. See SSA, POMS, "SI 02301.215 Summary of Posteligibility (PE) Suspension, Stop Payment and Termination Events by Payment Status Code (PSC)," February 18, 2016, http://policy.ssa.gov/poms.nsf/lnx/0502301215.

[180] SSA, POMS, "SI 00810.350 Income Break-Even Points General Information," November 6, 2017. http://policy.ssa.gov/poms.nsf/lnx/0500810350. The *combined $85 earned income exclusion* is the sum of the $20 general income exclusion and the $65 earned income exclusion.

[181] The example assumes the individual or couple does not receive a SSP.

[182] 2017 Annual Statistical Supplement, Table 7.D1.

are eligible for a reduced SSI payment of no more than $30 per month (or $60 per month for couples in certain situations).[183]

The reduced SSI payment, which is also known as a *personal needs allowance*, is used to pay for small comfort items not provided by the facility. Any countable income reduces the $30 payment for institutionalized individuals; however, the full FBR is used in determining their eligibility for SSI ($750 per month for an individual in 2018). The reduced SSI payment is not indexed to inflation and has remained at its current level since July 1988. In December 2016, 1.5% of SSI recipients received institutional care in an approved medical facility.[184]

Average and Total Monthly Payment Levels

As shown in Table 6, the average SSI payment in December 2017 was $542, which on an annualized basis was $6,504. That month, SSA made about $4.7 billion in payments. These amounts include federally administered SSPs but exclude state-administered SSPs. Payments are generally lower for seniors because some of them receive Social Security, which is counted as unearned income against the FBR (or the FBR *plus* the amount of the applicable federally administered SSP). Payments for children are typically higher because they often do not have income of their own.

Table 6. Average and Total Monthly Payment Amounts of SSI Recipients, by Type of Payment and Age Group, December 2017

Age Group	Number	Payment Amount	Total Monthly Payments (in thousands)
Total	8,227,676	$542	$4,754,456
Under 18 Years Old	1,182,593	647	810,752
Aged 18-64	4,805,112	564	2,959,560
Aged 65 or Older	2,239,971	437	984,144

Source: CRS, based on SSA, ORES, "SSI Monthly Statistics, 2017." January 2018, Tables 2, 6, and 7.

[183] Section 1611(e)(1)(B) of the Social Security Act; 42 U.S.C. §1382(e)(1)(B). See also 20 C.F.R. §§416.212 and 416.414. Some states supplement the reduced SSI payment.

[184] 2017 Annual Statistical Supplement, Table 7.E5.

When SSI Payments Start

Unlike SSDI benefits, SSI payments are not subject to a waiting period requirement. SSI payments begin (1) the first day of the month following the date the application is filed, or (2) the first day of the month following the date the individual becomes eligible for payments.[185] It is important to note that SSI recipients are not eligible for retroactive payments for months in which they met all other eligibility criteria *prior* to the month of application. Retroactive benefits are only available under the Social Security program. However, claimants may be owed past due payments for months in which they met all eligibility requirements *after* the month they filed an application through the month their claim is approved.

Medicaid

In addition to cash payments, most SSI recipients qualify for health coverage under Medicaid.[186] Established under Title XIX of the Social Security Act, Medicaid is a joint federal-state program that finances the delivery of primary and acute medical services, as well as long-term services and supports (LTSS), to certain needy populations, including the aged, blind, and disabled.[187] SSI recipients often have medical conditions that require significant health care resources. However, many SSI recipients are unable to work enough to gain health insurance through an employer or to pay for such insurance on their own. Medicaid provides most SSI recipients with health coverage, including some LTSS that private health insurance and Medicare do not cover, making it an important program for individuals with significant long-term care needs. In FY2015, estimated spending per disabled Medicaid enrollee under 65 years old

---

[185] Section 1611(c)(7) of the Social Security Act; 42 U.S.C. §1382(c)(7). See also 20 C.F.R. §416.501.

[186] See SSA, "Medicaid Information," https://www.ssa.gov/disabilityresearch/wi/medicaid.htm.

[187] 42 U.S.C. §§1396 et seq. See CRS Report R43357, *Medicaid: An Overview*.

(including children) was $19,500.[188] In 2016, approximately 94% of SSI recipients aged 1864 reported Medicaid coverage.[189]

SSI is a mandatory Medicaid eligibility pathway, which means that states are required by law to cover SSI recipients.[190] In general, individuals in receipt of SSI for a given month are also eligible for Medicaid for that month, provided they meet all other Medicaid eligibility requirements. SSI recipients typically become ineligible for Medicaid whenever their cash payments are suspended or terminated. However, states are afforded a certain degree of flexibility in this arrangement concerning (1) the Medicaid application process for SSI recipients and (2) the specific eligibility criteria applied to SSI recipients. Consequently, states are categorized into three groups with respect to Medicaid eligibility for SSI recipients:

- states that use SSI's eligibility criteria and do not require a separate application (i.e., "1634 states");
- states that use SSI's eligibility criteria but require a separate application (i.e., "SSI criteria states"); and
- states that use more restrictive eligibility criteria than SSI's criteria and require a separate application (i.e., "209[b] states").

The following subsections discuss the three groups in more detail.

---

188 HHS, Centers for Medicare & Medicaid Services (CMS), Office of the Actuary, *2016 Actuarial Report on the Financial Outlook for Medicaid*, Table 2, https://www.cms.gov/Research-Statistics-Data-and-Systems/Research/ActuarialStudies/Downloads/MedicaidReport2016.pdf. Estimate includes spending on disabled Medicaid enrollees under 65 years old who are eligible for Medicaid through non-SSI pathways.

189 CRS analysis of the 2017 CPS ASEC. A 2015 study that matched SSA administrative records to data from the Survey of Income and Program Participation (SIPP) found that 96.3% of SSI recipients under 18 years old and 96.0% of SSI recipients aged 18-64 reported Medicaid coverage in 2013. See Michelle Stegman Bailey and Jeffrey Hemmeter, *Characteristics of Noninstitutionalized DI and SSI Program Participants, 2013 Update*, Research and Statistics Note no. 2015-02, September 2015, Table 8, https://www.ssa.gov/policy/docs/rsnotes/rsn2015-02.html (hereinafter "Bailey and Hemmeter 2015").

190 Section 1902(a)(10)(A)(i)(II) of the Social Security Act; 42 U.S.C. §1396a(a)(10)(A)(i)(II).

1634 States

Thirty-four states and the District of Columbia grant Medicaid coverage automatically to individuals who become eligible for SSI. Section 1634 of the Social Security Act allows states to contract with SSA for the agency to perform Medicaid eligibility determinations for their SSI recipients as part of the SSI application process.[191] In other words, an SSI application in these states is also an application for Medicaid. States that elect to contract with SSA for these Medicaid determinations are known as *1634 states*. In December 2017, 85.8% of all SSI recipients resided in these areas.[192]

SSI Criteria States

Eight states and the Northern Mariana Islands use the same income, resource, and disability standards of the SSI program to determine Medicaid eligibility for SSI recipients but require them to file a separate application for Medicaid with the state or local Medicaid office. States that elect this option are known as *SSI criteria states*. The eight SSI criteria states are Alaska, Idaho, Kansas, Nebraska, Nevada, Oklahoma, Oregon, and Utah. In December 2017, 4.8% of all SSI recipients resided in these areas.[193]

209(b) States

The remaining eight states use more restrictive eligibility criteria than SSI's criteria to determine Medicaid eligibility for SSI recipients. Under Section 1902(f) of the Social Security Act, states may elect to use at least one eligibility criterion more restrictive than SSI's criteria in making Medicaid eligibility determinations for SSI recipients, provided any state established standard is no more restrictive than the standards used by the state's Medicaid program in 1972.[194] States that elect to apply more restrictive standards are known as *209(b) states*, after the section of the

---

[191] 42 U.S.C. §1383c. See also 20 C.F.R. §§416.2101-416.2176.

[192] 2017 Congressional Statistics, Table 2 for the applicable states.

[193] Ibid.

[194] Section 1902(f) of the Social Security Act; 42 U.S.C. §1396a(f).

Social Security Amendments of 1972 (P.L. 92603) that established the option. The eight 209(b) states are Connecticut, Hawaii, Illinois, Minnesota, Missouri, New Hampshire, North Dakota, and Virginia.[195] In December 2017, 9.4% of all SSI recipients resided in these areas.[196]

209(b) states may use a stricter definition of blindness or disability, a lower income or resource standard, a less generous methodology for counting income or resources, or some combination of those factors. For example, New Hampshire imposes a longer duration-of-impairment requirement for individuals with a disability other than blindness (48 months instead of SSI's 12- month standard),[197] while Virginia limits ownership of property contiguous to the individual's home (i.e., land other than the lot occupied by the home) to $5,000.[198] However, 209(b) states that use a more restrictive income standard than the SSI program must deduct incurred medical expenses from an SSI recipient's income in determining Medicaid eligibility.[199] This requirement allows SSI recipients to *spend down* their income to the state established income standard.

Since the enactment of the Patient Protection and Affordable Care Act (ACA; P.L. 111-148, as amended), three states have dropped their 209(b) status as part of larger efforts to reform their Medicaid programs. Specifically, Oklahoma elected to become a SSI criteria state effective October 1, 2015,[200] while Indiana and Ohio elected to become 1634 states effective June 1, 2014,[201] and August 1, 2016, respectively.[202]

---

195 Medicaid and CHIP Payment and Access Commission (MACPAC), *MACStats: Medicaid and CHIP Data Book*, December 2017, Exhibit 37, p. 109, https://www.macpac.gov/publication/macstats-medicaid-and-chip-data-book-2/.

196 2017 Congressional Statistics, Table 2 for the applicable states.

197 New Hampshire Revised Statutes §167:3-j.

198 Virginia Administrative Code 12VAC30-40-240.

199 42 C.F.R. §435.121. 209(b) states must also deduct the value of SSI and any optional SSP from an individual's income in determining Medicaid eligibility.

200 State of Oklahoma, Department of Human Services, "Library: Policy: 317:35-5-41.2. Miscellaneous Personal property," March 10, 2017, http://www.okdhs.org/library/policy/Pages/oac317035050041002.aspx.

201 State of Indiana, Family and Social Services Administration, "2014 Disability Eligibility Changes FAQ," https://www.in.gov/fssa/ddrs/4861.htm.

202 Letter from John B. McCarthy, director, Department of Medicaid, State of Ohio, to All Medicaid Eligibility Manual Holders, *Medicaid Eligibility Manual Transmittal Letter No. 116*, 2016, http://medicaid.ohio.gov/Portals/0/Resources/ Publications/Guidance/Medicaid Policy/Elig-Chip/MEMTL-116.pdf.

SNAP

Because SSI recipients are by definition low income, the Supplemental Nutrition Assistance Program (SNAP; formerly the Food Stamp Program) confers eligibility automatically to SSI eligible individuals in certain living situations. SNAP is a federally funded assistance program, administered jointly with the states, that provides benefits to eligible households on an electronic benefit transfer (EBT) card, which can be redeemed for foods at authorized retailers.[203] Under SNAP law, individuals living in pure SSI households those in which all members receive SSI payments are *categorically* eligible for SNAP.[204] SSI recipients living in mixed households may also qualify for SNAP if their household meets SNAP's *traditional* eligibility requirements.[205] In 2016, an estimated 52% of SSI recipients aged 1864 lived in households that received SNAP benefits.[206] (California provides SSI recipients with a higher federally administered SSP in lieu of SNAP benefits).[207]

---

[203] See CRS Report R42505, *Supplemental Nutrition Assistance Program (SNAP): A Primer on Eligibility and Benefits*, and CRS Report R42054, *The Supplemental Nutrition Assistance Program (SNAP): Categorical Eligibility*.

[204] 7 U.S.C. §2014(a) and 7 C.F.R. §273.2(j)(2)(D).

[205] Under Supplemental Nutrition Assistance Program (SNAP) law, the resources of SSI recipients in the household are deemed to meet the program's resource limitations for purposes of traditional eligibility (i.e., their resources are excluded). See 7 U.S.C. §2014(j) and 7 C.F.R. §273.8(e)(17). However, the SSI payments of household members are considered unearned income under SNAP's traditional eligibility rules and thus are included in the household income calculation. See 7 C.F.R. §273.9(b)(2)(i).

[206] CRS analysis of the 2017 CPS ASEC. A 2015 study that matched SSA administrative records to data from the SIPP found that 64.9% of SSI recipients under 18 years old and 64.6% of SSI recipients aged 18-64 lived in households that received SNAP benefits in 2013. See Bailey and Hemmeter 2015, Table 9.

[207] Under SNAP law, SSI recipients living in states that *cash out* the bonus value of the SNAP allotment are not considered to be a member of the household and thus are ineligible for SNAP benefits. See 7 U.S.C. §2015(g) and 7 C.F.R. §273.20. SSI recipients living in California receive an extra $10 in their monthly SSP in lieu of SNAP benefits. For more information on California's cash-out policy, see State of California, Legislative Analyst's Office (LAO), *The Potential Effects of Ending the SSI Cash-Out*, January 8, 2018, http://www.lao.ca.gov/Publications/Report/3729.

Financing

Federal SSI payments and administrative costs are financed from the general fund of the U.S. Treasury. SSPs are financed solely with state funds. States reimburse SSA for the cost of SSPs made to their eligible recipients and for the cost of administering their supplementation program. In FY2017, total federal SSI outlays were $58.7 billion, with $54.6 billion for benefit payments and $4.1 billion for administrative and other costs.[208] Spending on federally administered SSPs in FY2017 was $2.6 billion.[209] In 2016, about 93% of spending on federally administered SSPs was attributable to SSI recipients living in California.[210]

In their August 2017 report and under current law, SSA's actuaries project that spending on federal SSI payments will increase (in CPI-indexed 2017 dollars) from $54.6 billion in 2017 to $61.5 billion in 2041.[211] As a share of gross domestic product (GDP), SSA's actuaries project that spending on federal SSI payments will decrease from 0.28% in 2017 to 0.20% in 2041.[212] Under its April 2018 baseline and under current law, CBO projects that spending on federal SSI payments will increase (in nominal dollars) from $54.6 billion in FY2017 to $80.8 billion in FY2028.[213]

CONCURRENT DISABILITY BENEFICIARIES

(Hereinafter the term *SSDI beneficiary* refers to disabled workers, disabled widow[er]s, and disabled adult children of retired, disabled, or deceased insured workers. In addition, the term *SSI disability recipient* refers to blind or disabled SSI recipients under 65 years old).

---

208 SSA, *Justifications of Estimates for Appropriations Committees, Fiscal Year 2019,* February 12, 2018, Table i.7, https://www.ssa.gov/budget/.

209 Ibid.

210 2017 Annual Statistical Supplement, Table 7.B7.

211 2017 Annual Report of the SSI Program, Table IV.C3.

212 Ibid., Table IV.D1.

213 CBO, *Supplemental Security Income—CBO's April 2018 Baseline*, April 10, 2018, https://www.cbo.gov/sites/ default/files/recurringdata/51313-2018-04-ssi.pdf.

In December 2016, about 12.8 million adults aged 1864 received SSDI or SSI due to a qualifying impairment (Figure 3). Of those, more than 1.3 million (or 10%) received both types of disability benefits. About one in seven SSDI beneficiaries aged 18-64 received SSI concurrently. At the same time, about a quarter of SSI disability recipients aged 1864 also received SSDI. For this chapter, individuals who receive both SSDI and SSI due to a qualifying impairment are referred to as *concurrent disability beneficiaries*. Assuming they meet the applicable eligibility requirements, concurrent disability beneficiaries receive health coverage under Medicare and Medicaid. Individuals who qualify for both health care programs are known as *dual eligibles*.

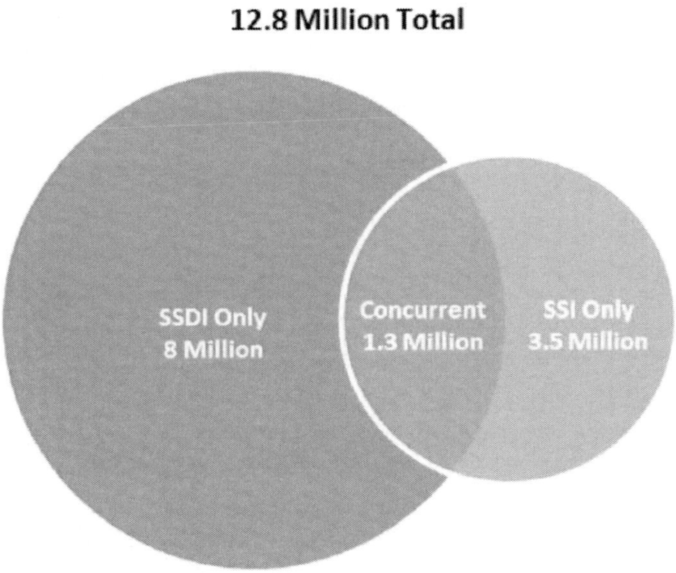

Source: CRS, adapted from SSA, ORES, Annual Statistical Report on the Social Security Disability Insurance Program, 2016, October 2017, Chart 12.

Notes: Subtotals may not equal totals due to rounding. The term SSDI includes disabled workers, disabled widow(er)s, and disabled adult children of retired, disabled, or deceased workers.

Figure 3. SSDI Beneficiaries and SSI Disability Recipients Aged 18-64, December 2016.

The average combined benefit for concurrent disability beneficiaries in December 2016 was $783 (Table 7). Of that amount, $538 was from SSDI and $245 was from SSI. Because average benefits for concurrent disability beneficiaries were below the FBR for an individual ($733 per month in 2016) and because SSDI benefits generally offset SSI payments on a dollar for dollar basis, *combined* benefit levels for each type of concurrent SSDI beneficiary were about the same. Thus, disabled workers (who have higher average SSDI benefit amounts) received lower average SSI payments, and disabled adult children (who have lower average SSDI benefit amounts) received higher SSI payments, resulting in roughly the same combined disability benefit amount across all three beneficiary types.

Table 7. Number of Concurrent Disability Beneficiaries Aged 18-64 and Average Benefit Amount, by Type of SSDI Beneficiary, December 2016

Type of SSDI Beneficiary	Number of Concurrent Beneficiaries	Average Monthly Benefit		
		Combined	SSDI	SSI
Total	1,310,459	$783	$538	$245
Disabled Workers	951,118	784	560	225
Disabled Widow(er)s	29,784	787	544	244
Disabled Adult Children	329,557	777	475	303

Source: CRS, based on SSA, ORES, *SSI Annual Statistical Report, 2016*, November 2017, Tables 15 and 16.

Notes: Subtotals may not sum to totals due to rounding. The term *SSDI* includes disabled workers, disabled widow(er)s, and disabled adult children of retired, disabled, or deceased workers.

As shown in Figure 4, the average benefit amount for concurrent disability beneficiaries is higher than that for SSI-only recipients but is lower than that for SSDI-only beneficiaries. The purpose of SSI for adults is generally twofold: (1) to provide cash assistance to aged, blind, or disabled individuals who have no income and (2) to supplement the incomes of those who have low Social Security benefits. For SSDI beneficiaries with minimal benefits and other income, SSI increases their overall monthly disability benefit from SSA.

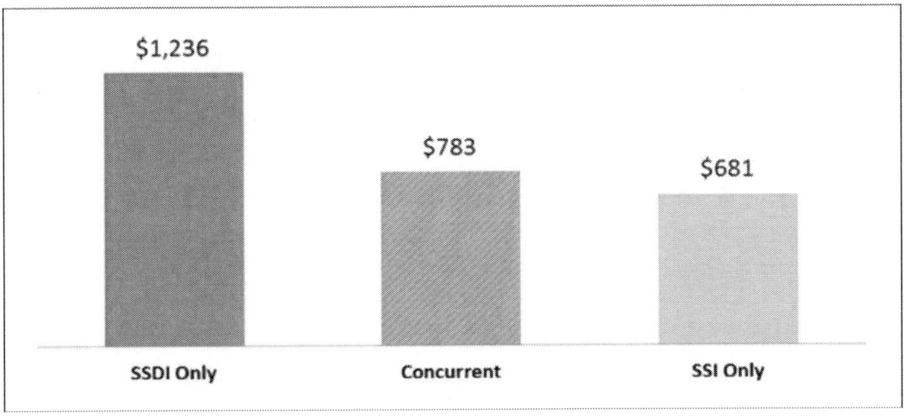

Source: CRS, based on SSA, ORES, Annual Statistical Report on the Social Security Disability Insurance Program, 2016, October 2017, Table 66.

Notes: The term *SSDI* includes disabled workers, disabled widow(er)s, and disabled adult children of retired, disabled, or deceased workers.

Figure 4. Average Monthly Benefit Amount for Disability Beneficiaries Aged 18-64, by Type of Disability Beneficiary, December 2016.

DEFINITION OF DISABILITY

SSDI and Adult SSI Claimants

SSDI and SSI use a total work-limiting definition of disability for adults; in other words, an individual's impairment(s) must significantly interfere with his or her ability to earn a living.[214] Most adults are considered disabled for SSDI and SSI eligibility purposes if they are "unable to engage in any substantial gainful activity by reason of any medically determinable physical or mental impairment that can be expected to result in death or that has lasted or can be expected to last for a continuous period of not less than 12 months."[215] Adults generally qualify

---

[214] The definition of blindness under the SSI program does not require an individual to be unable to perform substantial gainful activity (SGA).

[215] Sections 223(d)(1)(A) and 1614(a)(3)(A) of the Social Security Act; 42 U.S.C. §§423(d)(1)(A) and 1382c(a)(3)(A). Section 223(d)(1)(B) of the Social Security Act

as disabled for SSDI and SSI purposes if they have an impairment (or combination of impairments) of such severity that they are unable to perform any kind of substantial work that exists in significant numbers in the national economy, taking into consideration their age, education, and work experience. The work need not exist in the immediate area in which the claimant lives nor must a specific job vacancy exist for the individual.

Child SSI Claimants

The SSI program uses a special definition of disability for children because minors are generally not expected to work. Individuals under 18 years old must have "a medically determinable physical or mental impairment, which results in marked and severe functional limitations, and which can be expected to result in death or which has lasted or can be expected to last for a continuous period of not less than 12 months."[216] Children typically qualify as disabled if they have a severe impairment (or combination of impairments) that limits their ability to engage in age-appropriate childhood activities at home, in childcare, at school, or in the community. In addition, the child must be unable to perform substantial gainful activity (SGA).

Substantial Gainful Activity Earnings Limits

Under SSA's regulations for SGA, work activity is considered *substantial* if it involves doing significant physical or mental activities, even if it is done on a part time basis.[217] Work activity is considered *gainful* if an individual does it for pay or profit, regardless of whether the profit is realized or legal.[218]

---

provides an alternative definition of disability for blind individuals who are aged 55 or older.

[216] Section 1614(a)(3)(C) of the Social Security Act; 42 U.S.C. §1382c(a)(3)(C).

[217] 20 C.F.R. §§404.1572 and 416.972.

[218] Ibid.

SSA uses a monetary threshold to determine whether an individual's work activity constitutes SGA, which the agency adjusts annually to reflect changes in national earnings levels. For SSDI, the SGA earnings threshold in 2018 is $1,180 per month for most individuals and $1,970 per month for statutorily blind individuals.[219] Under the SSI program, SGA rules do not apply to statutorily blind individuals. Because of certain SSI work incentives, the nonblind SGA earnings threshold applies to individuals with a condition other than blindness only at the time of application for SSI.[220]

The SGA threshold for blind individuals under the SSDI program is specified in statute,[221] while the SGA threshold for nonblind individuals under the SSDI and SSI programs is specified in regulations by SSA.[222] The SGA threshold for blind individuals under the SSDI program is adjusted annually for average earnings growth in the economy, provided a COLA is payable for that year. On the other hand, the SGA threshold for nonblind individuals under both programs is adjusted annually for average earnings growth in accordance with the agency's regulations, regardless of whether a COLA is payable for the year. Thus, in years when a COLA is not payable, the SGA threshold for blind individuals under the SSDI program remains the same as the amount for the previous year, while the SGA threshold for nonblind individuals is adjusted according to the formula specified in regulations, which *may* result in a higher threshold.

---

[219] SSA, OCACT, "Substantial Gainful Activity," https://www.ssa.gov/oact/cola/sga.html.

[220] Section 1619(a) of the Social Security Act (42 U.S.C. §1382h[a]) provides for the continuation of cash payments for SSI recipients (but not for claimants) with substantial earnings that otherwise would disqualify them from the program. Under this provision, recipients who have earnings at or above the SGA threshold but whose countable income is less than the applicable FBR are eligible to receive special SSI payments in lieu of regular SSI payments. These special 1619(a) payments are calculated in the same manner as regular SSI payments and are payable for as long as an individual performs SGA and meets all other SSI eligibility criteria. 1619(a) effectively eliminates the SGA threshold for non-blind SSI *recipients*.

[221] 42 U.S.C. §423(d)(4)(A).

[222] 20 C.F.R. §§404.1574 and 416.974.

Drug Addiction and Alcoholism

Section 105 of the Contract with America Advancement Act of 1996 (P.L. 104121) amended the Social Security Act to bar SSA from considering an individual disabled if drug addiction or alcoholism (DAA) is a contributing factor material to the determination that the individual is disabled.[223] SSA's policy interpretation of this requirement is specified in Social Security Ruling (SSR) 132p.[224] *DAA* is a substance use disorder as defined in the latest edition of the Diagnostic and Statistical Manual of Mental Disorders (DSM). SSA considers an individual to have DAA if he or she has a medically determinable substance use disorder documented by objective medical evidence from an acceptable medical source. The DAA is considered *material* to the determination of disability if the individual would not meet the definition of disability if he or she were not using drugs or alcohol.[225] It should be noted that nothing in the Social Security Act precludes an individual from qualifying for SSDI or SSI for *using* drugs or alcohol (including medical and recreational marijuana).[226] The act simply prevents individuals from qualifying for benefits if their DAA is material to their disability determination or contributes to their inability to follow prescribed treatment (discussed below). In 2015, approximately 7.0% of all working age SSDI beneficiaries and SSI disability recipients reported drug or alcohol abuse in the past 12 months.[227]

---

[223] Sections 223(d)(2)(C) and [1614](a)([3])(J) of the Social Security Act; 42 U.S.C. §423(d)(2)(C) and 1382c(a)(3)(J). See also 20 C.F.R. §§404.1513(a)(5)(vi), 404.1535, 416.913(a)(5)(vii), and 416.935.

[224] SSA, "SSR 13-2p: Titles II and XVI: Evaluating Cases Involving of Drug Addiction and Alcoholism (DAA), February 20, 2013 (effective date March 22, 2013), https://www.ssa.gov/OP_Home/rulings/di/01/SSR2013-02-di01.html.

[225] 20 C.F.R. §§404.1535(b) and 416.935(b).

[226] See statement of Sarah-Schultz Lackey, spokesperson, SSA, in KTHV-TV, "Patients fear medical marijuana card could cost them their social security benefits," July 3, 2017, http://www.thv11.com/article/news/local/patients-fearmedical-marijuana-card-could-cost-them-their-social-security-benefits-11-listens/453909122.

[227] SSA, Office of Retirement and Disability Policy, Office of Research, Demonstration, and Employment Support, *National Beneficiary Survey: Disability Statistics, 2015*, March 2018, Table 8, p. 4, https://www.ssa.gov/policy/docs/ statcomps/nbs/2015/index.html.

Following Prescribed Treatment

The Social Security Act requires individuals to follow treatment prescribed from their medical source(s) if such treatment is expected to restore their ability to work (i.e., engage in SGA).[228] If an individual fails to follow the prescribed treatment without good reason, SSA will not consider the individual to be disabled for purposes of SSDI or SSI. In some instances, the individual's DAA may interfere with his or her ability to follow prescribed treatment. A 2015 report from SSA's Office of the Inspector General (OIG) noted the following case:

> An individual applied for disability benefits for seizures, high blood pressure, and poor eyesight. The medical evidence showed she was prescribed three doses of an anti-seizure medication per day; however, she only took two doses. She claimed she was taking only two doses to stretch the medication. However, because evidence in the file showed she was also using cocaine and marijuana, she had the means to purchase her medication as she had the means to purchase non-prescription drugs. The evidence showed that proper medication management should significantly reduce her seizure issues. Therefore, SSA denied the claim for failure to follow prescribed treatment.[229]

Comparisons with Other Program Definitions of Disability

The definitions of disability under Titles II and XVI of the Social Security Act are considered total and long term; neither program pays benefits to individuals with partial or short term impairments. SSA's all-or-nothing definitions of disability are different from other disability

---

[228] Sections 223(f) and 1614(a)(4) of the Social Security Act; 42 U.S.C. §§423(f) and 1382c(a)(4). See also 20 C.F.R. §§404.1513(a)(5)(vi), 404.1530, 404.1579(e)(4), 404.1586(c), 416.913(a)(5)(vii), 404.1594(e)(4), 416.930, 416.986(a)(3), and 416.994(b)(4)(iv).

[229] SSA, Office of the Inspector General (OIG), *Failure to Follow Prescribed Treatment,* A-01-15-50024, August 21, 2015, p. 8, https://oig.ssa.gov/audits-and-investigations/audit-reports/A-01-15-50024.

standards. For example, the VA provides partial or total disability benefits to veterans with qualifying impairments on a scale from 0% to 100% (in 10% increments).[230] In addition, state workers' compensation pays benefits for total or partial occupational-related injuries and illnesses that are permanent or temporary.[231] According to SSA, the Social Security Act's "purpose and specific eligibility requirements for disability and blindness differ significantly from the purpose and eligibility requirements of other programs."[232]

APPLICATION AND INITIAL DETERMINATION PROCESS[233]

The process begins when a claimant files an initial application for SSDI or SSI using one of four methods: (1) submitting an application in person at one of SSA's more than 1,200 nationwide field offices; (2) contacting a SSA teleservice representative over the phone and relaying the necessary information; (3) sending a paper application by mail; or (4) filing an electronic application on ssa.gov (for SSDI and certain concurrent claims only). If the agency requires more information to process the application, it will contact the claimant by phone or arrange for an in person interview at the local field office. Claimants must inform and submit all evidence to SSA related to their impairment as a condition of their application for benefits.[234]

Claims representatives at SSA's field offices screen claimants to make sure they meet the applicable nonmedical entitlement factors. For SSDI, nonmedical factors include disability insured status, the work activity test

---

[230] CRS Report R41289, *Disability Benefits Available Under the Social Security Disability Insurance (SSDI) and Veterans Disability Compensation (VDC) Programs*.

[231] CRS Report R44580, *Workers' Compensation: Overview and Issues*.

[232] SSA, "Revisions to Rules Regarding the Evaluation of Medical Evidence," 82 *Federal Register* 5848, January 18, 2017, https://www.gpo.gov/fdsys/pkg/FR-2017-01-18/pdf/2017-00455.pdf.

[233] This chapter describes the initial disability determination process for claims with a filing date on or after March 27, 2017. Claims with an earlier filing date are evaluated under somewhat different rules. See 20 C.F.R. §§404.1527 and 416.927.

[234] 20 C.F.R. §§404.1512 and 416.912.

(i.e., SGA earnings limit), and the claimant's relationship to certain family members. For SSI, such factors include income, resources, living arrangements, the work activity test (for nonblind claimants), citizenship, residency, and the requirement to apply for all other benefits. In general, claimants who do not meet the applicable nonmedical entitlement factors are found to be ineligible for benefits and do not receive a disability determination. SSA field office personnel notify claimants whose applications are denied due to nonmedical factors.

Applications that meet the applicable non-medical entitlement factors are forwarded to the disability determination services (DDS) office in the area that has jurisdiction for the disability determination (generally the state in which the claimant resides).[235] DDSs, which are fully funded by the federal government, are state agencies tasked with reviewing the medical and vocational evidence and issuing the disability determination for SSA.[236] Although DDS workers are state employees, they make the disability determinations based on federal law, regulations, and SSA's policy guidance. DDSs are located in the 50 states, the District of Columbia, Puerto Rico, Guam, and the Virgin Islands, and they employ approximately 15,000 state workers.

The disability determination for both types of benefits is made based on evidence gathered in an individual's case record. Disability examiners – with the help of medical or psychological consultants (who are licensed physicians, psychiatrists, or psychologists) typically use evidence collected from the claimant's own medical sources to evaluate the existence and severity of the claimant's impairment(s).[237] However, if the medical evidence is unavailable or insufficient to make a determination, disability examiners can schedule a physical or mental examination or test from a medical source to obtain the necessary information. In such cases, SSA

---

[235] See SSA, POMS, "DI 22501.002 Responsibilities for Case Development of Disability Claims," March 23, 2016, http://policy.ssa.gov/poms.nsf/lnx/0422501002.

[236] Sections 221(a) and 1633 of the Social Security Act; 42 U.S.C. §§421(a) and 1383b.

[237] See SSA, POMS, "DI 24501.001 The Disability Determination Services (DDS) Disability Examiner (DE), Medical Consultant (MC), and Psychological Consultant (PC) Team, and the Role of the Medical Advisor (MA)," December 8, 2017, http://policy.ssa.gov/poms.nsf/lnx/0424501001.

pays for the consultative examination (CE).[238] The initial review generally does not involve a face to face meeting between the claimant and the adjudicator (i.e., the claim is decided based solely on the evidence in the claims file). After considering all medical and other evidence, the DDS agency issues a disability determination and returns the case to the SSA field office. If the claim is approved, the SSA field office sends out the initial award notice and begins processing the claim. If the claim is denied, the DDS agency prepares a personalized disability explanation and notifies the claimant of the decision.

Disability Determinations for SSDI and Adult SSI Claimants

The Social Security Act gives the Commissioner of Social Security broad authority to promulgate regulations specifying the standards, administrative requirements, and procedures used in conducting disability determinations.[239] Under its regulations, SSA employs a fivestep sequential evaluation process to determine whether a claimant's medical condition meets the definition of disability prescribed in the act for SSDI and adult SSI claimants (Figure 5).[240]

Each step in the process is followed in a set order. If SSA finds a claimant disabled or not disabled at a given step, the initial disability determination process is completed and a decision by the agency is made. If SSA cannot find a claimant disabled or not disabled at a given step, the agency proceeds to the next step.

---

[238] SSA, "Consultative Examinations: A Guide for Health Professionals," https://www.ssa.gov/disability/professionals/ greenbook/ce-guidelines.htm.

[239] Sections 221, 223(d), and 1614(a)(3) of the Social Security Act; 42 U.S.C. §§421, 423(d), and 1382c(a)(3).

[240] 20 C.F.R. §§404.1520 and 416.920. See also Bernard Wixon and Alexander Strand, *Identifying SSA's Sequential Disability Determination Steps Using Administrative Data*, Research and Statistics Note no. 2013-01, June 2013, https://www.ssa.gov/policy/docs/rsnotes/rsn2013-01.html. Moreover, see Tom Johns, branch chief, Disability Quality Branch Office of Quality Performance, Dallas, *SSA's Sequential Evaluation Process for Assessing Disability*, https://www.ssa.gov/oidap/Documents/Social%20Security%20Administration.%20%20SSAs%20Sequential%20Evaluation.pdf.

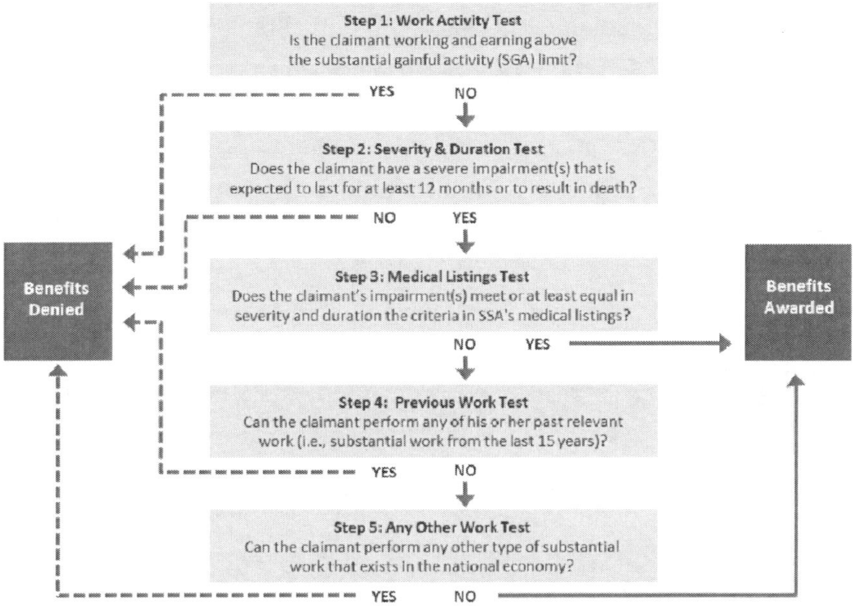

Source: CRS, based on Subpart P of 20 C.F.R. §404 and Subpart I of 20 C.F.R. §416.

Notes: The term *SSDI* includes disabled workers, disabled widow(er)s, and disabled adult children of retired, disabled, or deceased workers. In 2018, the SGA earnings limit is $1,180 per month for non-blind individuals and $1,970 per month for statutorily blind SSDI claimants.

Figure 5. Initial Disability Determination Process for SSDI and Adult SSI Claimants.

Step 1. Work Activity Test

The SSA field office assesses whether a claimant's level of work activity constitutes SGA.[241] In 2018, most claimants are found able to engage in SGA if their countable earnings average more than $1,180 per month.[242] *Countable earnings* equal gross earnings minus applicable exclusions. Blind SSDI claimants are found able to perform SGA if their countable earnings average more than $1,970 per month. (SGA rules do not apply to statutorily blind SSI claimants.)

---

[241] 20 C.F.R. §§404.1571-404.1576 and 416.971-416.976.

[242] SSA applies special rules in evaluating the countable income of self-employed claimants and the countable earnings or income of statutorily blind Social Security claimants who are aged 55 or older.

To determine countable earnings, SSA first documents a claimant's gross earnings for each month during the relevant period of work.[243] The agency then considers whether the claimant's work was performed under any special conditions, such as in sheltered employment or under certain government-sponsored job training or employment programs. Earnings or other compensation derived from work performed under special conditions may be deducted (in part or in whole) from gross earnings. Reasonable costs for certain impairment related work expenses (IRWE) – such as attendant care services or medical equipment – may also be deducted if the claimant needs such expenses to work. Once a claimant's countable earnings have been calculated and added together, SSA divides them over the number of months in the relevant review period to produce a monthly average. Claimants with countable monthly earnings at or below the applicable SGA limit proceed to the next step of the disability determination process. Those with countable monthly earnings above the applicable SGA limit are found not disabled, and their application is denied.

Step 2. Severity and Duration Test

The DDS agency determines whether available medical evidence establishes a physical or mental impairment (or combination of impairments) of sufficient severity to prevent the claimant from engaging in SGA and, if so, whether the impairment(s) can be expected to last for at least 12 months or to result in death. In making this determination, the DDS agency first verifies the existence of a medically determinable impairment using objective medical evidence (i.e., medical signs or laboratory findings) from the claimant's *acceptable medical sources*.[244] A claimant is considered to have a medically determinable impairment if such evidence shows the existence of one or more anatomical, physiological, or psychological abnormalities.

---

[243] Certain compensation is not counted as earnings for SGA purposes, such as vacation or sick pay.

[244] 20 C.F.R. §§404.1521 and 416.921. For more information on the terms used in this section, see 20 C.F.R. §§404.1502 and 416.902.

Once a medically determinable impairment has been established, the adjudicative team evaluates the severity of the impairment using all available evidence, including medical opinions and statements of symptoms from the claimant. *Symptoms*, such as pain or fatigue, are considered if the objective medical evidence from acceptable medical sources shows that the impairment(s) could reasonably be expected to produce the symptoms.[245] The DDS agency then evaluates the intensity and persistence of the claimant's symptoms to determine the extent to which such symptoms interfere with the claimant's ability to work. A claimant's impairment(s) is ultimately considered *severe* if it significantly limits his or her physical or mental ability to do basic work activities. *Basic work activities* include the following: walking, standing, sitting, lifting, pushing, pulling, reaching, carrying, or handling; seeing, hearing, and speaking; understanding, carrying out, and remembering simple instructions; use of judgment; responding appropriately to supervision, coworkers, and usual work situations; and dealing with changes in a routine work setting.[246] A claimant's impairment(s) is considered *not severe* if it has only a "minimal effect" on his or her ability to perform basic work activities required in most jobs.

In evaluating the claim at Step 2, the DDS agency is required to consider the combined effect of all the claimant's impairments without regard to whether any such impairment, if considered separately, would be of sufficient severity.[247] Thus, a claimant may meet the severity requirement if he or she has multiple non-severe impairments that when combined, have the same effect on the claimant's ability to function as a single severe impairment. Lastly, in addition to being severe, the claimant's medically determinable impairment(s) must be expected to result in death or have lasted or be expected to last for a continuous period

[245] 20 C.F.R. §§404.1529 and 416.929.

[246] 20 C.F.R. §§404.1522 and 416.922.

[247] Sections 223(d)(2)(B) and 1614(a)(3)(G) of the Social Security Act; 42 U.S.C. §§423(d)(2)(B) and 1382c(a)(3)(G). See also 20 C.F.R. §§404.1523(c) and 416.923(c).

of not less than 12 months.[248] Claimants who meet the severity and duration requirements proceed to the next step. Those who do not are found not disabled and their application is denied.

Step 3. Medical Listings Test

At Step 3, the DDS agency determines whether the claimant's medically determinable impairment(s) meets the medical criteria of an impairment specified in SSA's *Listing of Impairments* (also known as the *Blue Book*).[249] The listings describe medically determinable impairments for each body system that the agency considers severe enough to prevent a claimant from performing any gainful activity, regardless of the claimant's age, education, or work experience.[250] Most listed impairments are permanent or expected to result in death. All other listed impairments are expected to last for at least 12 months or for a specific duration.

The listings for adults (Part A) are categorized across 14 major body systems, with each category containing examples of common qualifying impairments as well as specific evaluative criteria for confirming their existence. Each listing outlines the impairments applicable to the body system, the medical and other documentation required to evaluate the claim, and the rules used to evaluate the specific impairment, including related symptoms, effects of treatment, and loss of function. For impairments that can be objectively measured, the listing may describe the minimum threshold for a particular diagnostic test. For those that are more subjective to measure, the listing may describe the minimum functional criteria. The listings were created to quickly screen relatively clear-cut cases, leaving adjudicators more time to evaluate more difficult cases at the latter stages of the process.

Claimants qualify at Step 3 of the disability determination process in one of two ways: (1) by meeting the criteria of a specific listing or (2) by equaling the criteria of a specific listing. For claimants to *meet a listing*,

---

[248] The Disability Determination Services (DDS) agency cannot combine two or more unrelated severe impairments to meet the 12-month duration requirement. The duration requirement does not apply to blind SSI claimants or to certain blind SSDI claimants aged 55 or older.

[249] Appendix 1 to Subpart P of 20 C.F.R. §404.

[250] 20 C.F.R. §§404.1525 and 416.925.

their medically determinable impairment(s) must satisfy *all* of the criteria described in the listing; a diagnosis alone is insufficient to meet a listing. In other words, claimants must have an impairment described in the listing, meet the objective medical and other findings, and meet the duration requirement.

If claimants are unable to meet a listing, they may be able to *equal a listing* if their medically determinable impairment(s) at least equals in severity and duration the criteria of any listed impairment.[251] Specifically, if the claimant's impairment(s) is described in the listings but he or she does not exhibit one or more findings specific for the listing (or one of the findings does not meet the specified severity), the DDS will find the claimant's impairment(s) medically equivalent to the listing, provided the claimant has other findings related to his or her impairment(s) that are at least of equal medical significance to the required criteria. If the claimant's impairment is not described in the listings but is closely analogous to a listed impairment, the DDS will find the claimant's impairment(s) medically equivalent to the analogous listing if the findings related to the claimant's impairment(s) are at least of equal medical significance to those of the listed impairment.[252]

Claimants with impairments that meet or equal a listing are found disabled and awarded benefits. Those with impairments that do not meet or equal a listing proceed to Step 4.

Step 4. Previous Work Test

Claimants with severe impairments that do not meet or equal a listed impairment proceed to an individual assessment that examines their remaining ability to work. To make this determination, the adjudicative team conducts a residual functional capacity (RFC) assessment, which is a function-by-function assessment of a claimant's ability to perform

---

[251] 20 C.F.R. §§404.1526 and 416.926.

[252] Claimants at this stage of the disability determination process are evaluated at a greater level of severity compared with those evaluated at the latter stages, insofar as awards at Step 3 are based on medical factors alone, whereas awards at the later stages take into consideration a claimant's vocational factors, such as age, education, and work experience. In addition, claimants at Step 3 must be unable to perform *any gainful activity*, which is a stricter standard than *any substantial gainful activity*.

sustained, work-related physical or mental activities despite the limitations and restrictions caused by his or her medically determinable impairment(s).[253] In general, RFC is a claimant's maximum remaining ability to do sustained work activities in an ordinary work setting on a regular and continuing basis (i.e., eight hours a day, five days a week, or an equivalent work schedule). The RFC assessment is based on all available evidence in the claimant's case record, such as objective medical evidence, activities of daily living (ADL), and statements provided by the claimant or other lay sources (e.g., family, friends, neighbors). In evaluating a claimant's RFC, the DDS agency considers the effects of pain and other symptoms, as well as any nonsevere impairments, on the claimant's ability to function in a work setting.

Once the assessment is complete, the DDS evaluates the claimant's RFC with the physical and mental demands of his or her past relevant work.[254] *Past relevant work* is defined as work performed in the past 15 years, at SGA, and which lasted long enough for the claimant to learn to do it.[255] The individual's past relevant work need not exist in significant numbers in the national economy.[256] If a claimant's medically determinable impairment(s) does not prevent him or her from performing past relevant work, the claimant is found not disabled and the application is denied. If the claimant is found unable to perform past relevant work, the case proceeds to the next step.

Step 5. Any Work Test

At the final stage of the disability determination process, the DDS agency considers whether the claimant can adjust to *any* other type of

---

[253] 20 C.F.R. §§404.1545 and 416.945.

[254] If there is insufficient evidence of a claimant's past relevant work, the DDS may expedite the claim to Step 5. See 20 C.F.R. §§404.1520(h) and 416.920(h).

[255] 20 C.F.R. §§404.1560 and 416.960.

[256] See SSA, POMS, "DI 25005.010 Whether Past Relevant Work Must Exist in Significant Numbers in the National Economy (SSR 05-1c) – U.S. Supreme Court Decision in the Case of Jo Anne B. Barnhart, Commissioner of Social Security v. Pauline Thomas," January 27, 2009, http://policy.ssa.gov/poms.nsf/lnx/0425005010.

work.[257] Specifically, the claimant must be unable to do not only his or her previous work but cannot, considering his or her age, education, and work experience, engage in any other kind of substantial gainful work that exists in the national economy.[258] *Work that exists in the national economy* means work that exists in significant numbers either in the region where the claimant lives or in several regions of the country.[259] It does not matter whether the work exists in the immediate area where the claimant lives, whether a specific job vacancy exists, or whether the claimant would be hired if he or she applied for such work.

At this stage, the DDS agency uses medical-vocational rules (also known as *the grids*) to relate the claimant's age, education, and work experience to his or her RFC to perform work related physical or mental activities.[260] The grids cross-reference the aforementioned vocational factors by certain exertional (i.e., strength demands) and skill levels to determine the limitations and restrictions imposed by the claimant's impairment(s) and related symptoms.[261] The DDS agency uses the Department of Labor's Dictionary of Occupational Titles (DOT) for information about the physical and mental demands needed for jobs in the national economy.[262] Claimants with impairments that prevent them from adjusting to any other work that exists in the national economy are found disabled and awarded benefits. Claimants with impairments that allow them to adjust to a significant number of jobs in the national economy are found not disabled and their application is denied.

---

[257] The DDS agency may find a claimant disabled if he or she meets the criteria outlined in SSA's special medical-vocational profiles, which describe specific combinations of vocational factors that are considered so unfavorable to a claimant that he or she is deemed unable to adjust to any other work. See 20 C.F.R. §§404.1562 and 416.962.

[258] Sections 223(d)(2)(A) and 1614(a)(3)(B) of the Social Security Act; 42 U.S.C. §§423(d)(2)(A) and 1382c(a)(3)(B).

[259] 20 C.F.R. §§404.1566 and 416.966.

[260] Appendix 2 to Subpart P of 20 C.F.R. §404. See also 20 C.F.R. §§404.1563-1565 and 416.963-416.965.

[261] The medical-vocational rules (i.e., the grids) were established in 1978. See 43 *Federal Register* 55349.

[262] The Dictionary of Occupational Titles (DOT) was last updated in 1991. SSA is working with the Bureau of Labor Statistics (BLS) to develop its own occupational information system. See SSA, "Occupational Information System Project," https://www.ssa.gov/disability research/occupational_info_systems.html.

In general, older individuals (i.e., those aged 50 or older) who have limited education and work experience are more likely to be awarded benefits than younger individuals or those who have more education or work experience. For example, all things being equal, a 59 year old coal miner with an 8th grade education and no other work experience is more likely to be awarded benefits than a 45 year old adjunct college professor who has worked several types of jobs in the past.

Disability Determinations for Child SSI Claimants

As noted earlier, because children are generally not expected to work, the SSI program uses a special definition of disability for minors. Individuals under the age of 18 must have a medically determinable physical or mental impairment, which results in *marked and severe functional limitations*, and which can be expected to result in death or which has lasted or can be expected to last for a continuous period of not less than 12 months. The first part of the disability determination process for child SSI claimants is similar to the one used for SSDI and adult SSI claimants (Figure 6).[263]

At Step 1, the DDS agency determines whether the child's countable monthly earnings average more than the nonblind SGA earnings limit. At Step 2, the DDS agency determines whether available objective medical evidence from acceptable medical sources establishes a medically determinable impairment, and, if so, whether all medical and other evidence demonstrates that such impairment (or combination of impairments) meets the severity and duration requirements. In determining the severity of the claimant's impairment(s), the DDS agency compares the claimant's functioning to that of children his or her own age who do not have impairments. A child's medically determinable impairment(s) is considered *not severe* if it is a slight abnormality (or a combination of slight abnormalities) that causes no more than minimal functional

[263] 20 C.F.R. §416.924.

limitations. At Step 3a, the DDS agency determines whether the child's medically determinable impairment(s) meets or medically equals the criteria of a specific listing. The listings for children (Part B) are categorized across 15 major body systems and like their adult counterparts, contain examples of common impairment for each body system and specific evaluative criteria for confirming the existence of a qualifying impairment.

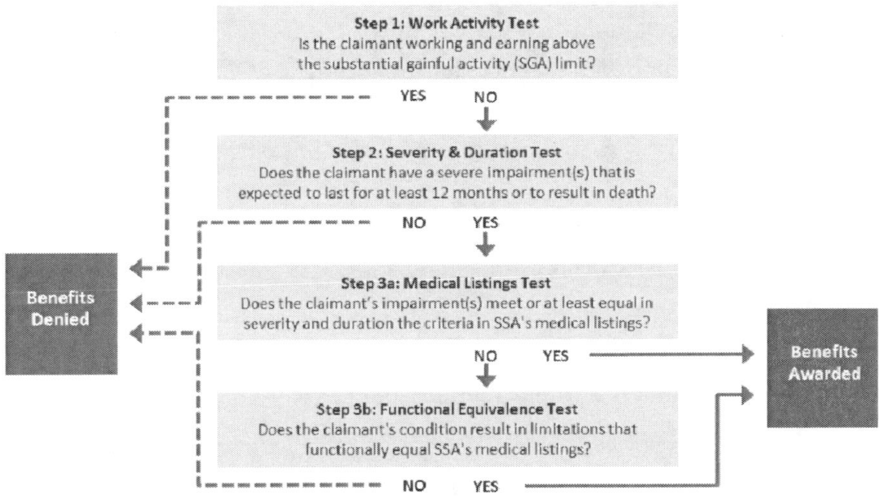

Source: CRS, based on Subpart P of 20 C.F.R. §404, Subpart I of 20 C.F.R. §416, and Chart 2 in Bernard Wixon and Alexander Strand, *Identifying SSA's Sequential Disability Determination Steps Using Administrative Data*, Research and Statistics Note no. 2013-01, June 2013, https://www.ssa.gov/policy/docs/rsnotes/rsn2013-01.html.

Notes: In 2018, the SGA earnings limit is $1,180 per month and applies only at the time of application.

Figure 6. Initial Disability Determination Process for Child SSI Claimants.

If a child has a severe impairment that does not meet or medically equal the criteria of a specific listing, then the case proceeds to Step 3b, where the DDS agency determines whether the impairment(s) results in limitations that *functionally equal* the listings.[264] During this process, the

[264] 20 C.F.R. §416.926a.

DDS agency assesses the extent to which a child's impairment(s) limits or restricts his or her day to-day functioning at home, in childcare, at school, or in the community. The DDS agency evaluates a child's functioning across six domains: (1) acquiring and using information; (2) attending and completing tasks; (3) interacting and relating with others; (4) moving about and manipulating objects; (5) self care; and (6) health and physical wellbeing. These domains are cross-referenced by age categories that describe age-appropriate functioning and behavior.

At this stage, a claimant's impairment (or combination of impairments) is not evaluated against a specific listing. Rather, it is evaluated on the basis of whether it causes functional limitations that are of listing-level severity, regardless of the nature of the impairment(s). A child's impairment(s) functionally equals the criteria in the listings if it results in marked limitations in at least two of the domains or an extreme limitation in one domain. A *marked limitation* in a domain occurs when a claimant's impairment(s) interferes seriously with his or her ability to independently initiate, sustain, or complete activities. An *extreme limitation* in a domain occurs when a claimant's impairment(s) interferes *very* seriously with his or her ability to independently initiate, sustain, or complete activities. Children are awarded benefits if their impairment(s) meets, medically equals, or functionally equals the listings.

Appeals Process

Individuals who are dissatisfied with SSA's initial determination or decision may request further review under the Social Security Act's administrative and judicial review provisions.[265] The appeals process affords claimants the opportunity to present additional evidence or arguments to support their case as well as to appoint a representative to act on their behalf, such as an attorney or a qualified nonattorney.[266] The

[265] Sections 205(b)(1) and 1631(c)(1)(A) of the Social Security Act; 42 U.S.C. §§405(b)(1) and 1383(c)(1)(A).

[266] 20 C.F.R. §§404.1705 and 416.1505.

claimant, his or her appointed representative, representative payee,[267] or other third party on behalf of the claimant can file a request for review. The request for further review must be made, in writing, within 60 days of the date the claimant received notice of the prior determination or decision (generally five days after the date on the notice), unless SSA determines that the claimant has good cause for failing to file a timely request.[268] Claimants may file their appeal using conventional SSA forms or online via the iAppeals system.

SSA's administrative appeals process is generally composed of three levels of review: (1) reconsideration of the case by a reviewer who did not participate in the initial determination; (2) a hearing before an administrative law judge; and (3) a request for review by the Appeals Council (Figure 7).[269] Individuals may elect to continue to receive benefit payment during this process under certain conditions.[270] At each step of the appeals process, the decisionmaker bases his or her decisions on provisions in the Social Security Act, SSA's regulations, and other agency guidance. Only after exhausting the administrative appeals process and receiving a final decision from SSA are claimants permitted to file a complaint against

---

[267] A *representative payee* is an individual appointed by SSA to receive the benefit payments of a Social Security beneficiary or SSI recipient who is unable to manage or direct the management of his or her benefit payments.

[268] SSA presumes the date that the individual receives the notice is five days after the date on the notice, unless the individual can demonstrate that he or she did not receive the notice within the five days.

[269] Sections 205(b) and 1631(c)(1)(A) of the Social Security Act require SSA "to make findings of fact, and decisions as to the rights of any individual applying for a payment" and to give denied claimants "reasonable notice and opportunity for a hearing." Since 1940, SSA's appeals process has consisted of an evidentiary hearing, as well as two additional levels of administrative reviewreconsideration prior to the evidentiary hearing (certain exceptions apply) and review by the Appeals Council (AC) after the evidentiary hearing has been conducted. See Social Security Board (SSB), 5 *Federal Register* 4169, October 22, 1940, https://cdn.loc.gov/service/ll/fedreg/fr005/fr005206/fr005206.pdf.

[270] SSDI beneficiaries and SSI disability recipients may continue to receive benefit payments pending appeal of a medical cessation determination at the reconsideration and hearing levels of the appeals process, provided they request an appeal and continuation of benefit payments no later than 10 days after the date they receive the notice of the prior determination or decision. However, if SSA later affirms the determination that the individual is not entitled to benefit payments, the individual must pay back any continued benefit payments that he or she received, subject to SSA's overpayment rules. See 20 C.F.R. §§404.1597a and 416.996.

the agency in federal court.[271] The following section describes each step of the appeals process in more detail.

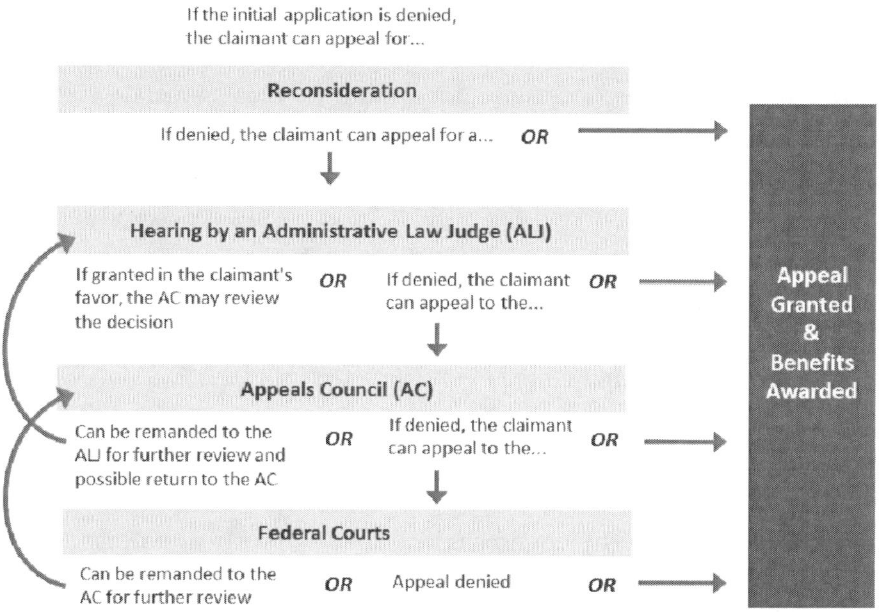

Source: CRS, based on Subpart J of 20 C.F.R. §404 and Subpart N of 20 C.F.R. §416.

Notes: Under the Disability Redesign Prototype Model, SSA eliminated the reconsideration step of the appeals process for disability issues in the following states: Alabama, Alaska, California (Los Angles North and Los Angeles West braches), Colorado, Louisiana, Michigan, Missouri, New Hampshire, New York, and Pennsylvania.

Figure 7. Appeals Process.

Step 1. Reconsideration

In general, reconsideration is the first mandatory step of the administrative appeals process that a claimant must initiate in order to

---

[271] Sections 205(g) and 1631(c)(3) of the Social Security Act; 42 U.S.C. §§405(g) and 1383(c)(3).

appeal an initial determination by SSA.[272] Reconsideration involves a thorough review of all evidence in the case record from the initial determination, along with any additional evidence submitted by the claimant. Reconsideration is effectively a new review of the case by the same DDS office that conducted the initial determination except that it is performed by an official who did not participate in the initial determination.[273] For cases involving the appeal of a medical determination, a new adjudicative team consisting of a disability examiner and a medical or psychological consultant reexamine the evidence from the initial determination and any new evidence submitted with the appeal. The team may request additional evidence or a new consultative examination. As with the initial level, the reconsideration level generally does not involve a face to face meeting between the adjudicator and the individual (i.e., *case review*).[274] However, if the individual received benefit payments (i.e., was a beneficiary or recipient) and contests an initial determination based on medical factors that he or she is not now blind or disabled, then the individual may request a *disability hearing*, which is a face to face reconsideration of the individual's last medical determination.[275] After the review has been completed, the adjudicator makes a determination based on the preponderance of the evidence in the case record. The claimant is later notified of the decision in writing.

In 1999, SSA eliminated the reconsideration level in the following states as part of the Disability Redesign Prototype Model: Alaska, Alabama, California (Los Angeles West and North Branches), Colorado, Louisiana, Michigan, Missouri, New Hampshire, New York, and

---

[272] 20 C.F.R. §§404.907-404.922 and 416.1407-416.1422.

[273] In general, state DDS agencies review medical and vocational issues, and SSA processing centers review all other issues.

[274] An individual who contests an initial determination of a *SSI non-medical* issue may request case review, informal conference, or formal conference. A *conference* is a face-to-face meeting between the individual and the official making the decision, during which the individual is given the opportunity to present his or her case. An *informal conference* allows an individual to present witnesses. A *formal conference* allows an individual who contests a nonmedical adverse action (i.e., a non-medical determination that the individual is no longer eligible for payments) to request that SSA subpoena adverse witnesses and documents and to cross-examine adverse witnesses. See 20 C.F.R. §§416.1413 and 416.1413c.

[275] 20 C.F.R. §§404.914-404.918 and 416.1414-416.1418.

Pennsylvania.[276] In these 10 states, claimants who appeal the initial determination skip the reconsideration level and proceed directly to the hearing level. As part of FY2019 President's budget request to Congress, the Trump Administration proposes to reinstate the reconsideration level in the 10 prototype states.[277] In addition to the legislative proposal, officials from SSA's Office of Budget informed CRS that the agency plans to use its regulatory authority to gradually reinstate the reconsideration step in the 10 prototypes over the next several years.[278]

Step 2. Hearing before an Administrative Law Judge

The second mandatory step of the administrative appeals process (or the first mandatory step for those who reside in one of the prototype states) is to request a hearing before an administrative law judge (ALJ).[279] An ALJ is an impartial hearing examiner who issues a *de novo* (i.e., fresh) decision with respect to the individual's claim for benefits.[280] The hearing level is often the first time that a claimant has the opportunity to appeal his or her case face to face (either in person or via video teleconferencing). During a

276 SSA, POMS, "DI 12015.100 Disability Redesign Prototype Model," January 16, 2014, http://policy.ssa.gov/ poms.nsf/lnx/0412015100.

277 SSA, *Justifications of Estimates for Appropriations Committees, Fiscal Year 2019,* February 12, 2018, p. 25, https://www.ssa.gov/budget/.

278 Information presented to CRS by SSA on February 15, 2018.

279 20 C.F.R. §§404.929-404.965 and 416.1429-416.1465. See SSA, "Information About Social Security's Hearings and Appeals Process," https://www.ssa.gov/appeals/.

280 Administrative law judges (ALJs) are authorized under the Administrative Procedure Act of 1946 (APA; 5 U.S.C. §511 et seq.). ALJs must meet certain minimum standards and pass a test administered by the Office of Personnel Management (OPM). Although the Social Security Act predates the APA and does not explicitly require SSA to use ALJs, the agency has used them (with few exceptions) to adjudicate SSDI and SSI hearings. SSA notes that ALJs "decide matters of fact and law in accordance with the Social Security Act, Administrative Procedure Act (APA), Social Security Administration (SSA) Regulations, Social Security Rulings, and other SSA policy pronouncements." See SSA, POMS, "DI 23020.020 Administrative Law Judge (ALJ) Hearing Cases," January 28, 2008, http://policy.ssa.gov/poms.nsf/lnx/0423020020. According to SSA, "[t]he Commissioner of Social Security has delegated the authority to hold hearings and issue decisions to administrative law judges (ALJ)." See SSA, Hearings, Appeals, and Litigation Law Manual (HALLEX), "I-2-0-2. Hearing OperationIn General," May 1, 2017, https://www.ssa.gov/ OP_Home/hallex/I-02/I-2-0-2.html.

hearing, an ALJ investigates the merits of an appeal by informally questioning the claimant, as well as any scheduled witnesses such as medical or vocational experts. A claimant or his or her appointed representative may also present additional evidence, examine evidence used in making the determination under review, introduce witnesses, question witnesses, and present oral or written arguments in support of a favorable decision. In general, all evidence, objections, or written statements must be submitted to SSA at least five business days before the date of the hearing.[281] Because SSA is not represented at the hearing, the proceeding is considered *inquisitorial* (i.e., non-adversarial). An ALJ issues a decision based on the preponderance of the evidence in the hearing record. In certain situations, the ALJ may dismiss a case without making a decision of its merits, such as when a claimant fails to appear for the hearing. The claimant is later notified in writing of the decision or dismissal.

Step 3. Appeals Council

The third mandatory step of the administrative appeals process is to request a review before the Appeals Council (AC).[282] The AC is made up of administrative appeals judges (AAJs), appeals officers (AO), and support personnel. The AC reviews ALJ decisions and orders of dismissal, as well as processes certain court actions.[283] The AC may dismiss or deny the request for review, or the AC may grant the request and either issue a decision or remand the case back to an ALJ for further proceedings. The AC may also review an ALJ decision or dismissal on its own motion

---

[281] 20 C.F.R. §§404.935(a) and 416.1435(a).

[282] 20 C.F.R. §§404.966-404.982 and 416.1466-416.1482.

[283] The AC reviews cases only under the following conditions: (1) there appears to be an abuse of discretion by the ALJ; (2) there is an error of law; (3) the action, findings or conclusions of the ALJ are not supported by substantial evidence; (4) there is a broad policy or procedural issue that may affect the general public interest; or (5) the AC receives additional evidence that is new, material, and relates to the period on or before the date of the hearing decision, and there is a reasonable probability that the additional evidence would change the outcome of the decision. See 20 C.F.R. §§404.970 and 416.1470.

within 60 days after the date of a decision or dismissal.[284] Once the AC decides to review an ALJ decision on its own motion, it may affirm, reverse, or modify the decision (including a favorable decision) or remand the case back to an ALJ for further proceedings. The claimant is notified in writing of the AC's decision or reason for denial of the review.

Step 4. Federal Courts

Only after exhausting the administrative appeals process and receiving a final decision from SSA may a claimant request judicial review by filing a civil action in a federal court.[285] The Social Security Act requires that such action be brought in the U.S. district court in the judicial district where the claimant resides (or has a principal place of business) or, if not applicable, the U.S. District Court for the District of Columbia. A district court may issue a decision or remand the case back to SSA for further action. Court remands are initially sent to the AC, which may assume jurisdiction and issue a decision or remand the case to an ALJ for further proceedings and a new decision. On rare occasions, disability cases are appealed beyond U.S. district court to the U.S. court of appeals and, ultimately, the U.S. Supreme Court.

Determinations of Continuing Eligibility

Continuing Disability Reviews

After SSA finds that a claimant is disabled, the agency evaluates his or her impairment(s) from time to time to determine if the individual is still

[284] 20 C.F.R. §§404.969 and 416.1469.

[285] Sections 205(g) and 1631(c)(3) of the Social Security Act; 42 U.S.C. §§405(g) and 1383(c)(3). See also 20 C.F.R. §§404.983-404.985 and 416.1483-416.1485.

medically eligible for payments on the basis of blindness or disability.[286] This evaluation is known as a *continuing disability review* (CDR). The frequency of a CDR depends on the beneficiary's prospective medical improvement. SSA's regulations specify three basic types of schedules or *diaries*.

- Medical Improvement Expected (MIE). If medical improvement is expected, then SSA schedules a review at intervals from 6 to 18 months following the most recent decision that the individual is disabled or that disability is continuing. Examples of impairments that fall into this category include traumatic injuries and severe bone fracture.
- Medical Improvement Possible (MIP). If medical improvement is possible but cannot be accurately predicted based on current experience and the facts of the case, then SSA schedules a review at least once every three years. Examples of impairments that fall into this category include heart failure and severe diabetes with end organ damage.
- Medical Improvement Not Expected (MINE). If medical improvement is unlikely due to the severity of an individual's condition, then SSA schedules a review once every five to seven years. Examples of impairments that fall into this category include intellectual disabilities, amyotrophic lateral sclerosis (ALS) which is sufficiently severe, and Parkinson's disease which is sufficiently severe. Individuals who receive this classification are considered *permanently disabled* by SSA.[287]

---

[286] Sections 223(i) and 1614(a)(4) of the Social Security Act; 42 U.S.C. §§423(i) and 1382c(a)(4). See also 20 C.F.R. §§404.1589, 416.989, and 416.989a.

[287] 20 C.F.R. §§404.1590 and 416.990.

As shown in Figure 8, few SSDI beneficiaries and SSI disability recipients are assigned a MIE diary.

SSA conducts two types of medical CDRs on individuals whose diaries mature: full medical CDRs and mailers.[288] A *full medical CDR* involves SSA sending the case to the state DDS agency for a full medical review. A *mailer* is a questionnaire sent to the individual in order to obtain additional information, which SSA uses to determine if a full medical CDR is appropriate.[289]

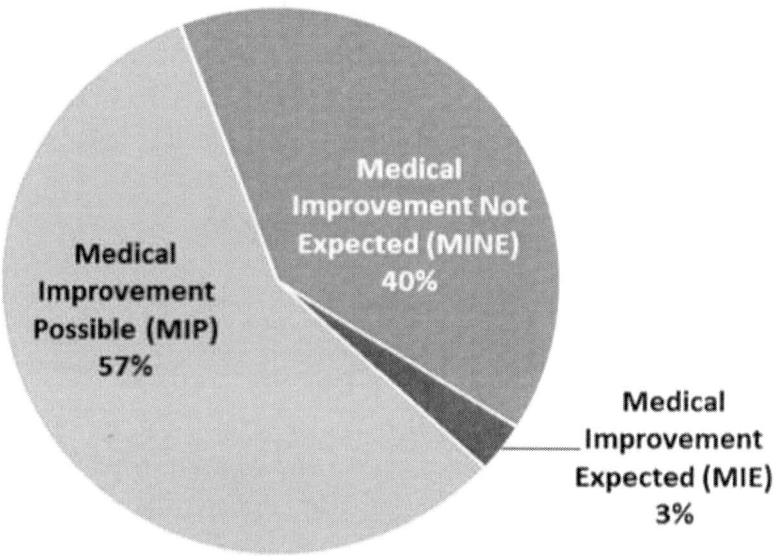

Source: CRS, based on unpublished data provided to CRS by SSA on August 10, 2017.

Notes: CDR = Continuing Disability Review. The term *SSDI* includes disabled workers, disabled widow(er)s, and disabled adult children of retired, disabled, or deceased workers. Data are for SSDI beneficiaries of any age and SSI disability recipients under 65 years old (including children).

Figure 8. CDR Diary Classification for SSDI Beneficiaries and SSI Disability Recipients, July 2017.

---

288 Applies to centrally processed cases.

289 SSA, POMS, "DI 13004.005 An Overview of Processing Continuing Disability Review (CDR) Mailer Forms SSA-455 and SSA-455-OCR-SM," September 23, 2016, http://policy.ssa.gov/poms.nsf/lnx/0413004005.

If the answers to the mailer do not indicate likely improvement, SSA may defer a full medical CDR.

Under current law, SSA must find substantial evidence of medical improvement during a CDR to find a SSDI beneficiary or SSI disability recipient no longer disabled and therefore ineligible for benefits.[290] The legal requirement for determining if disability continues during a CDR is called the *medical improvement review standard* (MIRS). Under a MIRS determination for adults, the agency generally considers a SSDI beneficiary or SSI disability recipient no longer disabled if the review finds considerable evidence that (1) there has been substantial medical improvement in the individual's impairment(s) related to his or her ability to work since the last favorable medical decision and (2) the individual has the ability to engage in SGA. For a child SSI recipient, SSA typically considers the child no longer disabled if the review demonstrates that there has been substantial medical improvement in the recipient's impairment(s) since his or her most recent favorable medical decision to the point in which the recipient's condition no longer meets or medically or functionally equals the severity in the listings. When a SSDI beneficiary or SSI disability recipient is found no longer disabled, he or she may appeal the decision using the process described previously.

Age-18 Disability Redeterminations

SSA reevaluates the eligibility of all child SSI recipients who attain the age of 18 under the adult standard for initial disability claims.[291] These reevaluations are known as *age-18 disability redeterminations*.

---

[290] Sections 223(f) and 1614(a)(4) of the Social Security Act; 42 U.S.C. §§423(f) and 1382c(a)(4).

[291] Section 1614(a)(3)(H)(iii) of the Social Security Act; 42 U.S.C. §1382c(a)(3)(H)(iii). See also 20 C.F.R. §416.987.

Because these reviews are a new disability determination under the adult criteria, the MIRS does not apply.[292]

Work CDRs

Under the SSDI program, SSA performs *work CDRs* to determine if a beneficiary's work activity represents SGA and if eligibility for benefits should continue. SSA typically initiates a work CDR if the agency becomes aware of the beneficiary's return to work. If a work CDR finds evidence that a beneficiary is engaging in SGA and is not participating in an approved SSA work incentive, the agency may find that the beneficiary's disability has ceased.

SSI Redeterminations

Under the SSI program, SSA conducts periodic *redeterminations* of a recipient's non-medical eligibility factors such as income, resources, and living arrangements to verify that a recipient is still eligible for SSI and receiving the correct payment amount.[293] There are two types of redeterminations: scheduled and unscheduled. *Unscheduled redeterminations* are conducted based on a report of a change in a recipient's circumstances that may affect program eligibility or payment amount. *Scheduled redeterminations* are performed at periodic intervals, depending on the likelihood of payment error: (1) annually if a change in a recipient's circumstances is likely to occur or (2) once every six years if a change in circumstances is unlikely to occur.

---

[292] SSA, POMS, "DI 33025.075 Age 18 Redetermination Cases Under P.L. 104-193," December 13, 2017, http://policy.ssa.gov/poms.nsf/lnx/0433025075.

[293] Section 1614(c) of the Social Security Act; 42 U.S.C. §1382c(c). See also 20 C.F.R. §416.204.

APPENDIX A. SIDE-BY-SIDE OF SSDI AND SSI

Table A-1. Comparison of the SSDI and SSI Programs

	Social Security Disability Insurance (SSDI)	**Supplemental Security Income (SSI)**
Type of Program	Work-related social insurance.	Need-based public assistance.
Type of Beneficiary	Disabled individuals under Social Security's full retirement age with significant past work.	Individuals with limited assets and little or no income who (1) are aged 65 or older or (2) have a qualifying impairment, regardless of age.
Definition of "Disability"	Inability to engage in substantial gainful activity (SGA) due to any medically determinable physical or mental impairment which has lasted or is expected to last for at least 12 months or to result in death. In 2018, the SGA earnings limit is $1,180 per month for most workers.	*Adults:* Same as SSDI. *Children:* Physical or mental impairment that causes marked and severe functional limitations with daily activities at home, in school, at daycare, or in the community. The impairment must be expected to last for at least 12 months or to result in death. The child's earnings must also be at or below the SGA limit at the time of application.
Work History and Contribution Requirements	Generally, must have worked and paid Social Security taxes for about 1/4 of adult life and for at least 5 years of the 10 years before the onset of disability.	None.
Nature of Cash Benefits	A share of a worker's career-average earnings in jobs covered under Social Security. The share of earnings replaced by SSDI is greater for workers with low lifetime wages than for high wage workers. The average disabled worker benefit in 2018 is $1,197 per month.	Maximum federal payment of $750 per month for an individual in 2018 ($1,125 for a couple). The payment is reduced by "countable income" (generally, half of earnings plus all other income). States may supplement this payment. The average SSI payment in 2018 is $552 per month.
Waiting Period	5 months.	None.
Health Coverage	Entitled to Medicare after 24 months of entitlement to cash benefits (generally 29 months after disability onset).	Automatically eligible for Medicaid in most states. Some states require a separate Medicaid application. Eight states use more restrictive eligibility criteria than SSI ("209[b] states")
Retroactive Benefits	Up to 12 months.	None.

Table A-1. (Continued)

	Social Security Disability Insurance (SSDI)	Supplemental Security Income (SSI)
Benefits for Family Members	Certain spouses and dependent children.	None.
Means Tested	No, but earnings must be within the SGA limit for a person to be considered disabled. (The SGA limit is an indirect test of disability.)	Yes. Must have "countable income" at or below the maximum benefit and no more than $2,000 in "countable assets" for an individual ($3,000 for a couple). Certain income and assets are not counted for eligibility and payment purposes
Financing	Primarily by payroll taxes credited to the Disability Insurance (DI) trust fund.	General revenues.

Source: CRS.

Appendix B. Certain Other Benefits Available to SSDI Beneficiaries and SSI Disability Recipients

Individuals who meet the blindness or disability standards of the SSDI or SSI programs may qualify for certain federal or state benefits. The following section discusses two federal benefits for which SSDI beneficiaries and SSI disability recipients may qualify.

Achieving a Better Life Experience Accounts

The Stephen Beck, Jr., Achieving a Better Life Experience Act (ABLE Act; Division B of P.L. 113-295) authorizes states to establish and maintain tax-advantaged savings plans through which contributions may be made to the investment account of a designated beneficiary to pay for qualified disability expenses.[294] *Qualified disability expenses* include costs

[294] 26 U.S.C. §529A. For more information, see CRS In Focus IF10363, *Achieving a Better Life Experience (ABLE) Programs*, and U.S. Congress, Senate Committee on the Budget, *Tax*

related to education, housing, transportation, employment training and support, assistive technology and personal support services, health and wellness (including longterm services and supports), financial management and administrative services, legal fees, expenses for oversight and monitoring, funeral and burial expenses, and other expenses identified in guidance published by the IRS. To qualify for an ABLE account, an individual must either be (1) entitled to Social Security or SSI benefit payments due to blindness or disability and such impairment occurred before the date the individual attained age 26 or (2) certified by a physician that his or her impairment meets the blindness or disability standards used for children under the SSI program, regardless of the individual's age, and such impairment occurred before the date the individual attained age 26.

There are three advantages to ABLE accounts. First, earnings in an ABLE account can grow tax free annually until they are withdrawn. Second, distributions (i.e., withdrawals) from an ABLE account are taxfree if they are used to pay for qualified disability expenses. Third, assets in and distributions from an ABLE account for qualified disability expenses are disregarded in determining a designated beneficiary's eligibility for and the amount of assistance provided by most federal assistance programs. Under the SSI program, however, only the first $100,000 in an ABLE account is excluded. The balance of an ABLE account above $100,000 is treated as a resource to the designated beneficiary and is counted against the program's resource limit. If a designated beneficiary becomes ineligible for SSI due solely to excess ABLE funds, his or her cash payments are suspended (without a time limit) until the balance of the ABLE account falls to or below $100,000. This suspension does not affect the beneficiary's eligibility for Medicaid. In addition, a distribution from an ABLE account for housing-related expenses is counted against the resource limit unless the distribution is spent in the month of receipt.

ABLE accounts allow SSI disability recipients to save for disability related expenses without such savings jeopardizing their SSI and Medicaid

---

Expenditures: Compendium of Background Material on Individual Provisions, committee print, prepared by the Congressional Research Service, 114th Cong., 2nd sess., December 2016, S.Prt. 114-31 (Washington: GPO, 2017), pp. 1011-1018, at https://www.gpo.gov/ fdsys/pkg/ CPRT-114SPRT24030/pdf/CPRT-114SPRT24030.pdf.

eligibility. Although ABLE accounts have no effect on an individual's entitlement to SSDI, the accounts may allow beneficiaries to save and establish or maintain their eligibility for other federal programs, such as Medicaid or SNAP. The Social Security Administration (SSA),[295] the Centers for Medicare & Medicaid Services (CMS),[296] and the Department of Agriculture's Food and Nutrition Service (FNS)[297] have all issued guidance on the treatment of ABLE accounts under SSI, Medicaid, and SNAP, respectively.

Total and Permanent Disability Discharge of Certain Federal Student Loans

SSDI beneficiaries and SSI disability recipients may have their federal student loans discharged if they meet the requirements of the Department of Education's (ED's) Total and Permanent Disability (TPD) discharge program.[298] The TPD discharge applies to obligations incurred under the following *federal* student loan programs: William D. Ford Federal Direct Loan (Direct Loan) program, the Federal Family Education Loan (FFEL) program, the Federal Perkins Loan program, and the Teacher Education Assistance for College and Higher Education (TEACH) Grant program. Borrowers qualify for the TPD discharge if they are determined to be totally and permanently disabled under any one of the following methods.

- VA Method. The borrower receives Department of Veterans Affairs (VA) disability compensation at the 100% rate due to one or more *service-connected* disabilities that the VA determined to

[295] SSA, POMS, "SI 01130.740 Achieving a Better Life Experience (ABLE) Accounts," April 2, 2018, at https://secure.ssa.gov/poms.nsf/lnx/0501130740.

[296] Letter from Brian Neale, Director, Center for Medicaid and CHIP Services, to State Medicaid Directors, *Implications of the ABLE Act for State Medicaid Programs*, September 7, 2017, https://www.medicaid.gov/federalpolicy-guidance/downloads/smd17002.pdf.

[297] 7 C.F.R. §273.8(e)(2)(ii).

[298] Sections 437(a), 455(a)(1), and 464(c)(1)(F) of the Higher Education Act of 1965 (HEA); 20 U.S.C. §§1087(a), 1087e(a)(1), and 1087dd(c)(1)(F). See also 34 C.F.R. §§674.51(aa), 674.61(b), 682.200(b), 682.402(c), 685.102(b), 685.213, and 686.42(b).

be (1) totally disabling under its rating schedule, or (2) less than totally disabling under its rating schedule but which prevent the individual from establishing or maintaining substantially gainful employment (known as an *individual unemployability* [IU] rating).[299]

- SSA Method. The borrower is entitled to SSDI or SSI and is scheduled to receive a medical review once every five to seven years (i.e., SSA assigns the individual a Medical Improvement Not Expected [MINE] continuing disability review [CDR] diary).[300]
- Certification Method. The borrower is certified by a physician that he or she is unable to engage in any substantial gainful activity due to any medically determinable physical or mental impairment that has lasted, or is expected to last, for at least 60 months or is expected to result in death (i.e., the individual meets the definition of disability for adults under the Social Security Act, except that the duration of the impairment must be for at least five years instead of one).

SSDI beneficiaries and SSI disability recipients with a MINE CDR diary may request a Benefits Planning Query (BPQY) statement from SSA

---

[299] The HEA provides that a qualifying loan may be discharged if the borrower is determined by the Department of Veterans Affairs (VA) to be unemployable due to a service-connected disability or condition. The Department of Education (ED) consulted with the VA and determined that there are two types of VA determinations that meet the requirements of the HEA for the Total and Permanent Disability (TPD) discharge. The first type of determination is that the veteran has one or more service-connected disabilities rated as totally disabling under the VA's rating schedule (i.e., a 100% rating). The second type of determination is that the veteran has one or more service-connected disabilities rated as less than totally disabling (i.e., a rating of less than 100%), but which, in the judgment of the VA, prevent the individual from securing or following a substantially gainful occupation. See ED, Financial Student Aid, "Procedures for discharging Title IV loans based on a determination by the Department of Veterans Affairs that a veteran is unemployable due to a service-connected condition or disability," May 15, 2009, https://ifap.ed.gov/dpcletters/GEN0907.html. For more information on the requirements for the aforementioned VA determinations, see 38 C.F.R. §§3.340, 3.4(b), 4.16, and 4.18.

[300] ED issued final regulations establishing the SSA method for the TPD discharge in November 2012 (effective July 2013). See ED, "Federal Perkins Loan Program, Federal Family Education Loan Program, and William D. Ford Federal Direct Loan Program," 77 *Federal Register* 66087, November 1, 2012, https://www.gpo.gov/fdsys/pkg/FR2012-11-01/pdf/2012-26348.pdf.

to demonstrate to ED that their medical review is scheduled once every five to seven years.[301] In July 2017, about 40% of all SSDI beneficiaries and SSI disability recipients had a MINE CDR diary (see Figure 8). SSDI beneficiaries and SSI disability recipients with a medical improvement expected (MIE) or medical improvement possible (MIP) CDR diary may still qualify for the TPD discharge if they are determined to be totally and permanently disabled under the VA method or the physician's certification method.

Borrowers awarded a TPD discharge based on a determination of totally and permanently disabled under the SSA method or the physician's certification method are subject to a three-year monitoring period from the date the discharge is initially granted.[302] During the *post-discharge monitoring period*, the borrower is required to have annual earnings at or below the Department of Health and Human Services' (HHS's) poverty guideline for a family of two, regardless of his or her actual family size. ED will reinstate the loan obligation if the borrower fails to meet any of the TPD discharge program's requirements during the postdischarge monitoring period. The post-discharge monitoring period does not apply to borrowers awarded a TPD discharge based on a determination of totally and permanently disabled under the VA method. For more information on the TPD discharge program, including the monitoring period, visit http://www.disabilitydischarge.com.

Computer Matching Agreements between ED and Other Federal Agencies to Improve the TPD Discharge Process

Some disability advocates and Members of Congress have expressed concern that the TPD discharge process is "cumbersome," in that it requires borrowers to independently determine whether they qualify for the discharge and to coordinate the sharing of information between federal

301 SSA, *Benefits Planning Query Handbook (BPQY)*, July 2012, https://www.ssa.gov/disabilityresearch/documents/BPQY_Handbook_Version%205.2_7.19.2012.pdf.

302 34 C.F.R. §§674.61(b)(6)-(7), 682.402(c)(6)-(7), and 685.213(b)(7)-(8).

agencies to verify that they meet the applicable requirements.[303] To address such concerns, President Barack Obama issued a memorandum in March 2015 that directed the Secretary of Education and the Director of the Office of Management and Budget (OMB), in consultation with the Commissioner of Social Security, to develop a plan to proactively identity student loan borrowers who receive SSDI and determine if they qualify for the TPD discharge.[304] Later that year, ED released a report that, among other things, advocated for the streamlining of the TPD discharge process by having federal agencies coordinate their efforts to notify borrowers automatically of their potential eligibility for the discharge.[305]

In April 2016, ED announced that it had conducted a data match with SSA to identify borrowers potentially eligible for the TPD discharge under the SSA method. The match identified 387,000 SSDI beneficiaries and SSI disability recipients with a combined loan balance of over $7.7 billion.[306] Shortly thereafter, borrowers who were positively identified in the match received a customized letter from ED's TPD servicer, Nelnet, explaining their eligibility for the discharge and how to apply for it. The number of individuals identified in the data match represented about 3% of the total SSDI beneficiary and SSI disability recipient population in July 2016, and about 7% of the total population with a MINE CDR diary that month. According to the Government Accountability Office (GAO), as of July 31,

---

[303] See, for example, Sen. Tammy Baldwin, in U.S. Congress, Senate Committee on Health, Education, Labor, and Pensions, *Strengthening the Federal Student Loan Program for Borrowers*, 113th Cong., 2nd sess., March 27, 2014, S.Hrg. 113-829 (Washington: GPO, 2016), p. 23.

[304] Executive Office of the President, "Student Aid Bill of Rights To Help Ensure Affordable Loan Repayment," 80 *Federal Register* 13473, March 4, 2015. See also 20 U.S.C. §1092 note.

[305] ED, *Strengthening the Student Loan System to Better Protect All Borrowers*, October 1, 2015, p. 12, https://www2.ed.gov/documents/press-releases/strengthening-student-loan-system.pdf.

[306] ED, Financial Student Aid, "Total and Permanent Disability (TPD) Match Process with Social Security Administration Begins (Updated May 9, 2016)," https://ifap.ed.gov/eannouncements/041216TPDMatchProcessSSABegins.html. See also ED, "U.S. Department of Education Acts to Protect Social Security Benefits for Borrowers with Disabilities," April 12, 2016, https://www.ed.gov/news/press-releases/usdepartment-education-acts-protect-social-security-benefits-borrowers-disabilities. Moreover, see ED, *Computer Matching Agreement between the Social Security Administration (SSA) and the U.S. Department of Education (ED) Federal Student Aid (FSA): Match #1100*, https://www2.ed.gov/about/offices/list/om/docs/pirms/ssa-mine-cma.pdf.

2016, "TPD discharge applications were sent to about 234,000 borrowers based on the data matching and slightly more than 19,000 applications had been submitted and approved."[307]

In April 2018, ED announced that it would conduct a similar data match with the VA to identify borrowers potentially eligible for the TPD discharge under the VA method.[308]

Recent Changes to the Federal Income Tax Treatment of Loans Discharged Under the TPD Discharge Program

Under prior law, the amount of student loan debt discharged under the TPD discharge program was included in the borrower's gross income for purposes of *federal* income tax in the year the discharge became final, which for borrowers approved under the SSA method or physician's certification method is at the close of the three year monitoring period and for borrowers approved under the VA method is the date that ED approves the discharge. This resulted in some borrowers having markedly high taxable income relative to their income exclusive of the discharged student loan indebtedness for the tax year. However, during debate on the 2017 tax revision (P.L. 11597), the Senate incorporated some of the provisions of the Stop Taxing Death and Disability Act (S. 405) into the legislation, which were ultimately enacted into law.[309] Section 11031 of P.L. 115-97

---

[307] U.S. Government Accountability Office (GAO), Social Security Offsets: Improvements to Program Design Could Better Assist Older Student Loan Borrowers with Obtaining Permitted Relief, GAO-17-45, December 19, 2016, p. 31, https://www.gao.gov/products/GAO-17-45. According to GAO, as of October 2016, an additional 7,000 borrowers were identified as being eligible for the TPD discharge via the SSA method.

[308] ED, "U.S. Department of Education and U.S. Department of Veterans Affairs Team Up to Simplify Student Loan Discharge Process for Disabled Veterans," April 16, 2018, https://www.ed.gov/news/press-releases/us-departmenteducation-and-us-department-veterans-affairs-team-simplify-student-loan-discharge-process-disabled-veterans. See also ED, *Computer Matching Agreement between the Veterans Administration (VA) and the U.S. Department of Education (ED) Federal Student Aid (FSA)*, https://www2.ed.gov/about/offices/list/om/docs/pirms/va-tpd-cma.pdf.

[309] See CRS Report R45092, *The 2017 Tax Revision (P.L. 115-97): Comparison to 2017 Tax Law*.

excludes the amount of the discharged indebtedness under the TPD discharge from the definition of gross income for federal income tax purposes.[310] These new provisions apply to loans discharged during the period from January 1, 2018, through December 31, 2025. Student loan debt discharged under the TPD discharge program may still be considered income for state income tax purposes.

[310] 26 U.S.C. §108(f)(5).

In: Social Security Disability
Editor: Michael Dimitriadis ISBN: 978-1-53615-747-5

Chapter 3

TRENDS IN SOCIAL SECURITY DISABILITY INSURANCE ENROLLMENT*

Zhe Li

ABSTRACT

The Social Security Disability Insurance (SSDI) program pays cash benefits to non-elderly workers and their dependents provided that the workers have paid into the Social Security system for a sufficient number of years and are determined to be unable to continue performing substantial work because of a qualifying disability. The total number of disabled-worker beneficiaries was approximately 2.7 million in 1985, peaked at approximately 9.0 million in 2014, and then declined over the last three years by nearly 0.3 million. In December 2017, 8.7 million disabled workers received SSDI benefits.

Multiple factors have contributed to the growth in the SSDI enrollment between 1985 and 2014. Some of the main factors are (1) the increased eligibility and rising disability incidence among women, (2) the attainment of peak disability-claiming years (between age 50 and full retirement age) among baby boomers (people born between 1946 and 1964), (3) the increase in full retirement age (FRA) from 65 to 66, (4)

* This is an edited, reformatted and augmented version of Congressional Research Service, Publication No. R45419, dated November 30, 2018.

fewer job opportunities during economic recessions, and (5) the legislative reform that expanded the eligibility standard in SSDI.

Some factors may have prolonged effects on SSDI benefit receipt. For example, the increase in the FRA from 65 to 66 has resulted in a larger proportion of SSDI beneficiaries who are ages 65 and older, and this proportion is likely to increase further as the FRA increases from 66 to 67 between 2020 and 2027. Another example is the consequence of the expansion in the eligibility criteria, which has resulted in more than half of the disabled-worker beneficiaries being enrolled into the program based on mental disorders or musculoskeletal disorders (typically back pain or arthritis). This trend is likely to persist in the future.

However, some of the effects on the growth in SSDI enrollment are likely to diminish over time. For example, the rise in labor force participation among women resulted in more women becoming eligible for SSDI benefits during the 1980s and the 1990s, but its positive effect on SSDI rolls became smaller as the female labor force participation rate stabilized and the disability incidence rate of women approached that of men.

In addition, some factors may have started to work in opposite directions. One example is the change in age distribution of the population. As the baby boomers reach their FRA (gradually increased from 65 to 66) between 2012 and 2031, there is expected to be a growing proportion of disabled workers who terminate disability benefits due to the attainment of FRA. About the same time, the lower-birth-rate cohorts (people born after 1964) started to enter peak disability-claiming years in 2015, which would likely reduce the size of the insured population between age 50 and the FRA and, consequently, result in a lower number of disability applications. Another example is the availability of more jobs during the post-Great Recession period. The increasing opportunity in employment may have made working more attractive than disability benefits for people who could qualify for SSDI, thus reducing the disability applications and awards after 2010. These factors are likely to contribute to a decline in the number of disabled-worker beneficiaries.

In addition to the change in the population age distribution and the availability of jobs in the market, some other factors may also be acting to decrease SSDI rolls in the recent three years. These factors are likely to include the prevalence of the Affordable Care Act (ACA) and the decline in the allowance rate (i.e., the share of applicants who are awarded disability benefits). The nationwide effects of the ACA on disability benefit receipt and the cause of the decreasing allowance rate are as yet unclear.

INTRODUCTION

Social Security Disability Insurance (SSDI)[1] is a federal social insurance program that provides monthly cash benefits to non-elderly disabled workers and their eligible dependents provided the worker paid into the system for a sufficient number of years[2] and is determined to be unable to perform substantial work because of a qualifying disability.

In the past three decades, the total number of disabled-worker beneficiaries continually increased from 2.7 million in 1985 to 9.0 million in 2014 and then started to decline to approximately 8.7 million in December 2017.[3] The size of the beneficiary population has a strong impact on SSDI expenditures and thus the solvency of the program's trust fund.

Multiple factors have contributed to the change in the number of SSDI beneficiaries over time. Understanding the importance of each competing factor helps inform predictions of SSDI solvency status and analysis of related legislation. This chapter analyzes the relative importance of factors affecting SSDI benefit receipts and terminations over the past 30 years.

TRENDS IN SSDI ENROLLMENT

Figure 1 shows that between 1985 and 2017 the total number of disabled-worker beneficiaries continually increased before 2014 and has declined for the last three years. The number of Social Security disabled-worker beneficiaries has experienced different growth rates in the last three decades. The disability rolls increased relatively slowly between 1985 and 1989 and then went through two faster-growing periods, 1989-1997 and

---

[1] For more information, see CRS In Focus IF10506, *Social Security Disability Insurance (SSDI)*.

[2] To achieve insured status, individuals must have worked in jobs covered by Social Security for about 10 years and for at least 5 of the 10 years immediately prior to the onset of disability. However, younger workers may qualify with less work experience based on their age.

[3] Benefits were also paid to 1.7 million dependents of disabled workers in December 2017. Social Security Administration, *Annual Statistical Supplement 2018*, Table 5.D3, https://www.ssa.gov/policy/docs/statcomps/ supplement/2018/5d.html#table5.d3.

2000-2010. The number of disabled-worker beneficiaries grew slowly again after 2010 and has declined since 2014. Among disabled workers, the proportion of female beneficiaries increased from 33% in 1985 to nearly 50% in 2017.

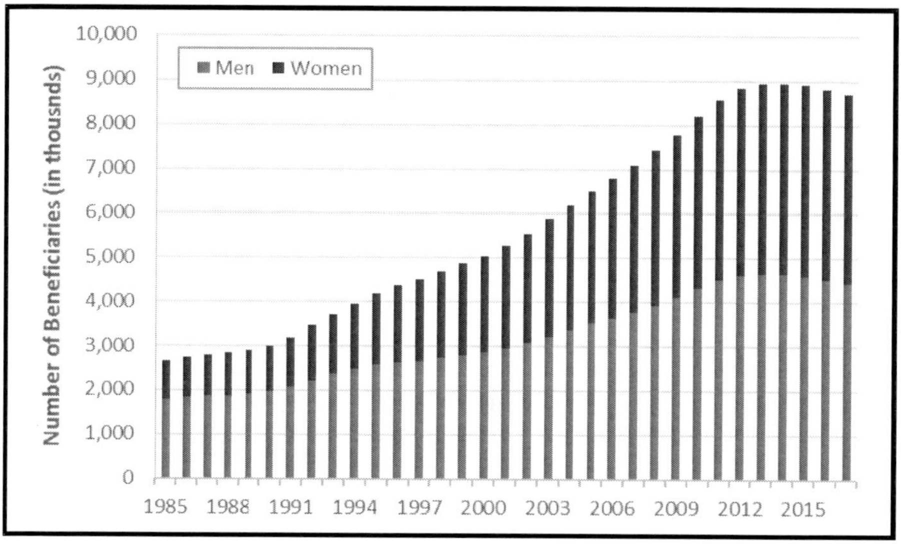

Source: Social Security Administration, *Annual Statistical Supplement 2018*, Table 5.D3, https://www.ssa.gov/policy/docs/statcomps/supplement/2018/5d.html #table5.d3.

Figure 1. Number of Social Security Disabled-Worker Beneficiaries, 1985-2017 (in thousands).

The number of disabled-worker beneficiaries in current payment status increases with new disability awards and declines with benefit terminations. In general, to qualify for SSDI, workers must be (1) insured in the event of disability, (2) statutorily disabled,[4] and (3) younger than Social Security's full retirement age (FRA), which is 65-67, depending on

---

[4] To meet the statutory test of disability, insured workers must be unable to engage in any *substantial gainful activity* (SGA) due to any medically determinable physical or mental impairment that is expected to last for at least one year or result in death. The Social Security Administration (SSA) uses a monetary threshold to determine whether an individual's work activity constitutes SGA, which is adjusted annually for earnings growth. In 2018, the SGA earnings limit for most workers is $1,180 per month.

the year of birth.[5] A disabled worker's SSDI benefits are terminated when they (1) die, (2) attain FRA (the age at which unreduced Social Security retired-worker benefits are first payable),[6] (3) medically improve (i.e., no longer meet the statutory definition of disability), or (4) return to work.

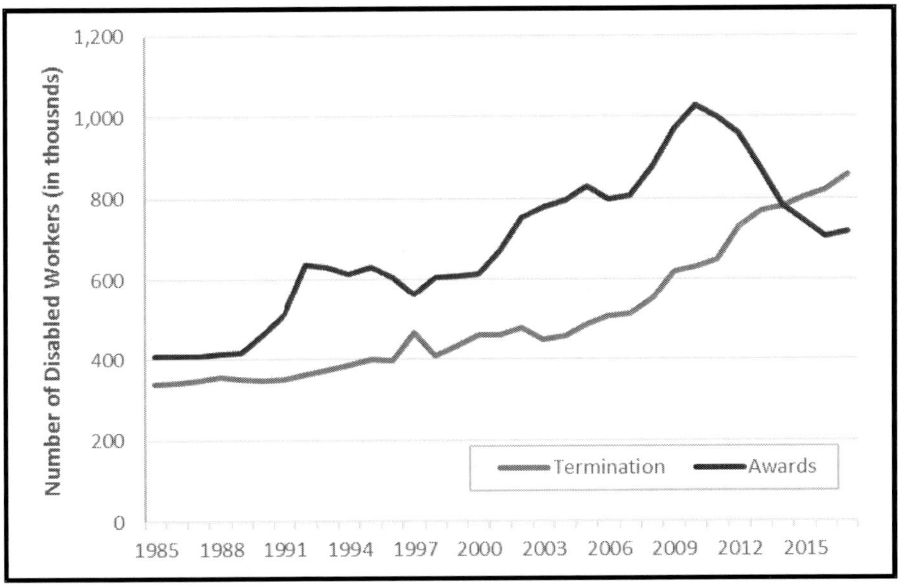

Source: Social Security Administration, *Annual Statistical Supplement 2018*, Table 6.C2 and Table 6.F1, https://www.ssa.gov/policy/docs/statcomps/supplement/2018/6c.html#table6.c2, and https://www.ssa.gov/policy/docs/statcomps/supplement/2018/6f.html#table6.f1.

Figure 2. Terminations and Awards to Disabled Workers, 1985-2017 (in thousands).

The main reason for the decline in the number of SSDI beneficiaries is the decrease in disability benefit awards, which dropped down below the number of terminations starting in 2014 (see Figure 2).

---

[5] The FRA increases gradually from 65 to 67 for workers born in 1938 or later. Under the scheduled increases enacted in 1983 (P.L. 98-21), the FRA increases to 65 and two months for workers born in 1938. The FRA continues to increase by two months every birth year until it reaches 66 for workers born in 1943-1954. Starting with workers born in 1955, the FRA increases again in two-month increments until it reaches 67 for workers born in 1960 or later.

[6] At FRA, SSDI beneficiaries are transferred from the Disability Insurance (DI) program to the Old-Age and Survivors Insurance (OASI) program.

The number of new awards to disabled workers in the SSDI program grew from approximately 416,100 in 1985 to more than 1 million in 2010. However, this trend was reversed in 2011, with a gradual decline in new disability awards to approximately 716,000 in 2017. From 1985 to 2017, the number of disabled-worker beneficiaries whose benefits were terminated rose from 340,000 to 859,000, which was higher than the number of new disability awards in the recent three years. Multiple factors may have contributed to the trends in SSDI benefit receipts and terminations. The following sections examine the effects of different factors and discuss the relative importance of competing factors at different time periods.

Factors Affecting SSDI Enrollment

Several factors may affect the change in the number of SSDI disabled-worker beneficiaries, including changes in demographic characteristics of the insured population, changes in employment and compensation, and changes in program rules and implementation. This section discusses the impact of those factors on SSDI benefit awards and terminations, as well as the roles they have played over time.

Changes in the Demographic Characteristics of the Insured Population

The number of SSDI disabled-worker beneficiaries depends in part on the size of the working-age population who are disability insured—the workers who have paid into the Social Security system for a sufficient number of years. From 1985 to 2017, the SSDI insured population grew from 109 million to 155 million at an average rate of about 1.6% per year during 1985-2007 and 0.4% per year in the more recent 10 years.[7] Two factors—increased eligibility among female workers and the aging of the workforce—may play important roles in the relatively faster growth in the insured population between 1985 and 2007. However, because the share of women in the workforce was no longer increasing and the baby boom generation (people born between 1946 and 1964) was aging out of the disability insurance program, the growth in the insured population slowed after 2007.[8] Starting in 2003, the increase in full retirement age, combined with the aging of the baby boomer generation, also contributed to the growth of the disability-insured population.

Female Labor Force Participation

Some studies have shown that increased eligibility for the SSDI program and the rising incidence of disability among women played an important role in disability benefit receipt during the 1980s and the 1990s.[9] Some experts attribute the increase in beneficiaries to increased labor force participation of women, which resulted in more women becoming potentially eligible for SSDI.[10] Between 1985 and 2005, the proportion of women who participated in the labor force increased from 54% to 60%, and the proportion of women who were insured for disability increased from 49% to 59% (see Figure 3). During this period, the female proportion of disabled worker beneficiaries increased from 33% to 46% (see Figure 1).

---

[7] CRS calculation based on SSA, *Annual Statistical Supplement 2018*, Table 4.C2, https://www.ssa.gov/policy/docs/ statcomps/supplement/2018/4c.html#table4.c2.

[8] The economic recession between December 2007 and June 2009 may also contribute to the slower growth in the insured population after 2007.

[9] Jeffrey B. Liebman, "Understanding the Increase in Disability Insurance Benefit Receipt in the United States," *Journal of Economic Perspectives*, vol. 29, no. 2 (2015), pp. 123-149; see also Congressional Budget Office (CBO), *Social Security Disability Insurance: Participation and Spending*, June 2016, https://www.cbo.gov/publication/51443 (hereinafter "CBO SSDI Report 2016").

[10] Testimony of Virginia P. Reno, "Securing the Future of the Social Security Disability Program," House Committee on Ways and Means, Subcommittee on Social Security, December 2, 2011, https://waysandmeans.house.gov/UploadedFiles/Reno_Testimonyss 122.pdf; and CBO SSDI Report 2016.

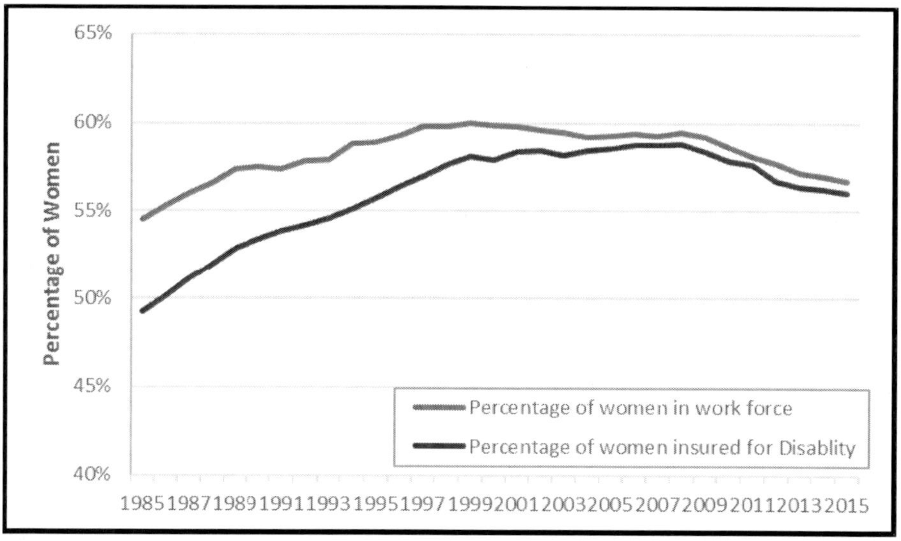

Source: Bureau of Labor Statistics, "Women in the Labor Force: A Databook," April 2017, Table 2, https://www.bls.gov/opub/reports/womens-databook/2016 home.htm; and Social Security Administration, *Annual Statistical Supplement 2018*, Table 4.C2, https://www.ssa.gov/policy/docs/statcomps/supplement/2018/ 4c.html#table4.c2.

Figure 3. Percentages of Women in the Workforce and Percentages of Women Insured for Disability, 1985-2015.

The SSDI incidence rate—the ratio of new disability awards to the number of disability insured who are not already receiving benefits (i.e., disability-exposed population)—increased substantially for women, from 2.97 per 1,000 disability-insured women in 1985 to 5.89 in 2005 (see Table 1). During the same time, the incidence rate for men has been relatively steady after adjusting for the population age distribution and the business cycle. The difference between SSDI incidence rates for men and women became negligible in and after 2005 (see Table 1). In 1984, approximately 11/2 non-elderly males were receiving SSDI for every non-elderly female. By 2008, this ratio was close to parity.[11]

[11] Report to the Social Security Advisory Board, "2015 Technical Panel on Assumptions and Methods," September 2015, http://www.polsim.com/SSAB-TP15.pdf#page=37.

Table 1. SSDI Disability Incidence Rates, by Sex and Age Group, Selected Years (awards per 1,000 disability-exposed population)

	1985	1995	2005	2017
Total	**3.76**	**4.97**	**5.70**	**4.63**
Sex				
Men	4.51	5.51	6.05	4.95
Women	2.97	4.70	5.89	4.87
Age Group				
Less than age 50	1.23	1.66	1.71	1.10
Age 50 and above	7.73	7.83	6.56	5.02

Source: CRS calculation using Social Security Administration, *Annual Statistical Supplement 2018*, available at https://www.ssa.gov/policy/docs/statcomps/supplement/2018/.

Notes: Disability-exposed population is the number of disability insured who are not already receiving benefits. Because of differences in data sources and calculation methods, statistics reported in this table may differ from those reported by the Social Security Trustees Report 2018, Figure V.C3.

The effect of female labor force participation on the growth in SSDI enrollment diminished after 2010. The female labor force participation rate remained relatively stable for 10 years between 2000 and 2010 and then started to go down after the conclusion of the Great Recession in 2010 (see Figure 3). The share of women among disabled-worker beneficiaries and the share of women in the workforce both stabilized around 46% after 2005.[12] The incidence rate for women peaked in 2010 and then declined to 4.7 in 2017.[13] Some argue that those developments have contributed to slower growth in SSDI enrollment in recent years.[14]

The Change in Age Distribution of the Population

Another factor that contributes to the trends in SSDI enrollment is the aging of the workforce.

---

[12] CRS calculation using Bureau of Labor Statistics, "Women in the Labor Force: A Databook," April 2017, Table 2, and SSA, *Annual Statistical Supplement 2018*, Table 6.C2.

[13] CRS calculation using SSA, *Annual Statistical Supplement 2018*, https://www.ssa.gov/policy/docs/statcomps/ supplement/2018/.

[14] CBO SSDI Report 2016.

The aging of the baby boom generation (people born between 1946 and 1964) has an effect on the composition of the overall working-age population. Some argue that as baby boomers reached their peak disability-claiming years (usually considered between age 50 and FRA),[15] the number of disability beneficiaries rose,[16] and as baby boomers convert from disability benefits to retirement benefits and are replaced by lower-birth-rate cohorts in the peak disability-receiving ages, the disability enrollment rates will likely fall.[17]

The baby boom generation reached the age of 50 between 1996 and 2014, during which time the share of disabled workers between age 50 and FRA increased from 56% to 73%.[18] As the baby boomers continue to reach their FRA between 2012 and 2031, there is expected to be a growing proportion of disabled workers who terminate disability benefits due to the attainment of FRA. Since 2000, between 7% and 10% of disabled worker beneficiaries have been terminated from the SSDI rolls each year.[19] The overall number of disabled worker terminations increased from 460,351 to 859,020 between 2000 and 2017 (an increase of 87%), while the number of disabled workers who attained FRA more than doubled during this period (from 212,948 to 494,651). Before 2012, the proportion of disabled workers terminated due to attainment of FRA stayed relatively constant at approximately 50%. However, starting in 2012, the proportion gradually rose, reaching approximately 58% at the end of 2017 (see Figure 4). Statistics from the Social Security Administration (SSA) show that the

---

[15] In December 2017, 76% of disabled workers were between age 50 and FRA. CRS calculation using SSA, *Annual Statistical Supplement 2018*, Table 5.D4, https://www.ssa.gov/policy/docs/statcomps/supplement/2018/ 4c.html#table4.d4.

[16] Reno, "Securing the Future of the Social Security Disability Program."

[17] CBO SSDI Report 2016 and Social Security Board of Trustees, 2018, *The 2018 Annual Report of the Board of Trustees of the Federal Old-Age and Survivors Insurance and Federal Disability Insurance Trust Funds*, https://www.ssa.gov/OACT/TR/2018/index.html (hereinafter "Social Security Trustees Report 2018").

[18] SSA, *Annual Statistical Report on the Social Security Disability Insurance Program 2016*, released October 2017, Table 39, https://www.ssa.gov/policy/docs/statcomps/di_asr/2016/sect03c.html#table39.

[19] CRS calculation using *Annual Statistical Supplements* (2001-2018) from SSA.

share of new disability insurance awardees who are between age 50 and FRA started to decline in 2017.[20]

In addition to the reason of attaining FRA, there was a declining proportion of disabled workers who terminated benefits due to death, medical improvement (i.e., no longer meeting the statutory definition of *disability*), or returning to work. Among these terminations, death accounted for about one-third of the overall terminations, with the proportion decreasing from 36.7% in 2000 to 29.3% in 2017, and medical improvement and returning to work accounted for approximately 10% of all the terminations between 2010 and 2017.[21]

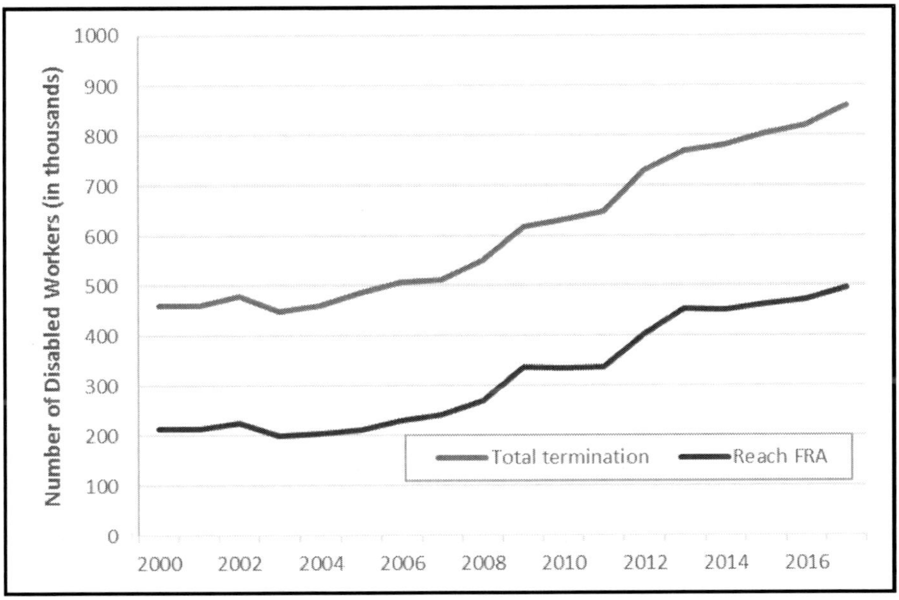

Source: CRS calculation using *Annual Statistical Supplements* (2001-2018) from SSA.

Figure 4. Termination of Benefits Among Disabled Workers, 2000-2017. Total termination and termination due to attainment of FRA (in thousands).

---

[20] SSA, *Annual Statistical Supplement 2018*, Table 6.C2, https://www.ssa.gov/policy/docs/statcomps/supplement/2018/ 6c.html#table6.c2.

[21] The proportion of disabled workers who terminated benefits due to medical improvement and returning to work remained slightly above 10% during 2000 to 2006, dropped down below 10% between 2007 and 2014, and then went up above 10% after 2015. See *Annual Statistical Supplements* (2001-2018) from SSA.

The aging of the population also impacts the incidence rate (i.e., the ratio of new awards to the disability-exposed population) of the SSDI program. The left graph of Figure 5 shows the gross and age-sex-adjusted incidence rate from 1985 to 2017. The gross incidence rate is unadjusted, which was affected by the changing age-sex distribution of the disability-exposed population, while the age-sex-adjusted incidence rate assumes that the age and the sex distributions of the population were constant at its 2000 level. The age-sex-adjusted incidence rate was higher than the gross incidence rate between 1985 and 2000 as the baby boom generation swelled the size of the younger-age population, whose disability incidence is generally lower than that in older populations. After 2000, the age-sex-adjusted rate was lower than the gross rate as the baby boom generation moved into an age range where disability incidence peaks. SSA projects that the gross incidence rate will generally decline as the baby boom generation moves above the FRA and the lower-birth-rate cohorts of the 1970s enter prime disability ages (50 to FRA).[22]

The right graph of Figure 5 shows the age-sex-unemployment-adjusted incidence rate from 1985 to 2017, which is the predicted age-sex-adjusted incidence rate, under the counterfactual assumption that unemployment rates were constant at the 1985-2017 mean value of 6.02% for the entire period.[23] Compared with the age-sex-adjusted incidence rate, the age-sex-unemploymentadjusted incidence rate appeared to be relatively stable after 1992. The effect of business cycles on the disability incidence rate will be discussed in the section "Business Cycle and Unemployment Rate."

---

[22] Social Security Trustees Report 2018, p. 133.

[23] The predictions use coefficients obtained from regressing the annual incidence rate on the contemporaneous unemployment rate and a one-year lag in the unemployment rate using a methodology similar to that from Liebman, "Understanding the Increase in Disability Insurance Benefit Receipt in the United States." The method is also similar to that of the Social Security Technical Advisory Panel, Technical Panel on Assumptions and Methods, 2011, https://www.ssab.gov/Details-Page/ArticleID/216/2011-Technical-Panel-on-Assumptions-and-Methods-A-Report-tothe-Board-September-2011.

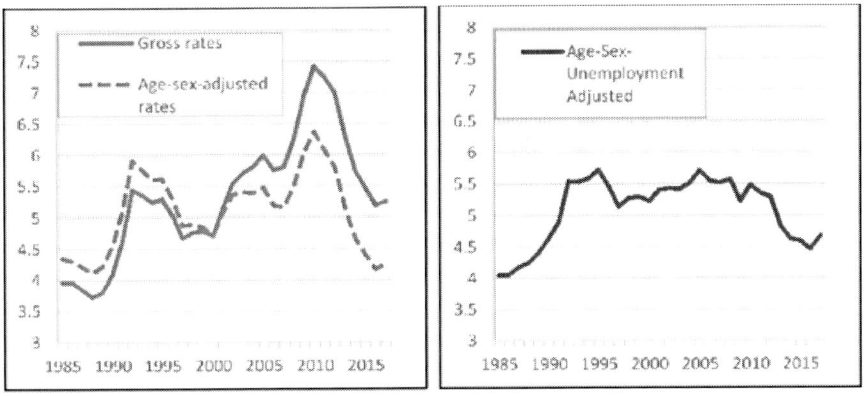

Source: CRS calculation and Social Security Trustees Report 2018, Figure V.C3.

Notes: The graph on the left shows the actual incidence rate, along with an age-sex-adjusted rate that holds the age and the sex distributions of the population constant at its 2000 level, while the graph on the right shows the predicted age-sex-adjusted incidence rate, under the counterfactual assumption that unemployment rates were constant at the 1985-2017 mean value of 6.02% for the entire period. The counterfactual unemployment rate in the right graph was chosen using the method discussed in Jeffrey B. Liebman, "Understanding the Increase in Disability Insurance Benefit Receipt in the United States," *Journal of Economic Perspectives*, vol. 29, no. 2 (2015), pp. 123-149.

Figure 5. Gross and Adjusted Incidence Rates, 1985-2017. Awards per 1,000 disability-exposed population.

The Change of the FRA

Under the scheduled increases enacted by Social Security Amendments of 1983 (P.L. 98-21), the FRA increases gradually from 65 to 67 for workers born in 1938 or later. Between 2003 and 2009, the FRA gradually increased in two-month increments until it reached 66 for workers born between 1943 and 1954, and then between 2020 and 2027, it will gradually increase again until it reaches 67 for workers born in 1960 and later.

Raising the FRA increased the size of the SSDI program. From 2002 (the year prior to the FRA increase) to 2017, the number of new awards for workers ages 65-FRA increased from 750 to 6,136, and the share of SSDI beneficiaries who were ages 65-FRA increased from 1% to 11%.[24] In December 2017, there were about 495,600 disabled workers between ages 65 and FRA.[25]

In addition, the rise in the FRA increased the value of SSDI cash benefits relative to early retirement benefits. When a worker claims benefits before the FRA, there is an actuarial reduction in monthly benefits.[26] The earliest a worker can claim retirement benefits is age 62. For a worker with an FRA of 65, claiming benefits at 62 results in a 20% reduction in the monthly benefit. The reduction rises to 25% if the FRA is 66 and will be 30% for a FRA of 67. Since SSDI benefits are approximately the same as full retirement benefits,[27] the SSDI program has become relatively more attractive for the later birth cohorts whose FRA—and penalty for early retirement benefits—is larger. Although some studies suggest that an increase in the value of disability benefits relative to early retirement benefits induces more individuals to apply for SSDI benefits, researchers are divided over whether such individuals are actually awarded benefits.[28]

---

[24] SSA, *Annual Statistical Supplement 2018*, Table 6.C2, https://www.ssa.gov/policy/docs/statcomps/supplement/2018/ 6c.html#table6.c2.

[25] SSA, *Annual Statistical Report on the SSDI Program 2016*, Table 4, https://www.ssa.gov/policy/docs/statcomps/ di_asr/2016/sect01b.html#table4.

[26] See CRS Report R44670, *The Social Security Retirement Age*.

[27] SSDI benefits are based on the highest earnings in the applicable computation period (up to five of the lowest-earning years can be dropped), while full retirement benefits are based on highest 35 years of covered earnings. See CRS Report R44948, *Social Security Disability Insurance (SSDI) and Supplemental Security Income (SSI): Eligibility, Benefits, and Financing*, and CRS Report R43542, *How Social Security Benefits Are Computed: In Brief*.

[28] See Norma B. Coe and Kelly Haverstick, "Measuring the Spillover to Disability Insurance Due to the Rise in the Full Retirement Age," *Center for Retirement Research at Boston College*, December 2010, pp. 9-14, http://crr.bc.edu/ working-papers/measuring-the-spillover-to-disability-insurance-due-to-the-rise-in-the-full-retirement-age/. In addition, see Mark Duggan et al., "Aching to Retire? The Rise in the Full Retirement Age and its Impact on the Disability Rolls," *National Bureau of Economic Research*, Working Paper 11811, December 2005, http://www.nber.org/papers/ w11811. Using aggregate data, Duggan et al. found that the 1983 amendments increased SSDI enrollment by 0.58 percentage points for men (ages 45-64) and 0.89 percentage points for women (ages 45-64) between 1983 and 2005. Using disaggregate data, Coe and Haverstick found that a one percentage point decrease in the ratio of retirement to disability benefits resulted in a 0.28 percentage point increase in the two-year SSDI application rate for individuals born between 1938 and 1943. However, the researchers found no evidence that the increase in the FRA resulted in a rise in the incidence of SSDI receipt among individuals ages 55-FRA born between 1938 and 1941. (The 1942 and 1943 cohorts had not reached FRA).

In summary, many researchers show that demographic changes account for the bulk of the SSDI program's growth. Although results may differ in the measure of time period and calculation methods, most analysis suggests that more than half of the growth in SSDI enrollment before 2014 stems from factors of a growing share of working women eligible for DI, an aging population, and the increase in Social Security's full retirement age.[29]

Changes in Employment and Compensation

The opportunity of employment and the relative value of compensation over disability benefits may also contribute to the change in SSDI enrollment. In deciding whether to apply for SSDI benefits, workers typically compare the value of SSDI benefits (cash payments, health coverage, and the amount of leisure and family time) with their opportunities for work and compensation. This section discusses how employment opportunities and the earnings and benefits associated with working are likely to affect SSDI benefit receipts.

Business Cycle and Unemployment Rate

Figure 6 displays the number of SSDI applications (left axis) and the national unemployment rate (right axis) for each year between 1985 and 2017. The shaded areas mark the three economic recessions that took place July 1990-March 1991, March 2001-November 2001 and December 2007-June 2009 as dated by the National Bureau of Economic Research. In all

---

[29] Statement of Stephen C. Goss, Chief Actuary, SSA, before the House Committee on Ways and Means, Subcommittee on Social Security, March 14, 2013, https://www.ssa.gov/legislation/testimony_031413a.html; David Pattison and Hilary Waldron, "Growth in New Disabled-Worker Entitlements, 1970-2008," *Social Security Bulletin*, vol. 73, no. 4 (2013), https://www.ssa.gov/policy/docs/ssb/v73n4/v73n4p25.html; Kathy A. Ruffing, "How Much of the Growth in Disability Insurance Stems From Demographic Changes?," Center on Budget and Policy Priorities, 2014, https://www.cbpp.org/sites/default/files/atoms/files/1-27-14ss.pdf; and Mary C. Daly et al., "The Future of Social Security Disability Insurance," *Economic Letter*, Federal Reserve Bank of San Francisco, 2013, https://www.frbsf.org/economic-research/publications/economic-letter/2013/june/future-social-security-disability-insurance-ssdi/.

three cases, SSDI applications rose during the recession and peaked after the official end of the recession.

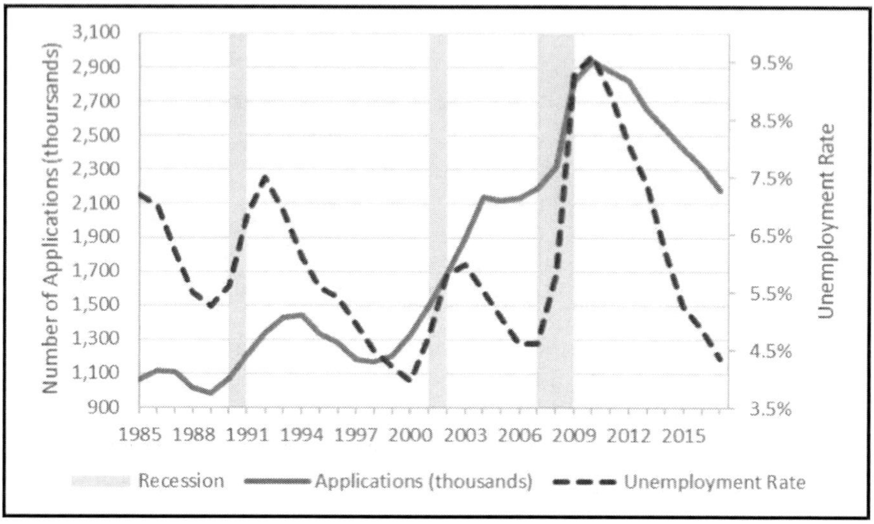

Source: SSA, *Annual Statistical Supplement, 2018*, Table 6.C7, https://www.ssa.gov/policy/docs/statcomps/ supplement/2018/6c.html; and Bureau of Labor Statistics, Unemployment Rate retrieved on July 31, 2018, https://data.bls.gov/pdq/SurveyOutputServlet.

Figure 6. Annual SSDI Applications and Unemployment Rate, 1985-2017.

One explanation for these business cycle effects is that they are driven by conditional disability applicants—those who would prefer to remain in the labor force but would apply for SSDI benefits if they lost their present jobs.[30] When opportunities for employment are plentiful, some people who could qualify for disability insurance benefits find working more attractive, and when employment opportunities are scarce, some of those people apply to the SSDI program instead of looking for work.[31] Some studies find that SSDI applications during recessions have higher past earnings and

[30] David H. Autor and Mark G. Duggan, "The Rise in the Disability Rolls and the Decline in Unemployment," *Quarterly Journal of Economics*, vol. 118, no. 1 (2003), pp. 157-206.

[31] CBO SSDI Report 2016.

more recent work experience than those during other time periods.[32] Researchers also find that the percentage of claims that are allowed drops under conditions of high unemployment.[33]

Despite the higher number of denials among disability insurance applications, the incidence rates (both gross and age-sex-adjusted) generally increase during and after economic recessions (see the left graph of Figure 5). The right graph of Figure 5 displays the predicted incidence rate under the assumption that unemployment rates were constant at 6.02% for the entire period, the mean value between 1985 and 2017. Compared with the fluctuation in the gross and age-sex adjusted incidence rates, the relatively stable unemployment-adjusted incidence rate after 1990 indicates that business cycles are likely to explain some of the trends in the SSDI enrollment.

The Value of SSDI Benefits Relative to Earnings

Some studies show that average preapplication earnings of disability insurance applicants have been declining over time relative to nonapplicants.[34] A possible reason might be that more low-wage earners are incentivized to apply for SSDI since the value of disability insurance benefits relative to earnings has been steadily rising for low-wage workers.[35] The initial amount of SSDI benefits is tied to the growth in average national earnings, which are growing faster than earnings for low-wage workers. Historical data show that the cumulative growth in real wages from 1979 to 2017 was 34.3% for the 90th percentile (high-wage

---

[32] Norma B. Coe and Matthew S. Rutledge, "How Does the Composition of Disability Insurance Applicants Change Across Business Cycles?," *Center for Retirement Research at Boston College*, Working Paper 2013-5, 2013; and Stephan Lindner and Clark Burdick, "Characteristics and Employment of Applicants for Social Security Disability Insurance over the Business Cycle," *Center for Retirement Research at Boston College*, Working Paper 2013-11, 2013.

[33] Stephen C. Goss et al., "Disabled Worker Allowance Rates: Variation Under Changing Economic Conditions," SSA, Office of the Chief Actuary, August 2013, https://www.ssa.gov/oact/NOTES/pdf_notes/note153.pdf.

[34] Till von Wachter et al., "Trends in Employment and Earnings of Allowed and Rejected Applicants to the Social Security Disability Insurance Program," *American Economic Review*, vol. 101, no. 7 (2011), pp. 3308-3329.

[35] CBO SSDI Report 2016.

earners), 6.1% for the 50th percentile (middle-wage earners), but 1.2% for the 10th percentile (low-wage earners).[36]

Availability of Health Insurance Coverage

One possible reason for people to apply for the disability insurance program might be the availability of Medicare to participants in SSDI (after a two-year waiting period).[37] Some studies show that Medicare availability has encouraged some people to apply for disability insurance benefits, because many people with disabilities did not have access to health insurance coverage otherwise.[38]

Beginning in 2014, the Affordable Care Act (ACA) provided more options for people with disabilities to obtain insurance. By enabling access to private health insurance and expanding access to subsidized public health insurance, the ACA may alter disability claiming decisions. The effect of the ACA on SSDI enrollment is not yet clear.[39]

Some researchers find that people who have an alternative source of health insurance coverage (from a spouse's employer or retiree coverage) are more likely to apply for SSDI benefits.[40] They argue that the Medicare's two-year waiting period for SSDI beneficiaries may deter disability applications from workers who have health insurance through their jobs but no alternative source of health coverage after leaving work. The availability of the ACA improves coverage options for those with disabilities, which may cause the number of disability applications to rise.

---

[36] See CRS Report R45090, *Real Wage Trends, 1979 to 2017*.

[37] See CRS Report RS22195, *Social Security Disability Insurance (SSDI) and Medicare: The 24-Month Waiting Period for SSDI Beneficiaries Under Age 65*.

[38] Alice R. Levy et al., "The Potential Employment Impact of Health Reform on Working-Age Adults with Disabilities," *Journal of Disability Policy Studies*, vol. 24, no. 2 (2013), pp. 102-112. The study argues that employer-sponsored health insurance may not be available to many people with disabilities who work in low-skill or part-time employment. In addition, private health insurance plans are less likely to offer comprehensive benefit packages for people with disabilities, and the premiums are likely to be high for persons with disabilities.

[39] Marcus Dillender, "The Potential Effects of Affordable Care Act on Disability Insurance and Workers' Compensation," in *The Economics of Health*, pp. 81-102, https://research.upjohn.org/up_press/238/.

[40] Jonathan Gruber and Jeffrey Kubik, "Health Insurance Coverage and the Disability Insurance Application Decision," *National Bureau of Economic Research*, Working Paper No. 9148, 2002.

In addition, by providing greater access to health care, the ACA may make it easier for people to obtain the documentation necessary to prove they have a disability, thus resulting in more people applying for disability insurance or an increase in the acceptance rate.[41]

Others suggest that by creating good health insurance opportunities, the ACA may lower the value of the disability program, causing fewer people to apply for disability and more SSDI beneficiaries to return to work. Although the actual effect of the ACA on disability applications is hard to examine due to the short length of time since implementation, some studies using state-level data show that disability applications are likely to decrease with the introduction of the ACA.[42] Researchers suggest that the ACA, with reasonable health care costs through the income-adjusted premium, may reduce dependency on health insurance coverage (i.e., Medicare) for some disabled-worker beneficiaries and allow them to return to work, thus reducing the number of people receiving disability benefits.[43] Some analytical results also indicate that the ACA may cause SSDI recipients to be healthier, which has the potential to lower the likelihood that people become disabled while at work[44] and increase their likelihood of exiting the disability rolls.[45]

---

[41] Dillender, "The Potential Effects of Affordable Care Act on Disability Insurance and Workers' Compensation."

[42] Nicole Maestas et al., "Effects of Health Care Reform on Disability Insurance Claiming," RAND Corporation, RB9769, 2014, https://www.rand.org/pubs/research_briefs/RB9769.html.

[43] Norma Coe and Kalman Rupp, "Does Access to Health Insurance Influence Work Effort among Disability Cash Benefit Recipients?," Center for Retirement Research at Boston College, Working Paper 2013-10, 2013.

[44] Charles J. Courtemanche and Daniela Zapata, "Does Universal Coverage Improve Health? The Massachusetts Experience," *Journal of Policy Analysis and Management*, vol. 33, no. 1 (2014), pp. 36-69.

[45] Robert R. Weathers II and Michelle Stegman, "The Effect of Expanding Access to Health Insurance on the Health and Mortality of Social Security Disability Insurance Beneficiaries," *Journal of Health Economics*, vol. 31, no. 6 (2012), pp. 863-875; and Charles Michalopoulos et al., "The Effects of Health Care Benefits on Health Care Use and Health: A Randomized Trial for Disability Insurance Beneficiaries," *Medical Care*, vol. 50, no. 9 (2012), pp. 764-771.

Changes in Policy Rules and Implementation

Some of the observed trends in SSDI enrollment were the result of changes in policies. This section examines how changes in eligibility criteria for disability determination and continuing disability reviews (CDRs) affected SSDI benefit awards and terminations.

Policy Changes in Eligibility Criteria

In 1984, the Disability Benefits Reform Act (P.L. 98-460) expanded the ways in which a person could medically qualify for disability insurance benefits. Some researchers argue that, under this legislation, the SSA relaxed its screening rules of mental disorders and placed more weight on applicants' reported pain and discomfort.[46] Applicants were able to qualify on the basis of the combined effect of multiple medical conditions, each of which might not have met the criteria if considered alone.[47] Some studies claim that these changes made it easier for some applicants to qualify for benefits due to certain difficult-to-verify impairments, such as back pain or depression.[48]

One study shows that eligibility standards expanded significantly after the 1984 legislation but have been relatively stable since the early 1990s.[49] The age-sex-unemployment-adjusted incidence rate increased from 4.1% in 1985 to approximately 5.6% in the early 1990s, and there has been no increase since then (see the right graph in Figure 5). After controlling for the effect of rising incidence among women and the aging of the workforce, analysis shows that the 1984 legislative reform still contributed

[46] David H. Autor and Mark G. Duggan, "The Growth in Social Security Disability Rolls: A Fiscal Crisis Unfolding," *Journal of Economics Perspectives*, vol. 20, no. 3 (2006), pp. 71-96, http://dx.doi.org/10.1257/jep.20.3.71.

[47] CBO SSDI Report 2016.

[48] Liebman, "Understanding the Increase in Disability Insurance Benefit Receipt in the United States"; and Wachter et al., "Trends in Employment and Earnings of Allowed and Rejected Applicants to the Social Security Disability Insurance Program."

[49] Liebman, "Understanding the Increase in Disability Insurance Benefit Receipt in the United States."

a significant proportion of the increase in the incidence rate from 1985 to the early 1990s.[50]

The 1984 act has resulted in some compositional changes in the SSDI beneficiary population. First, the change in eligibility criteria has contributed to a shift in the types of disabilities for which beneficiaries qualify. The share of disabled-worker beneficiaries with mental disorders or musculoskeletal system and connective tissue disorders (typically back pain or arthritis) has increased from 30% of newly awarded disabled workers in 1983 (the year before the legislation was enacted) to 52% in 2004 and remained around this level for more than 10 years from 2005 to 2016.[51] Researchers argue that in conjunction with labor market developments that increased the incentive for low-wage workers to apply for benefits,[52] these new program rules likely led to an increase in disability receipts, although the extent of the increase is unclear.[53]

Second, because mental disorders may have an early onset[54] and low age-specific mortality, SSDI beneficiaries with those diagnoses are likely to experience relatively long durations on the program.[55] The proportion of disabled workers who died in 1983 was 4.9%; 2.9% died in 2017.[56] Although it is conceivable that medical progress has reduced mortality for a wide range of conditions, researchers claim that it seems likely that a portion of the decline in mortality rates among SSDI recipients is the result of a change in the composition of the beneficiary population.[57]

---

[50] Liebman, "Understanding the Increase in Disability Insurance Benefit Receipt in the United States."

[51] Social Security Administration, *Annual Statistical Report on the Social Security Disability Insurance Program, 2016*, October 2017, Table 40, at https://www.ssa.gov/policy/docs/statcomps/di_asr/2016/sect03c.html#table40.

[52] See "The Value of SSDI Benefits Relative to Earnings."

[53] Autor and Duggan, "The Growth in Social Security Disability Rolls."

[54] Ronald C. Kessler et al., "Age of Onset of Mental Disorders: A Review of Recent Literature," *Curr Opin Psychiatry*, vol. 20, no. 4 (2007), pp. 359-364. The study shows that roughly half of all lifetime mental disorders in most studies start by the mid-teens and three-fourths by the mid-20s.

[55] Autor and Duggan, "The Growth in Social Security Disability Rolls."

[56] CRS calculation using *Annual Statistical Supplements* (1983-2005) from SSA.

[57] Liebman, "Understanding the Increase in Disability Insurance Benefit Receipt in the United States."

Third, incidence rates at younger ages have increased relative to rates at older ages. Table 1 shows that the difference between the incidence rates of disabled workers below and above age 50 became smaller over time. One possible explanation is that young disabled workers are more likely to be on the rolls due to mental disorders, which tend to have an early onset.[58] Some statistical results show that successive birth cohorts have been increasingly entering SSDI at younger ages, and, combined with a declining mortality rate, the average duration of disability benefit receipts has lengthened.[59] These phenomena are likely to result in a further increase in SSDI rolls and program spending.

Changes in Program Integrity Workloads

Continuing disability reviews (CDRs) are periodic reviews conducted by SSA to determine whether SSDI beneficiaries continue to meet the definition of *disability* under the Social Security Act. Disabled beneficiaries whose medical conditions are determined to no longer be disabling are generally terminated from the SSDI rolls.

Due to the high number of initial disability applications since 2003, SSA dedicated resources to processing initial applications rather than conducting CDRs. As a result, SSA has had a backlog of full medical CDRs[60] since FY2002. Between 2003 and 2009, the backlog increased to about 1.5 million full medical CDRs.[61] With increased program integrity funding from FY2014 to FY2018, SSA has increased the number of full medical CDRs completed, and the backlog decreased to about 64,000 cases at the end of FY2017.[62] SSA completed all available CDRs, eliminating the

---

[58] Testimony of Stephen C. Goss, Chief Actuary, SSA, "The Foreseen Trend in the Cost of Disability Insurance Benefits," July 24, 2014, https://www.ssa.gov/legislation/testimony_072414a.html.

[59] Yonatan Ben-Shalom et al., "Trends in SSDI Benefit Receipt: Are More Recent Birth Cohorts Entering Sooner and Receiving Benefits Longer?," *Mathematica Policy Research*, Working Paper 55, February 2018.

[60] SSA considers the cases for which it does not conduct a timely (three-year) periodic CDR as backlogged until the CDR for those cases can be initiated.

[61] SSA, Office of the Inspector General, *The Social Security Administration's Completion of Program Integrity Workloads*, p. 8, http://go.us.gov/cQpz9.

[62] SSA, Office of the Inspector General, *Fiscal Year 2017 Inspector General Statement on the Social Security Administration's Major Management and Performance Challenges*, https://www.ssa.gov/finance/2017/ OIG%202017%20Mgmt%20Challenges.pdf.

backlog, by the end of FY2018.[63] This is a possible reason that the number of disabled workers who no longer meet the medical requirement in 2017 was more than 150% higher than in 2014.[64] The recovery rate (medical improvement and return to work) was 18.2 per 1,000 beneficiaries for 2017 and projected to go down to 11.0 per 1,000 beneficiaries with the elimination of the backlog.[65]

Changes in Allowance Rates

The total allowance rate is the proportion of SSDI claimants who are ultimately allowed benefits (excluding applicants disqualified for nonmedical reasons—that is, technical denials).[66] The initial disability determination is made by the Disability Determination Services. Individuals who are dissatisfied with SSA's initial determination may request a further review, an appeals process that is generally composed of three levels: (1) reconsideration of the case by a reviewer who did not participate in the initial determination, (2) a hearing before an administrative law judge (ALJ), and (3) a request for review by the Appeals Council.[67]

Figure 7 shows the final outcome of disabled-worker applications from 1992 to 2016. The allowance rate at all adjudicative levels (the initial determination and the appeals process) reached a peak of 62% in 2001 and then declined steadily to 48% in 2016. Considered separately, the allowance rate for disabled-worker applicants at the initial determination level decreased from 40% to 33% between 2001 and 2016, the allowance rate at the reconsideration level declined from 13% to 9%, and the

---

[63] Social Security News, "We Can't Answer Our Phones but We're Up to Date in Cutting People Off Benefits," August 22, 2018, https://socsecnews.blogspot.com/2018/08/we-cant-answer-our-phones-but-were-up.html.

[64] CRS calculation using *Annual Statistical Supplement* (2015-2018) from SSA, Table 6.F2.

[65] Social Security Trustees Report 2018, p. 135.

[66] Nonmedical factors in disability insurance decisions may include insured status, the SGA test, and the claimant's relationship to certain family members.

[67] 20 C.F.R. §§404.900, 416.1400.

allowance rate at the hearing level or above declined from 73% to 46% during the same time period.[68]

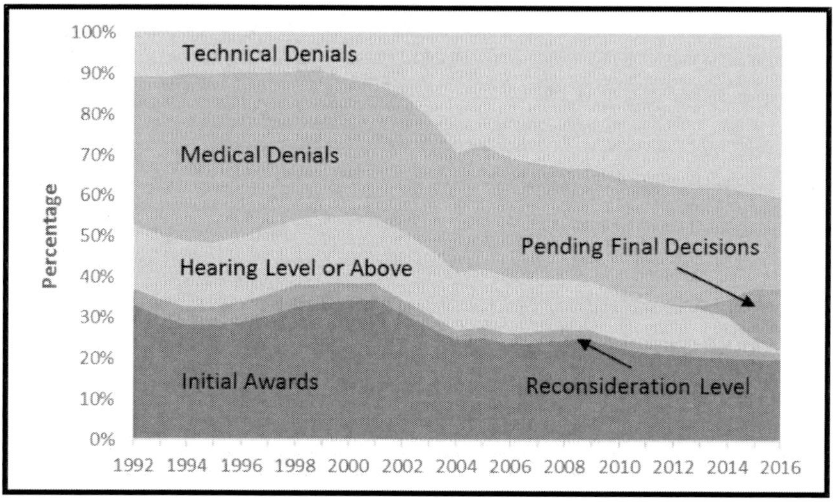

Source: Social Security Administration, Annual Statistical Report on the SSDI Program, 2017, at https://www.ssa.gov/policy/docs/statcomps/di_asr/2017/sect04.html, Table 60-63.

Notes: Technical denials include both nonmedical decision technical denials and medical decisions that were subsequently denied for technical (nonmedical) reasons. Because a number of applications remain pending for more recent years, the allowance rates will change over time. Cases can be pending at the initial or appeal levels and can include either medical or technical issues.

Figure 7. Final Outcome of Disabled-Worker Applications, 1992-2016.

Thus far, it is unclear what causes the decline in the total allowance rate among disabled-worker applications. Some researchers claim that the total allowance rate is generally countercyclical: SSDI applications increase when the unemployment rate rises but the allowance rate generally falls after one to two years of recession, likely because a larger share of the applications filed during a recession is motivated by financial

---

[68] The allowance rate at each adjudicative level is defined as the proportion SSDI claimants at each level who are allowed benefits, excluding applicants disqualified for nonmedical reasons. Because a number of applications remain pending for more recent years, the allowance rates will change over time. Cases can be pending at the initial or appeal levels and can include either medical or technical issues.

hardship. Those researchers suggest that the decline in allowance rates since 2001, and particularly after 2009, is attributable to fluctuations in the unemployment rate.[69] Some others believe that the persistent low total allowance rates would indicate a "regime shift" in the SSDI determination process, and they also show that more recent cohorts of ALJs at the hearing level have lower allowance rates than did earlier ALJ cohorts with the same level of experience.[70]

EXPLAINING THE RECENT DECLINE IN SSDI ENROLLMENT

The number of SSDI beneficiaries has experienced large growth in the past 30 years, but the trend was reversed starting in 2014. The decline in SSDI rolls was driven by two forces: the decrease in new disability awards since 2011 and the continuous increase in the termination of disability benefits. Based on the previous discussion, this section summarizes the possible causes of the recent decline in SSDI enrollment.

The Decrease in New Disability Awards

Since 2010, new awards to disabled workers have decreased every year, dropping from 1 million to 762,100 in 2017. Although there has been no definitive cause identified, four factors may explain some of the decline in disability awards.

1. Availability of jobs. The unemployment rate was as high as 9.6% in 2010 and then gradually decreased every year to about 4.35% in 2017. The opportunities for employment make working more attractive than disability benefits for people who could qualify for

---

[69] Goss et al., "Disabled Worker Allowance Rates."

[70] Report to the Social Security Advisory Board, "2015 Technical Panel on Assumptions and Methods," pp. 37-40.

SSDI. If the unemployment rate were kept at 6.02%—the average level between 1985 and 2017—the age-sex-adjusted incidence rate would have been 3.5% (0.35 per 1,000 disability-exposed population) higher in 2016. Thus about 50,000 more disabled-worker benefits would have been awarded in that year.[71]

2. Aging of lower-birth-rate cohorts. The lower-birth-rate cohorts (people born after 1964) started to enter peak disability-claiming years (usually considered ages 50 to FRA) in 2015, replacing the larger baby boom population. This transition would likely reduce the size of the insured population who are ages 50 and above, as well as the number of disability applications. As the baby boomers reached age 50 between 1996 and 2014, the growth rate of the insured population ages 50 to FRA has been consistently around 5% from 1997 to 2008. The growth rate started to decrease in 2009, dropped down below 1% in 2014, and became negative (no growth) in 2018.[72]
3. Availability of the Affordable Care Act (ACA). The ACA expanded health insurance opportunities beginning in 2014. The availability of health insurance under the ACA may lower the incentive to use SSDI as a means of access to Medicare, thus reducing the number of disability applications. The nationwide effect of the ACA on disability benefit receipt is still unclear.
4. Decline in the allowance rate. The total allowance rate at all adjudicative levels declined from 62% in 2001 to 48% in 2016. While this decline may in part reflect the impact of the Great Recession (since SSDI allowance rates typically fall during an economic downturn),[73] the Social Security Advisory Board

---

[71] CRS calculation based on predicated incidence rates in Figure 5 and the numbers of the insured population and SSDI beneficiaries from SSA 2018 *Annual Statistical Supplement*.

[72] CRS calculation using SSA 2018 *Annual Statistical Supplement*, Table 4.C2, https://www.ssa.gov/policy/docs/ statcomps/supplement/2018/4c.html#table4.c2.

[73] Kalman Rupp, "Factors Affecting Initial Disability Allowance Rates for the Disability Insurance and Supplemental Security Income Program: The Role of the Demographic and Diagnostic Composition of Applicants and Local Labor Market Conditions," *Social Security Bulletin*, vol. 72, no. 4 (2012).

Technical Panel suspects that the declining initial allowance rate may be a result of the change in the SSDI adjudication process.[74]

In addition to the factors contributing to a decline in SSDI applications and awards, some others may have the opposite effect of pushing disability benefit receipt upward. Some of those factors may include the increase in the FRA, the growth in applications from low-wage workers, and higher incidence rates among young applicants resulting from an expansion of SSDI eligibility rules. But the effect of those factors was smaller than the ones that decreased new SSDI awards between 2011 and 2017.

The Increase in Disability Terminations

The number of benefit terminations among disabled workers has been increasing from 2001 to 2017 (see Figure 2), and the share of total disabled-worker beneficiaries who terminated benefits also increased from 8% to almost 10%. The following factors are likely to contribute to the increase in disability terminations.

- Baby boomers reached FRA. As the relatively large baby boomer population reaches its FRA (gradually increased from 65 to 66) between 2012 and 2031, there is expected to be a growing proportion of disabled workers who terminate disability benefits due to the attainment of FRA. As shown in the previous section, the proportion of terminations that were due to attainment of FRA was about 50% before 2012, but the ratio gradually increased to nearly 60% in 2017. The potential increase in the number of terminations may slow down due to the scheduled increase in the FRA from 66 to 67 between 2020 and 2027, which will result in fewer disabled workers exiting the SSDI program due to the attainment of FRA.

---

[74] Report to the Social Security Advisory Board, "2015 Technical Panel on Assumptions and Methods," p. 37.

- Efforts in CDRs. With increased program integrity funding in recent years, SSA has increased the number of full medical CDRs completed, and the backlog was reduced to about 64,000 cases at the end of FY2017. Between 2013 and 2017, about 147,000 benefits were terminated after CDRs.[75] The effect of CDRs on SSDI terminations will become relatively smaller, as the SSA eliminated the backlog by the end of FY2018.
- Availability of the ACA. The prevalence of the ACA after 2014 is likely to cause some SSDI recipients to return to work for two reasons. First, the ACA may reduce beneficiary reliance on SSDI as a path to Medicare access. Second, the ACA may improve the health conditions of disabled-worker beneficiaries. The actual magnitude of the effect awaits further analysis.

Some factors may work in the opposite direction to decrease disability terminations. Examples include the scheduled further increase in FRA from 66 to 67 and the declining mortality rate among disabled-worker beneficiaries.[76]

---

[75] SSA Data for Periodic Continuing Disability Reviews Cases Processed and Backlog, https://www.ssa.gov/open/data/Periodic-Continuing-Disability-Reviews.html.

[76] In the Social Security Trustees Report 2018, the Office of the Chief Actuary at SSA estimates that the death rates among disabled beneficiaries will continue to decline through 2095.

In: Social Security Disability
Editor: Michael Dimitriadis
ISBN: 978-1-53615-747-5

Chapter 4

SOCIAL SECURITY DISABILITY INSURANCE: INFORMATION ON POTENTIAL IMPLICATIONS OF EXPANDING PRIVATE DISABILITY INSURANCE*

United States Government Accountability Office

ABBREVIATIONS

ACLI	American Council of Life Insurers
ADA	Americans with Disabilities Act
AHIP	America's Health Insurance Plans
BLS	Bureau of Labor Statistics
DOL	Department of Labor
EBEI	evidence-based early intervention
EBRI	Employee Benefit Research Institute

* This is an edited, reformatted and augmented version of United States Government Accountability Office; Report to Congressional Requesters, Publication No. GAO-18-248, dated April 2018.

ERISA	Employee Retirement Income Security Act of 1974
FECA	Federal Employees' Compensation Act
OASI	Old-Age and Survivors Insurance
PDI	private disability insurance
SOA	Society of Actuaries
SSA	Social Security Administration
SSDI	Social Security Disability Insurance
SSI	Supplemental Security Income
TTW	Ticket to Work

WHY GAO DID THIS STUDY

SSDI, which is administered by SSA, provides financial and other assistance to qualifying individuals who are unable to work due to their disabilities. SSDI is primarily funded by employee and employer payroll taxes that are placed in the Disability Insurance Trust Fund, which is currently projected to not be able to pay full benefits starting in 2028. While there are a number of ways to address the fiscal condition of the Disability Insurance Trust Fund, some researchers have proposed expanding employer-provided PDI. GAO was asked to review whether expanding PDI could result in potential savings to the Disability Insurance Trust Fund.

This chapter examines (1) what is known about how coverage and key features of SSDI and PDI compare, and (2) the potential implications of three distinct proposals to expand employer-sponsored PDI on the Disability Insurance Trust Fund and various stakeholders.

GAO analyzed data on SSDI and PDI coverage from SSA and BLS for 2016 and 2017; reviewed relevant federal laws, regulations, and guidance; reviewed three PDI policies that three large insurers we selected described as typical for their companies; reviewed three distinct proposals to expand PDI identified through a literature review; and interviewed SSA and Department of Labor officials, authors, researchers, and representatives of insurance, employer, employee, and disability groups for a range of perspectives.

WHAT GAO FOUND

GAO's analysis found that coverage and key features of Social Security Disability Insurance (SSDI) and long-term employer-sponsored private disability insurance (PDI) differ in a number of ways. Key differences include the number of workers covered; characteristics of covered workers; and eligibility, benefits, and return to work assistance. For example:

According to GAO's analysis of Bureau of Labor Statistics and Social Security Administration (SSA) data, SSDI covers an estimated 96 percent of workers, while 33 percent of workers have PDI coverage through their employers. Also, PDI coverage is more prevalent among workers with higher wages (e.g., management positions) and in certain business sectors (e.g., finance).

GAO's review of SSDI and PDI policies found that some PDI policies may pay benefits for medical conditions that SSDI would not. However, these PDI policies may time limit payments for mental health and musculoskeletal disorders, while SSDI does not. In addition, while both SSDI and PDI policies include features designed to help beneficiaries return to work, PDI policies may provide such supports more quickly than SSDI.

GAO's review of the literature identified three distinct proposals for expanding PDI that the proposals' authors believe would address SSDI's fiscal challenges. Specifically, all three proposals suggest that cost savings for the Disability Insurance Trust Fund could be expected by expanding PDI. According to the proposals, this would happen because expanding PDI would provide workers earlier access to cash and employment supports, which would reduce the number of SSDI claims or the length of time SSDI benefits are paid to claimants. However, GAO's review of the three proposals noted that none of them provide enough information to assess how SSDI enrollment and costs might be affected with an expansion of PDI. Therefore, it is unclear whether cost savings to the Disability Insurance Trust Fund would actually be realized. For example, the proposals do not provide information on the type and timing of return-to-work services that would be provided under expanded PDI, nor do they take into account the differences in the populations served by SSDI and PDI policies. Moreover, stakeholders that GAO interviewed about these proposals raised a number of issues about other implications of PDI expansion that the proposals do not explicitly or fully address. For example:

Insurers told GAO that is was unclear how expanding PDI would affect PDI premiums and the impact this would have on enrollment.

Employers told GAO they were concerned about potential additional requirements or administrative burdens that would be placed on them if PDI were expanded.

Employee and disability advocacy groups told GAO they were concerned about whether PDI expansion would provide standard services or employee protections currently available under SSDI, especially with respect to PDI expansion proposals that would replace SSDI for 2 years.

April 10, 2018

The Honorable Orrin Hatch
Chairman
Committee on Finance
United States Senate

The Honorable Mike Lee
United States Senate

The Disability Insurance Trust Fund, primarily funded by employers and workers through payroll taxes and administered by the Social Security Administration (SSA), is used to provide cash benefits to people no longer able to work as a result of their disabilities and to their dependents. In calendar year 2016, SSA paid $142.7 billion in Social Security Disability Insurance (SSDI) benefits to more than 10.6 million beneficiaries. Over time, demographic and other factors have reduced the Disability Insurance Trust Fund's reserves and the fund's projected depletion in 2016 was delayed when Congress passed a law that temporarily reallocated a share of payroll tax revenues from the trust fund for the Old-Age and Survivors Insurance (OASI) to the Disability Insurance Trust Fund. As of July 2017, the Social Security Board of Trustees projects that the Disability Insurance Trust Fund will be depleted in 2028, at which time incoming payroll tax revenues may not be sufficient to support paying full benefits.

In prior work, we identified various types of proposals made by researchers and others to address the fiscal condition of the Disability Insurance Trust Fund and related challenges, including proposals to slow the flow of people applying for SSDI; target finite resources more efficiently and effectively; and better align SSDI eligibility criteria with changes in the labor market, advances in medicine and technology, and modern concepts of disability.[1] We also previously reported that some researchers have suggested that one way to help address the fiscal condition of the Disability Insurance Trust Fund is to expand employer-sponsored private disability insurance (PDI). We reported that to the extent PDI expansion options encourage workers to forgo applying for SSDI or limit the amount of time workers receive SSDI, they also have the potential to reduce the number of SSDI beneficiaries and program costs. You requested that we review the potential savings to the Disability Insurance Trust Fund and other implications associated with proposals to expand PDI coverage.

This chapter describes: (1) what is known about how coverage and key features of SSDI and PDI compare, and (2) the potential implications of three distinct proposals to expand employer-sponsored PDI on the Disability Insurance Trust Fund and various stakeholders.

To compare access to and features of SSDI and PDI, we reviewed relevant federal laws, regulations, and guidance; analyzed SSDI data and

---

[1] GAO, *Social Security's Future: Answers to key questions*, GAO-16-75SP (Washington, D.C.: October 2015).

Bureau of Labor Statistics data on disability insurance coverage; and reviewed insurance industry surveys on PDI coverage. Our work mainly focused on employer-sponsored, long-term PDI—which we refer to as PDI in this chapter—because it most closely mirrors the SSDI program.[2] We requested and reviewed PDI policies from three large insurance companies, which company representatives told us were typical policies for their companies, and we interviewed SSA and Department of Labor (DOL) officials, as well as representatives of an association and a nonprofit organization that conduct insurance industry surveys, and insurance associations and insurance companies.

To understand the potential implications of expanding PDI, we conducted a literature search to identify any proposals to expand PDI and that evaluated the potential effect of expansion on the number of SSDI beneficiaries and the amount of SSDI expenditures. We identified three proposals that evaluated long-term, employer-provided PDI. We interviewed the authors of the proposals and assessed the proposals for the soundness of their methodologies, the reliability of any data used, and limitations. We also spoke with SSA and DOL officials, as well as other researchers in the disability field to get their views on the identified proposals. To understand the potential implications of the three proposals to expand PDI for stakeholders, we spoke with representatives of groups that might be affected by such proposals, including insurance associations and insurance companies, employer associations and employers, unions and employee/disability advocacy groups, a states' insurance association and organization, and DOL and SSA officials.[3]

---

[2] Employers may also offer short-term disability insurance; however, this typically covers a period before SSDI benefits would begin. Also, individuals can purchase individual disability insurance outside of their employment, but we do not address this in this chapter because the focus of this chapter is on proposals to expand employer-sponsored disability insurance.

[3] We spoke with representatives of two insurance associations, three employer associations, three employee advocacy/disability groups, two unions, a states' insurance association, and a states' insurance organization. We also spoke with representatives of eight employers and five insurance companies who participated in discussion groups (two employer groups and two insurance company groups) that we organized at the Disability Management Employer Coalition Annual Conference on August 2, 2017.

This chapter does not examine the extent to which the provisions in pension plan disability benefits or other disability protections may promote work and help lower SSDI take-up rates or costs. Rather, we focus on the relationship between SSDI and long-term employer-sponsored PDI, which were the focus of the proposals we examined and because PDI most closely mirrors the SSDI program.

We conducted this work from November 2016 to April 2018 in accordance with generally accepted government auditing standards. Those standards require that we plan and perform the audit to obtain sufficient, appropriate evidence to provide a reasonable basis for our findings and conclusions based on our audit objectives. We believe that the evidence obtained provides a reasonable basis for our findings and conclusions based on our audit objectives.

BACKGROUND

Social Security Disability Insurance (SSDI)

In recent decades, economic and demographic factors have contributed to an increase in the number of SSDI beneficiaries and increased program costs, which has reduced the size of the Disability Insurance Trust Fund reserves from a peak of $215.8 billion in 2008 to $46.3 billion in 2016. Over the past 26 years, the total number of SSDI beneficiaries more than doubled, from 4.2 million in calendar year 1990 to nearly 11 million in calendar year 2016. By contrast, during that same time, the number of workers covered by SSDI increased by less than a third—from 133 million to 171 million. In calendar year 2016, around 8.8 million workers with disabilities and 1.8 million dependents (spouses and children) received SSDI payments, totaling $142.7 billion, of which $133.6 billion was paid to the workers and $9.1 billion to their dependents.

As we have reported previously, the growth in the number of SSDI beneficiaries to date can be mostly attributed to demographic factors such as the aging of the working population, the increase in the percentage of women in the workforce who are insured for SSDI benefits, and the growth in disability incidence rates for women to a level similar to men.[4] Since 2010, these demographic factors have begun to stabilize, resulting in much smaller projected increases in the number of SSDI beneficiaries in the future. However, few beneficiaries exit the program once they have qualified for benefits, and beneficiaries generally receive benefits until they reach retirement age or die. According to SSA's 2016 Annual Statistical Report, of the 8.8 million individuals receiving SSDI benefits in calendar year 2016, about 9 percent (820,372) exited the program that year. Of those exiting SSDI, more than half (470,320 or 57.3 percent) exited because they reached the full retirement age and began receiving Social Security retirement benefits instead, fewer than a third (251,492 or 30.7 percent) exited because they died, and a relatively small portion (47,887 or 5.8 percent) exited the program due to earnings exceeding the allowable limit. Of the rest of those who exited the program (50,673 or 6.2 percent), most did so because their medical condition improved[5]

Private Disability Insurance (PDI)

In most cases, long-term employer-sponsored private disability insurance (PDI) is paid for by the employer and provided as part of a package of benefits for employees, although sometimes employees are required to pay some of or the entire PDI premium. According to one industry survey (the most recent available), in 2013, 19 PDI companies

---

[4] The proportion of the insured population receiving SSDI benefits has increased even when adjusting for demographic factors such as age and sex. Researchers have suggested various non-demographic factors that may have contributed to this increase, but consensus is lacking. For example, changes in program eligibility rules and employment opportunities may have increased the pool of workers likely to apply for SSDI. See GAO-16-75SP.

[5] SSA. "Annual Statistical Report of the Social Security Disability Insurance Program, 2016." (Washington, D.C.: October 2017.) Other SSA-funded research, using longitudinal data rather than measures from only one point in time, found that 3.7 percent of SSDI's beneficiaries who entered the program in 1996 had left the program after finding work by 2006. See Liu, Su and David Stapleton. "How Many SSDI Beneficiaries Leave the Rolls for Work? More Than You Might Think." *Disability Policy Research Brief* Number 10-01. (Washington, DC: Mathematica Policy Research, April 2010).

covering about 75 percent of the PDI market policies provided PDI benefits to around 653,000 individuals, with annual payments totaling around $9.8 billion.[6]

Another industry survey estimated that the five largest insurers in the PDI market held about half of the market share of premiums paid.[7] PDI policies can be offered either on an opt-in basis, in which employees who choose to pay for PDI receive it, or on an opt-out basis, where employees are automatically enrolled in PDI, but can decline (opt-out of) the insurance.[8]

Other Disability Protections for Workers

Beyond the insurance market for PDI, workers may be eligible for other types of disability protection through their employment. For example, 38 percent of workers have employer-sponsored short-term disability coverage according to BLS, but unlike SSDI, this coverage typically lasts 6 months. In addition, state workers' compensation programs generally provide payments and assistance to individuals who are injured on the job, while both SSDI and PDI are designed to replace lost income from the onset of any disability regardless of whether it was work-related.[9] Also, some workers may be eligible for disability payments through defined benefit pension plans. These benefits, commonly known as disability retirement benefits, provide eligible workers with early retirement payments if they can no longer work because of the onset of a

---

[6] Council for Disability Awareness. *2014 Long Term Disability Claims Review*. 2014 (Portland, Maine: Council for Disability Awareness).

[7] LIMRA. *U.S. Group Disability Insurance 2016 Annual Review*. 2017 (Hartford, Connecticut: LIMRA).

[8] A large insurer with whom we spoke told us that opt-out PDI plans were increasingly common, but still a small percentage—around 2 percent—of its applicable PDI plans.

[9] In addition, the Federal Employees' Compensation Act (FECA) provides compensation benefits to civilian employees of the United States for disability due to personal injury sustained while in the performance of duty or to employment-related disease. See 5 U.S.C. §§ 8101-8193.

disability.[10] According to BLS data, many workers covered by defined benefit pension plans are state and local workers, though these data do not show what portion of them are not covered by SSDI.[11]

Proposals to Expand PDI

From our literature review, we identified three distinct proposals for expanding PDI in order to potentially alleviate financial challenges facing the SSDI program. These proposals were made in studies authored by: David Babbel and Mark Meyer (Babbel and Meyer) of Charles River Associates, Rachel Greszler (Greszler) of The Heritage Foundation, and David Autor and Mark Duggan (Autor and Duggan) for The Center for American Progress and the Hamilton Project.[12] While the proposals differed in how PDI expansion might be achieved, each proposal assumes or requires that PDI coverage would provide vocational assistance, workplace accommodations, and partial income replacement to employees with work-limiting disabilities.[13] Each proposal assumed that PDI expansion would result in the provision of effective return–to-work assistance earlier than would occur under SSDI. According to the authors, their proposals would slow the growth of the SSDI program by increasing

---

[10] We previously reported that coverage through defined-benefit pension plans has decreased in recent decades. GAO, *The Nation's Retirement System: A Comprehensive Re-evaluation Is Needed to Better Promote Future Retirement Security*, GAO-18-111SP (Washington, D.C.: Oct., 2017).

[11] According to BLS officials, in 2016 about 13.4 million state and local workers and in 2014 about 9.6 million private sector workers had a disability retirement option in their pension plan.

[12] We identified a fourth proposal that would—in addition to giving employers and insurers an expanded role in providing disability benefits in lieu of SSDI for a 2 year period— change SSDI benefits from permanent to temporary and provide SSDI partial disability awards, as well. Since the proposal was not solely focused on expanding PDI and its provisions for expanding PDI were similar to other proposals we identified, we did not include it in our review. See Jason J. Fichtner and Jason S. Seligman, "Beyond All Or Nothing: Reforming Social Security Disability Insurance To Encourage Work and Wealth" (chapter 13) in *SSDI Solutions: Ideas To Strengthen The Social Security Disability Insurance Program*, by Jim McCrery and Earl Pomeroy (West Conshohocken, PA: Infinity Publishing, March 2016).

[13] Based on discussions with insurers and our review of three sample policies, PDI may provide vocational assistance and workplace accommodations or reimburse the employer for such services.

work attachment of potential applicants or beneficiaries of SSDI and reversing the decline in employment rates of work-capable adults with disabilities, thereby improving the long-term solvency of the Social Security system.[14] Two of the proposals suggested piloting the approaches to assess potential savings and implementation issues.

SSDI Covers a Much Larger Portion of the Workforce Than PDI, and Features of Coverage Differ

SSDI Covers Almost All Workers, Whereas PDI Covers About One-Third of Workers, Who Are Generally Higher-Paid

According to our analysis of SSA and BLS data, nearly all American workers pay Social Security taxes and are potentially covered by SSDI, while only a third of workers have PDI coverage. For SSDI, an estimated 96 percent of American workers, along with their employers, pay Social Security payroll taxes, a portion of which are used to fund SSDI.[15] Of individuals aged 20 or older in 2016, 87 percent met the SSA work requirements to be eligible for benefits in the event of a disability.[16]

---

[14] The proposals also cited additional benefits beyond potential savings for SSDI. For example, all three proposals cited potential gains in financial security for the individual, two cited potential psychological benefits or individual well-being benefits, and one cited potential improvements to the overall economy and an increase in government revenue.

[15] The remaining 4 percent not covered by SSDI are mostly public sector workers in state and local government. About one-fourth of public-sector employees do not pay Social Security taxes on the earnings from their government jobs. Also, individuals who began working for the federal government starting in 1984 have been covered by Social Security though federal employees hired before 1984 are generally not covered. See GAO, *Social Security: Issues Regarding the Coverage of Public Employees*, GAO-08-248T (Washington, D.C.: Nov. 6, 2007).

[16] In order to be eligible for SSDI payments, an individual generally needs 40 quarters of credits, 20 of which were earned in the last 10 years ending with the year the individual becomes disabled. In 2017, a work credit is earned for each $1,300 of wages or self-employment income. Up to four credits can be earned each year.

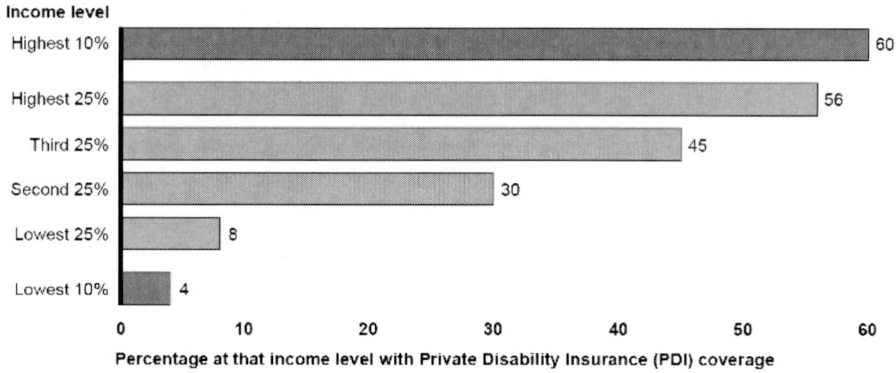

Source: GAO analysis of Bureau of Labor Statistics National Compensation Survey Data. | GAO-18-248.

Note: PDI totals in this figure refer to employer-sponsored long-term private disability insurance, as reported in the National Compensation Survey. This survey includes workers in civilian nonfarm industries (except those employed in private households and workers in the federal government). This survey does not include PDI plans where the employer does not pay any of the cost of the premiums.

Figure 1. Private Disability Insurance (PDI) Participation Rates by Income Category, 2017, Paid In Whole or In Part by Employers.

By contrast, as of March 2017, the Bureau of Labor Statistics (BLS) estimates that approximately 33 percent of the workforce is insured by employer-sponsored PDI where the employer pays at least some of the premium.[17] Employees may also pay the entire premium of employer-sponsored PDI—and researchers we interviewed from three private sector organizations that survey the PDI market told us that these plans are a minority of the PDI market. However, neither BLS nor industry surveys comprehensively track the extent of PDI coverage where employees pay 100 percent of the premium cost.[18]

---

[17] BLS also tracks employee access to PDI, which is defined as the number of employees who have a PDI benefit that is available for their use. For March 2016, BLS reported that 34 percent of workers had access to PDI and that 33 percent of workers participated in PDI, a 97 percent take-up rate.

[18] Benefits that are employer-sponsored but that are paid for entirely by employees are not captured as part of the National Compensation Survey conducted by BLS, and therefore are not included in these totals. Other industry surveys include queries regarding employer-sponsored PDI that is paid entirely by employees, but the nationwide proportion of employees that pay the entire premium is not fully captured by these surveys. For example,

In addition, while SSDI coverage is higher across all industries and income levels, PDI coverage is much more prevalent at higher wage levels and in certain occupations and industries than others. In particular, as of March 2017, 60 percent of those in the highest 10 percent of wage earners had PDI, whereas 4 percent of those in the lowest 10 percent did (see Figure 1).

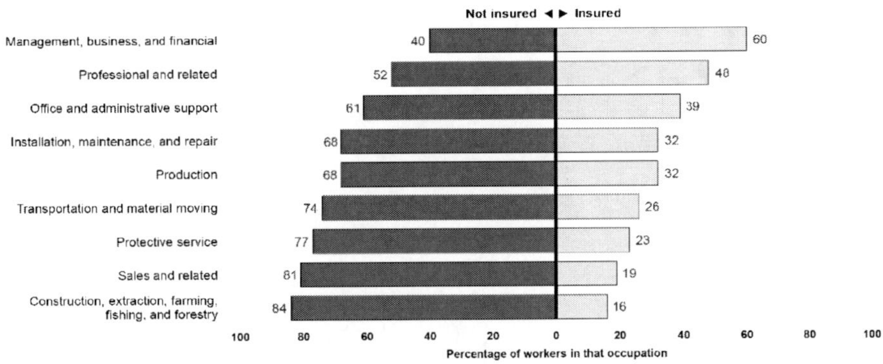

Source: GAO analysis of Bureau of Labor Statistics National Compensation Survey Data. | GAO-18-248.

Note: PDI totals in this figure refer to employer-sponsored long-term private disability insurance, as reported in the National Compensation Survey. These occupational categories were selected because they correspond to the high-level occupational categories used in the survey. These occupation data include workers employed in the civilian nonfarm industries (except those in private households and workers in the federal government). Workers in agricultural occupations in nonfarm industries, such as those on a farm operated by a non-profit organization, are included in the survey.

Figure 2. Percentage of Civilian Workers with Private Disability Insurance (PDI) Paid In Whole or In Part by Employers, for Selected Occupations, March 2017.

---

the Employee Benefit Research Institute (EBRI) surveys employees about benefits and asked employees who pays for PDI, regardless of whether the employee participated in PDI. According to EBRI researchers with whom we spoke, among those surveyed and who have an employer-sponsored PDI policy, 21 percent of employees said that the employer pays nothing toward their PDI premium. LIMRA, which is a private-sector research firm, has reported that for insurers that can break out their premium data, 23 percent of the premiums insurance companies receive for employer-sponsored PDI policies were from employees that paid the entire premium.

Our analysis of BLS data found that differences in PDI coverage also exist by occupation and industry. Specifically, 60 percent of workers in business and financial operations occupations have PDI coverage, compared to 16 percent of workers in construction, extraction, farming, fishing, and forestry occupations that have PDI (see Figure 2). Broad differences in PDI coverage also exist by industry; for example, 83 percent of workers in utilities have PDI, but only 5 percent of workers in leisure and hospitality have PDI (see Figure 3). According to researchers from one organization with whom we spoke, the higher rates of PDI coverage reflect areas where labor markets are more competitive, leading employers to offer PDI to attract employees.

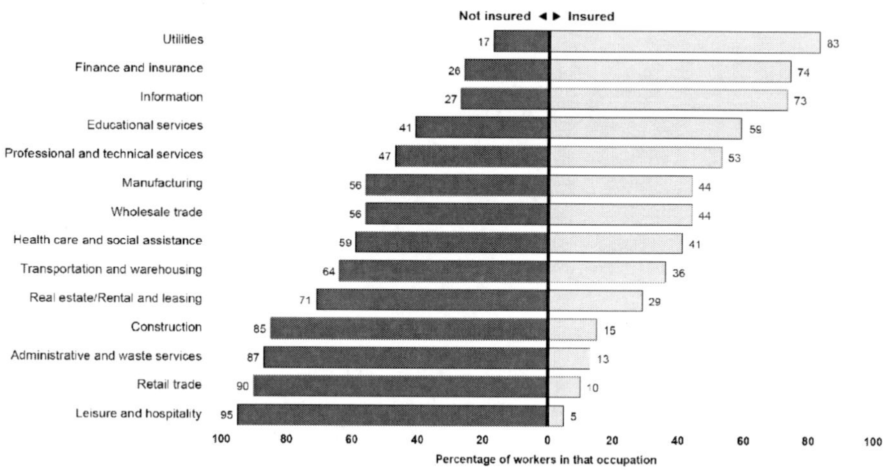

Source: GAO analysis of Bureau of Labor Statistics National Compensation Survey Data. | GAO-18-248.

Note: PDI totals in this figure refer to employer-sponsored long-term private disability insurance, as reported in the National Compensation Survey. These industry categories were selected because they correspond to high-level industry categories used in the survey. These data include workers employed in private nonfarm industries except those in private households.

Figure 3. Percentage of Private-Sector Workers with Private Disability Insurance (PDI) Paid In Whole or In Part by Employers, for Selected Industries, March 2017.

SSDI and PDI Differ in Many Respects, Including Eligibility, Benefit Level, and Approach to Return to Work

Eligibility

Our review of SSDI program rules and PDI policies indicates that eligibility for PDI is similar in some ways to eligibility for SSDI. For example, both allow individuals with many types of disabilities to receive benefits until retirement, recovery, or death. However, there are also some significant differences, as SSDI and PDI have different definitions and employment requirements. According to SSDI program rules, to meet SSDI's definition of disability, an individual must have a medically determinable physical or mental impairment that (1) has lasted or is expected to last at least 1 year or to result in death and (2) prevents the individual from engaging in substantial gainful activity.[19] SSA uses a list of medical conditions—established in regulations—that it considers severe enough to entirely prevent an individual from working. Benefits can also be provided for medical conditions that are not on the list if the medical condition or combination of medical conditions meets or equals the severity of those on the list.[20] SSA also considers additional factors— such as an individual's residual functional capacity, relevant past work, age, education, and work experience. SSA can determine that the medical conditions combined with the applicable factors preclude the individual from performing his or her prior work or any other work in the national economy.[21]

---

[19] 42 U.S.C. § 423(d). Substantial gainful activity is generally work activity involving significant physical or mental activities that are done for pay or profit, whether or not a profit is realized. 20 C.F.R. § 404.1572. The substantial gainful activity earnings amount in 2018 is $1,180 per month or $1,970 if blind.

[20] However, on March 29, 1996, Congress passed the Contract with America Advancement Act of 1996, which amended the Social Security Act to specify that an individual shall not be considered to be disabled for purposes of SSDI payments if alcoholism or drug addiction would be a contributing factor material to the individual's disability determination.

[21] See 20 C.F.R. § 404.1520.

Eligibility for granted SSDI benefits continues until retirement or death, or until SSA deems that the underlying medical conditions have sufficiently improved or that the individual has become gainfully employed.

In contrast, typical PDI policies have provisions related to inability to work that may compensate workers in a wider range of circumstances than SSDI does, although these provisions become more strict after 2 years.[22] For the first 2 years of PDI benefits, policies generally define disability as the inability of an individual to work his or her own occupation. For disabilities that last for more than 2 years, a typical PDI policy changes how it defines disability from the inability to work in one's previous occupation, to the inability to work in any occupation offering a reasonable income, which was 60 percent of pre-disability earnings in the three sample policies we examined. Similar to SSDI, PDI benefit payments generally continue for the length of the disability or until retirement; however, unlike SSDI, benefits paid for certain conditions, such as mental health conditions, are generally limited to 2 years. Also unlike SSDI, PDI policies typically include a pre-existing condition provision, whereby benefits are not paid if the applicant received treatment, services, or consultation or took medication for the condition in the 3 months prior to being insured.[23]

The requisite time period between the onset of a disability and when benefits can begin is comparable between SSDI and PDI, according to our review of SSDI program rules and PDI policies; however, the time it takes to process and make decisions on claims may run longer for SSDI.

---

[22] Our description of PDI features refers to employer-sponsored long-term private disability insurance and is based on our review of three PDI policies that three large insurers identified as typical, a literature review, and interviews with agency officials and various industry stakeholders

[23] Generally, based on PDI policies we reviewed, after someone has been covered under a policy for 12 consecutive months and has not made a claim, the pre-existing exclusion no longer applies.

For both SSDI and PDI, benefits do not usually start immediately upon disability onset. SSDI and PDI applicants must apply for benefits and usually wait for a period of time—known as a waiting period for SSDI and as an elimination period for PDI—for payments to begin.[24] The waiting period for SSDI benefits is 5 months after disability onset. For the PDI policies we examined, the elimination period ranged from 3 to 6 months after onset.[25] Another factor affecting the time to receipt of benefits is the time it takes to award the benefit. For PDI, federal regulations under the Employee Retirement Income Security Act of 1974 (ERISA) that govern claims in ERISA-covered plans, including disability claims, generally require initial claims to be decided within 45 days after receipt of the claim by the plan, with some ability to extend for two 30 day periods based on reasons beyond the plan's control.[26] PDI claimants may also appeal the initial decision.[27] On the other hand, based on our review of SSDI program rules, claims for SSDI are not subject to timing requirements established by law.[28] Further, denied claimants may appeal the initial decisions. The average decision time for appeals before Administrative Law Judges in fiscal year 2017 was 605 days, according to SSA's fiscal year 2017 performance report.[29]

---

[24] In this chapter, we use the term elimination period to encompass both the SSDI "waiting period" and the PDI "elimination period." PDI policies we examined use the term "waiting period" differently, to describe a period before coverage begins. Therefore, to avoid confusion we use the term elimination period throughout this chapter to describe the time before benefits may begin.

[25] For policies we examined, PDI benefits would begin when either the elimination period or, if applicable, short-term PDI coverage ended.

[26] ERISA applies to most private sector employee benefit plans, including welfare plans (plans established or maintained to provide benefits such as health benefits or disability benefits) and retirement plans (plans established or maintained to provide retirement income or defer income until a later time).

[27] Normally a claimant must complete the plan's internal claims procedures before filing an action in court.

[28] SSA does track timeliness against performance targets. In its fiscal year 2017 performance report, SSA reported that SSDI initial decisions in fiscal year 2017 took 111 days on average from the date of application, thereby meeting its target for average disability claims processing time of 113 days in fiscal year 2017.

[29] SSA program rules generally allow for four levels of appeal: reconsideration, hearing by an administrative law judge, review by the Appeals Council, and Federal Court review. According to SSA, individuals approved for SSDI at any of these levels are eligible for retroactive payments.

Our review of SSDI program rules and PDI policies also indicates that individuals are required to have longer employment periods for SSDI eligibility than for PDI, but PDI is generally not portable if the individual leaves the employer offering PDI. According to SSA guidance, individuals become eligible to receive SSDI payments after they have paid the Social Security payroll tax long enough—about 10 years for many—and recently enough to accumulate the required number of credits.[30] In contrast, the three sample PDI policies we reviewed contained 30-day waiting periods for coverage to begin. Further, part-time status and job changes affect PDI more than SSDI eligibility. SSDI's program rules generally allow for the work credits that an individual has accumulated to continue to count toward SSDI eligibility even if the individual is working part-time, changes jobs, or becomes unemployed or otherwise leaves the workforce. In comparison, PDI coverage, which is offered at the discretion of employers, is not generally portable, and may exclude part-time workers altogether—as was the case for the three "typical" PDI policies we reviewed.[31] Nationally, PDI coverage is much more prevalent among full-time workers than part-time workers. According to BLS data, 42 percent of full-time workers and 5 percent of part-time workers have PDI where the employer pays for all or part of the premiums. See Table 1 for a comparison of SSDI and PDI eligibility features.

---

[30] The requisite number of work credits depends on the individual's age when they become disabled. Specifically, workers aged 31 and older generally must have 40 quarters of work credits with at least 20 quarters of coverage during the 40 calendar quarter period ending with the quarter in which their disability began. Workers under age 31 need quarters of coverage in at least one-half (not less than six) of the quarters in the period beginning with the quarter after the quarter they attained the age of 21 and ending in the quarter in which their disability began.

[31] For PDI, individuals become eligible under the terms of the contract between their employer and an insurance provider, which define which employees are eligible for coverage. According to industry groups with which we spoke, employers may also choose PDI optional features in addition to standard features. These options can include different eligibility standards, cost-of-living adjustments, and different benefit levels.

Table 1. Comparison of Eligibility Features of Social Security Disability Insurance (SSDI) and Typical Private Disability Insurance (PDI) Policies

Eligibility features	SSDI program rules	PDI (typical policy)
Employment requirements	Must have enough and recent qualifying quarters of employment paying the relevant payroll tax—changes depending on age at onset of disability. Coverage continues if individual changes employers. Covers part-time workers.	Waiting period—typically 30 days—before coverage begins. Coverage generally ends if individual changes employers. Excludes part-time workers.
Exclusions	Conditions for which drug addiction or alcoholism are a contributing factor material to the determination of disability. Conditions that arise in connection with the commission (after October 19, 1980) by an individual of an offense which constitutes a felony under applicable law and for which such individual is subsequently convicted, or which is aggravated in connection with such an offense (but only to the extent so aggravated).	Pre-existing conditions and conditions that arise from risky behaviors (such as self-inflicted injuries, participation in a riot, committing criminal acts).
Benefit period	Benefits last until retirement, recovery, or death.	Benefits generally last until retirement, recovery, or death, but are time-limited for certain conditions, such as drug and alcohol illness, mental health conditions, musculoskeletal or connective tissue illnesses, chemical and environmental illness, fibromyalgia, and chronic fatigue.
Definitions of disability	Inability to engage in any substantial gainful activity—perform any work that exists in the national economy and (in 2018) earn no more than $1,180 a month or $1,970 if blind—due to a medically determined impairment that has lasted or is expected to last at least 1 year or to result in death.	Inability to perform work in their prior occupation. After 2 years of receiving benefits, unable to work any occupation and earn 60 percent of pre disability income.

Table 1. (Continued)

Eligibility features	SSDI program rules	PDI (typical policy)
Elimination period	5 months after disability onset[a]	3 to 6 months after disability onset, or after a short-term disability policy ends, whichever is longer

Source: GAO analysis of federal laws and regulations, Social Security Administration guidance; interviews with insurance representatives and sample PDI policy documents. | GAO-18-248

[a]This 5-month waiting period can be applied retroactively, but for no more than 17 months from the time of the application.

Note: Our description of PDI features refers to employer-sponsored long-term private disability insurance and is based on our review of three PDI policies that three large insurers identified as typical, a literature review, and interviews with agency officials and various industry stakeholders.

Benefit Level

Our review of SSDI program rules and PDI policies indicates that SSDI benefit levels for individuals are generally lower than PDI but are designed to provide more income replacement for low-income workers than higher-income workers. Under federal law, SSA determines benefit amounts using a progressive formula, whereby low-income beneficiaries receive relatively higher benefit payments based on their average monthly earnings over the course of their career.[32] For calendar year 2018, the formula pays 90 percent of the first $896 of the individual's average monthly earnings, plus 32 percent of the earnings between $896 and $5,399, plus 15 percent of earnings over $5,399. (See Figure 4 for the amount of benefits SSA paid in 2018 according to prior income levels.) Using the formula, we calculated that at an average indexed annual earnings of $44,000, the monthly benefit would be $1,693, which is 46 percent of prior average monthly earnings.[33] Under the formula, workers earning less would receive a higher proportion of their prior average, while

[32] SSDI's benefit formula averages a worker's highest 35 years of earnings, which are indexed to reflect the change in general wage levels that occurred during the worker's years of employment. For further details, see GAO-16-75SP.

[33] The percentage of the insured worker's earnings replaced would also be higher under certain circumstances if a minor dependent child, spouse, and/or adult dependent were included as beneficiaries.

workers earning the taxable maximum (set at $128,400 for 2018) or more would be eligible to receive $3,042 per month, which is at most 28 percent of their earnings.[34] Under federal law, disabled workers with qualifying dependents may receive additional SSDI payments, up to 50 percent of their individual benefit amount.[35] Therefore, according to our calculations, the maximum family benefit for average annual indexed earnings of $44,000 would be $2,540, which is 69 percent of prior average monthly earnings.[36]

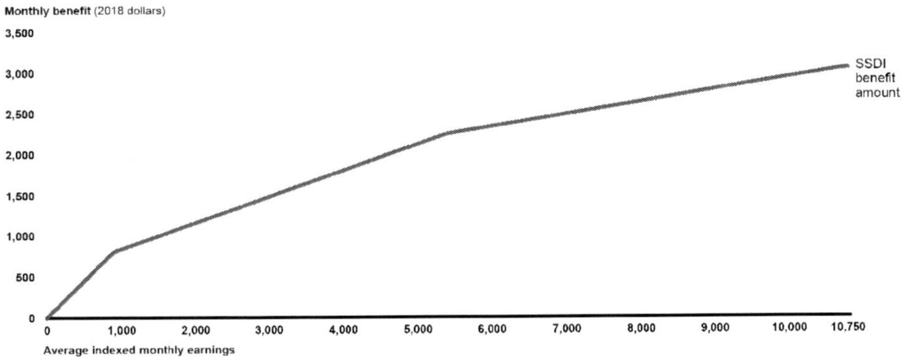

Source: GAO analysis of Social Security Disability Insurance. (SSDI) data. | GAO-18-248.

Figure 4. Social Security Disability Benefit Amounts at Different Income Levels.

By contrast, up to certain income levels, PDI policies typically replace 60 percent of an employee's current salary if the employee is unable to continue working his or her prior job.[37] Therefore, a worker earning $44,000 annually in their prior job would receive $2,200 per month. For

[34] Social Security limits the amount of earnings subject to taxation for a given year. The same annual limit also applies when those earnings are used in a benefit computation. This limit changes each year with changes in the national average wage index.

[35] According to SSA data, around a million disabled workers received dependent benefits in 2016, and most of them received the maximum family benefit amount. More than half (649,321) of these families were families with one dependent child.

[36] Under federal law, for lower-income beneficiaries, maximum family benefits are capped at the workers' individual benefit amount. As benefits replace less income, the maximum is the smaller of either 85 percent of the workers' average monthly earnings or 150 percent of their individual benefit amount, but cannot be less than the individual's benefit amount.

[37] When calculating a covered individual's current salary. PDI policies may not include commissions, bonuses, and overtime.

high-income workers, PDI policies typically have a monthly maximum payment. In one PDI policy we reviewed, this monthly maximum was $5,000. Employers and employees pay for SSDI through payroll taxes on employees' wages and salaries, so the cost to employers and employees only varies based on employees' wages and salaries. Federal law also determines the part of the payroll tax that is allocated for SSDI, half of which is contributed by the employee and half by the employer.[38] For PDI, either employers, employees, or a combination of the two make premium payments, depending on the policy negotiated between the insurer and the employer. According to industry representatives with whom we spoke, premiums may vary based on many factors, such as wages and salaries, the length of the elimination period, rate of income replacement, type of industry, and a company's prior claim experience.[39]

Another difference between SSDI and PDI benefit levels is their treatment of partial benefits or partial disability determinations. SSDI program rules do not provide partial payments to individuals who have lost some but not all of their ability to earn income in the national economy. In contrast, some PDI policies may pay benefits for a partial disability. For example, in one of three policies we examined, workers could qualify for partial benefits, at lower levels, if they were partially unable to achieve their previous earnings because of a disability.

PDI policies generally require beneficiaries to apply for SSDI and, if found eligible, PDI payments are typically adjusted downward (offset) by the amount of SSDI payments.[40] There is no similar requirement

---

[38] For 2016 through 2018, the combined payroll tax rate allocated for SSDI is 2.37 percent. This is the result of a temporary reallocation of the Social Security payroll tax rate between the OASI and Disability Insurance Trust Funds. For 2019 and later, the Disability Insurance Trust Fund share is scheduled to return to its 2015 level of 1.80 percent.

[39] We did not obtain current premium information for PDI, although a 2016 industry survey of 30 disability insurance companies reported average in-force annual premiums of $256 per person and new sales annual premiums per person of $233.

[40] One policy we reviewed required individuals who are or become eligible for such income (either from SSDI or other benefits) to apply; another policy required the PDI beneficiary to provide proof that they applied for SSDI benefits.

or payment adjustment for SSDI beneficiaries.[41] In cases where PDI

Table 2. Comparison of Benefit Features of Social Security Disability Insurance (SSDI) and Typical Private Disability Insurance (PDI) Policies

Benefit features	SSDI program rules	PDI (typical policy)
Rate of Income Replacement	Progressive formula based on average indexed earnings, which results in proportionally higher benefits (up to 90 percent of prior earnings) Or lower-income beneficiaries.	60 percent of the salary of the applicant's last occupation (may not include commissions, bonuses, and overtime). Monthly benefits capped for higher earners.
Partial benefits	Not available.	May be available for individuals whose disabilities affect some but not all of their ability to earn income.
Effect of SSDI and PDI Payments on the Other	SSDI payment is not affected by PDI payments.	PDI payment is reduced by the amount of any SSDI payments to worker, spouse, and dependents. Minimum PDI payment of $100 per month.
Coverage of dependents	Spouses, children, and widows and widowers may be eligible for benefits. Benefits for a disabled worker plus dependent family members are capped at 150 percent of the worker's individual benefit.	Not covered.
Medical benefits	Medicare eligibility conferred after 2 years.	Not included.
Cost of Coverage	Payroll tax on employees' wages and salaries, paid by employers and employees.	Annual premiums paid by employers and/or employees. Premiums vary based on multiple factors

Source: GAO analysis of federal laws and regulation, Social Security Administration guidance, interviews with insurance representatives, and sample PDI policy documents. | GAO-18-248.

Note: Our description of PDI features refers to employer-sponsored long-term private disability insurance and is based on our review of three PDI policies that three large insurers identified as typical, a literature review, and interviews with agency officials and various industry stakeholders.

[41] SSDI benefits may be adjusted for other sources of income, though not for PDI payments. For example, according to SSA guidance, SSDI beneficiaries in most states may be subject to a reduction in their SSDI payments if they also receive workers' compensation or other public disability benefits and the total amount of these benefits would exceed 80 percent of the worker's average earnings before the worker became disabled. In this situation, SSDI benefits would be reduced so the benefits from these sources would not exceed the threshold.

beneficiaries are not required to or do not apply for SSDI, PDI policies we reviewed would still reduce their PDI payment by the SSDI amount that the beneficiaries may have been entitled to receive. The PDI payments would be reduced for the full amount of the SSDI payments, including any SSDI payments for the worker's spouse and dependents, but will typically maintain a minimum PDI benefit. The three PDI policies we reviewed provide a minimum $100 monthly benefit when the SSDI offset would otherwise totally eliminate the PDI benefit or reduce it below $100 a month. According to insurers we interviewed and PDI policies we reviewed, insurers will assist PDI beneficiaries with their SSDI applications, and if necessary, provide legal assistance for SSDI appeals processes. According to one industry survey, 72 percent of PDI beneficiaries also qualified for SSDI.[42]

PDI benefits may also be reduced by the amount of income from other sources such as workers' compensation payments, sick leave, or severance pay from an employer. Additionally, under federal law, SSDI confers Medicare eligibility after 2 years. In contrast, insurance associations and our review of PDI policies indicate that PDI policies do not typically provide health care benefits. Table 2 provides a summary of SSDI and PDI benefit features.

Return to Work Incentives and Assistance

Both SSDI and PDI policies include incentives to return to work, such as allowing beneficiaries to retain some earnings when they return to work, but PDI policies may provide return-to-work services sooner than SSDI. As long as they continue to meet SSDI's eligibility criteria, beneficiaries can earn up to the substantial gainful activity amount each month, without any impact on their SSDI benefit, according to SSDI program rules.[43] SSDI

---

[42] Council for Disability Awareness, *2014 Long Term Disability Claims Review* (Portland, Maine: Council for Disability Awareness).

[43] According to Mathematica an estimated 11.4 percent of beneficiaries in December 2011 were working with earnings under the substantial gainful activity amount while receiving SSDI

program rules also provide work incentives in the form of a trial work period, which allows the beneficiary to receive full disability benefits while potentially earning more than the substantial gainful activity amount, for up to 9 months.[44] SSDI beneficiaries who earn above the substantial gainful activity threshold after 9 months of a trial work period will no longer receive SSDI cash benefits, but will continue to receive Medicare coverage, if enrolled, for up to 7 years and 9 months. After the trial work period ends, the 36-month extended period of eligibility begins, during which SSDI beneficiaries are entitled to receive benefits so long as they continue to meet the definition of disability and their earnings are below the substantial gainful activity monthly earnings limit. Moreover, individuals whose benefits stopped due to work may have their benefits reinstated under an expedited reinstatement if for medical reasons they are unable to work again at some point within 5 years. Under this expedited reinstatement, beneficiaries receive up to 6 months of temporary cash benefits while SSA conducts a medical review. Despite these SSDI provisions, participants of a 2013 Social Security Advisory Board Forum have criticized the SSDI program for having poorly structured work incentives,[45] and we have previously reported that complex SSDI rules

---

benefits. See *Employment, Earnings, and Primary Impairments Among Beneficiaries of Social Security Disability Programs,* Mathematica Policy Research (Washington, D.C.: November 7, 2013).

[44] For 2018, a month in which an SSDI beneficiary earns more than $850 or works more than 80 hours in self-employment is considered a "month of services" for that beneficiary's trial month period. During the trial work period, the beneficiary receives full SSDI benefits, regardless of how high their earnings might be as long as they report their work activity and have a disabling impairment. The 9 months of the trial work period do not need to be consecutive, but must take place within the same 60 month period. As an additional financial incentive, when SSA assesses a beneficiary's gross earnings to determine if they have reached substantial gainful activity, the beneficiary can deduct the cost of impairment-related work expenses, which are items and services that because of impairment the beneficiary needs to work. For example, service animals, structural or operational modifications to a vehicle, and medical devices such as a wheelchair or a respirator can count as expenses that enable a beneficiary to work. See Social Security Administration, *2016 Red Book: A Summary Guide to Employment Supports for Persons with Disabilities Under the Social Security Disability Insurance (SSDI) and Supplemental Security Income (SSI) Programs*. (Baltimore, MD: 2016).

[45] In particular, participants of the forum cited the marked reduction in SSDI benefits— referred to as the "cash cliff"—after completion of the trial work period. See Social Security Advisory Board, *2013 Forum Summary. Social Security Disability: Time for Reform*. (Washington, D.C.: March 8, 2013). For additional details on SSDI's work incentives, see

related to these work incentives may result in overpayments to beneficiaries.[46]

PDI policies we reviewed also provide for continued payments while beneficiaries participate in the insurer's return-to-work program or find other employment. However, in contrast to what is referred to as SSDI's "cash cliff," PDI payments are gradually reduced in some ways to account for the beneficiaries' earnings. For example, in one policy we reviewed, if the beneficiary participates in the insurer's return-to-work program, the beneficiary may continue receiving benefit payments in addition to any employment earnings. However, unlike SSDI, the combination of the employment earnings plus the PDI payment would be capped at 110 percent of the beneficiary's pre-disability earnings. Under this same policy, after the first 12 months that the beneficiary is disabled and working at a reduced capacity, the partial PDI payment decreases proportionally as the employment earnings increase until the beneficiary earns 80 percent of their pre-disability earnings, at which point they are no longer considered to be disabled. The other two policies we reviewed provided pro-rated PDI payments as soon as a beneficiary had some work earnings, until those earnings reach a threshold, such as 80 or 100 percent of their pre-disability earnings.[47]

Both SSDI and PDI policies offer services and supports to beneficiaries to help them return to work, but PDI policies may focus more on early provision of services and, depending on the policy, earlier intervention and case management. SSDI program rules allow beneficiaries access to return-to-work services and supports through the Ticket to Work

---

Social Security Administration, *2016 Red Book: A Summary Guide to Employment Supports for Persons with Disabilities Under the Social Security Disability Insurance (SSDI) and Supplemental Security Income (SSI) Programs*. (Baltimore, MD: 2016).

[46] See Disability Insurance: SSA Could Do More to Prevent Overpayments or Incorrect Waivers to Beneficiaries, GAO-16-34 (Washington, D.C.: Oct. 29, 2015). In that report, we recommended that SSA take steps to enhance beneficiary understanding of program requirements, including clarifying work reporting requirements provided to beneficiaries and increasing the frequency of reporting reminders to SSDI beneficiaries so that they are more similar to those available to Supplemental Security Income beneficiaries. SSA has not implemented this recommendation.

[47] In one policy we examined, work earnings used to reduce PDI benefits would take into account commissions, bonuses, and overtime, even though these types of earnings are not be included when initially determining PDI benefits levels.

(TTW) program, which helps interested beneficiaries transition to self-sufficiency through work.[48] When individuals become eligible for SSDI, SSA guidance calls for sending them information about public or private employment networks or state vocational rehabilitation agencies. According to SSA's guidance, beneficiaries can choose to work with one of these service providers and develop a plan for work goals that may involve services such as training, career counseling, vocational rehabilitation, and job placement. The TTW program then pays for those services and ensures that participating beneficiaries will not be subject to a review of their disability while they continue to work with the service provider. However, the SSA Office of the Inspector General reported that fewer than 3 percent of beneficiaries were participating in TTW in 2015.[49] In addition, SSA-funded evaluations have found that TTW has had limited success in returning SSA beneficiaries to work and reducing their dependence on SSDI.[50]

In addition to return-to-work services through TTW, SSA officials told us that beneficiaries may use services provided through or by other federal, state, and local programs or provider networks, such as the Department of Labor's Stay-at-Work/Return-to-Work initiative. However, we have previously reported that the large number of federal agencies and programs

---

[48] The Ticket to Work and Self Sufficiency Program, established in 1999, provides eligible beneficiaries (ticket holders) with a ticket they may assign to SSA-approved public or private providers (referred to as employment networks) or from traditional state vocational rehabilitation agencies. Employment networks or state agencies are to provide employment services, vocational rehabilitation services, or other support services to help ticket holders obtain and retain employment and reduce dependence on SSA benefits. See also, GAO, *Social Security Disability: Ticket to Work Participation Has Increased, but Additional Oversight Needed*, GAO-11-324 (Washington, D.C.: May 6, 2011).

[49] See Social Security Administration Office of the Inspector General, *The Ticket to Work Program: Informational Report* (Baltimore, MD: September 2016). According to this chapter, 436,613 beneficiaries participated in the Ticket to Work (TTW) program in 2015, and SSA paid around $237 million for these services, which averaged $543 per participant. This chapter also noted that, of the 65,702 beneficiaries who participated in the Ticket to Work program in 2004, 13,277 had earned enough income to have their benefits suspended for at least 1 month between 2004 and 2014.

[50] A SSA-funded series of evaluations of Ticket to Work found that although it is targeting individuals interested in employment, rigorous impact analyses failed to provide strong evidence of its impact on employment. However, the evaluators also noted that changes in Ticket to Work regulations and the national unemployment rate may influence the impact of the program in the future. Mathematica Policy Research, *Executive Summary of the Seventh Ticket to Work Evaluation Report*. (Washington, D.C: July 20, 2013).

providing employment supports to individuals with disabilities represents a fragmented system of services, and little is known about their effectiveness.[51]

In contrast, according to insurance representatives and the three PDI policies we reviewed, PDI policies may provide early interventions, funding for workplace accommodations, and case management to help beneficiaries return to work. For example, one policy we reviewed explicitly offered an early intervention program to covered employees even when the PDI insurer was not also the short-term disability insurer, to identify workers who might benefit from vocational analyses and rehabilitation services before they are eligible for long-term disability benefits.[52] Separately, this policy also had a return-to-work program with case managers who coordinate services and refer beneficiaries to clinical specialists, such as nurse consultants, psychiatric clinical specialists or vocational rehabilitation consultants. According to this policy, if the insurer determined that beneficiaries were capable of participating in the return-to-work program, but did not, their benefits could cease.

Information on how many PDI beneficiaries receive work assistance, such as worksite modifications, and insurers' aggregate expenditures for such assistance is also generally unknown. While participation in and the impact of SSA's TTW program has been extensively evaluated, the insurance representatives and researchers with whom we spoke could not provide us with data or studies showing the extent or cost of work assistance provided by PDI insurers, so the impact of these investments is not publicly known. See Table 3 for a comparison of SSDI and PDI policies' work incentives and assistance.

---

[51] GAO, *Employment for People with Disabilities: Little Is Known about the Effectiveness of Fragmented and Overlapping Programs*, GAO-12-667 (Washington, D.C.: June 29, 2012).

[52] According to an employer group with which we spoke, employers with long-term PDI often also offer short term disability coverage, which may provide such assistance before the long-term PDI policy becomes effective.

Table 3. Comparison of Selected Return-to-Work Features of Social Security Disability Insurance (SSDI) and Typical Private Disability Insurance (PDI) Policies

Selected Return-to-work features	SSDI program rules	PDI (typical policy)
Work incentives	Full payments continue if beneficiary has earnings below Substantial Gainful Activity, and for 9 months during a trial work period. Post-trial work period: payments cease but Medicare coverage continues for up to 7 years and 9 months; individual is entitled to a 36-month extended period of eligibility if the individual continues to meet the disability definition and earn less than the substantial gainful activity monthly earnings limit; and may qualify for expedited reinstatement for 5 years.	Payments may continue during a return-to-work period—on a pro-rated and/or capped basis according to the beneficiary's earnings—until the beneficiary reaches a pre-disability earnings threshold set by the policy.
Work assistance	The Ticket to Work (TTW) program funds work assistance provided by state vocational rehabilitation agencies and other employment networks.	Rehabilitative services and workplace accommodation assistance for return- to-work available at insurer's discretion. Insurers may have case management staff and/or early intervention efforts as part of standard benefits

Sources: GAO analysis of federal laws and regulations, Social Security Administration guidance, interviews with insurance representatives, and sample PDI policy documents. | GAO-18-248.

Note: Our description of PDI features refers to employer-sponsored long-term private disability insurance and is based on our review of three PDI policies that insurers identified as typical, a literature review, and interviews with agency officials and various industry stakeholders.

IMPLICATIONS OF PROPOSALS TO EXPAND PRIVATE DISABILITY INSURANCE CANNOT BE ASSESSED DUE TO INCOMPLETE INFORMATION

Our literature review identified three distinct proposals to expand PDI— through some type of federal action—as a way to provide savings for SSDI; however, we were unable to assess the implications of these proposals on SSDI. Based on our review, there is an array of complex factors that could influence PDI expansion and SSDI cost savings—factors for which data, methods, and assumptions for projecting SSDI savings are either unreliable and unsupported, or unavailable. In addition, insurer, employer, and employee stakeholders we spoke with identified other implications of expanding PDI—but these implications cannot be ascertained because the proposals are not sufficiently detailed.[53]

PDI Expansion Proposals Foresee Savings

The three distinct PDI expansion proposals we identified include the following:

- David Babbel and Mark Meyer (Babbel and Meyer) of Charles River Associates proposed that voluntary employer-sponsored PDI coverage could be extended to more working Americans through congressional action and the federal government facilitating education and outreach efforts.[54] Specifically, they recommended the enactment of legislation to make it clear to employers that automatic enrollment with "opt-out" arrangements under employer-sponsored group disability plans is legal. The authors

---

[53] We have previously reported that in evaluating reform proposals it is important to consider implementation, administration, and public understanding because they have the potential to delay—if not derail—reforms if not specifically taken into account in the proposals. For example, reforms that are not well understood could face difficulties in achieving broad public acceptance and support. See, GAO, *Social Security: Criteria for Evaluating Social Security Reform Proposals,* GAO/T-HEHS-99-94 (Washington D.C.: March 25, 1999).

[54] See David F. Babbel and Mark F. Meyer, "Expanding Private Disability Insurance Coverage to Help the SSDI Program" (chapter 9) of *SSDI Solutions: Ideas to Strengthen the Social Security Disability Insurance Program*, The McCrery-Pomeroy SSDI Solutions Initiative, A Project of the Committee for a Responsible Federal Budget (West Conshohocken, PA: Infinity Publishing, March 2016). The study was prepared and submitted at the request of and with funding by America's Health Insurance Plans (AHIP) and the American Council of Life Insurers (ACLI). The proposal used a similar analysis to establish that PDI results in SSDI cost savings in a previous paper prepared by these authors on behalf of AHIP, *Private Disability Insurance and Return-to-Work: Cost Savings to SSDI and Other Federal Programs.*

believe this will address confusion and uncertainty that is holding employers back from providing PDI.

- Rachel Greszler (Greszler) of The Heritage Foundation proposed encouraging employers to voluntarily provide PDI in exchange for a payroll tax credit.[55] Under this proposal, participating employers would qualify for the tax credit by covering the first 2 or 3 years of PDI benefits at least equivalent to SSDI benefits to employees. Workers awarded benefits under the employers' PDI would transfer to the SSDI program if their disability continued beyond the first 2 or 3 years and they qualified for SSDI. PDI would then cease to provide benefits, unless employers chose to extend the PDI policies. According to the author, if an individual is denied PDI benefits, the individual could apply for SSDI.
- David Autor and Mark Duggan (Autor and Duggan) proposed extending coverage of PDI to all workers through a statutory mandate.[56] Employers would be required to provide PDI benefits for 2 years to individuals with disabilities who are unable to work. At the end of this period, PDI benefits would cease and SSDI would provide benefits for individuals qualifying for SSDI. Under the proposal, individuals with extremely disabling conditions with very limited prospects of returning to work (e.g., stroke, late stages of certain cancers, etc.) would be eligible to apply for SSDI at the onset of their disability, in lieu of PDI.[57]

Table 4 summarizes key features of the three proposals to expand PDI that we identified.

---

[55] See, Rachel Greszler, *BACKGROUNDER: Private Disability Insurance Option Could Help Save SSDI and Improve Individual Well-being* (Washington, D.C.: The Heritage Foundation, July 2015).

[56] See David H. Autor and Mark Duggan, *Supporting Work: A Proposal for Modernizing the U.S. Disability Insurance System* (Washington, D.C.: Center for American Progress and The Hamilton Project, December 2010).

[57] Under this proposal, conditions covered by SSA's list of Compassionate Allowance Conditions would be eligible for immediate SSDI application at the onset of the disability. According to the authors, the PDI policy should not shoulder claims costs except during the relatively brief Compassionate Allowance determination period.

Table 4. Key Features of Proposals to Expand Private Disability Insurance (PDI)

Three proposals to expand PDI			
Key feature	Babbel and Meyer	Greszler	Autor and Duggan
PDI Expansion Mechanism	Voluntary. Encourage employers to cover workers through auto enrollment.	Voluntary. Encourage employers to cover workers in lieu of Social Security Disability Insurance (SSDI) for a time, through financial incentives.	Mandatory. Require employers to cover workers in lieu of SSDI for a time.
Employee Premium Contribution	Not specified	Not specified	Up to 40 percent of premium
Employer Payroll Tax Credit	No	Yes	No
Required Period of PDI Benefits	Not specified	2 – 3 years	2 years
Restriction on Applying for SSDI	No. Individuals can receive SSDI and PDI concurrently.	Yes, for 2-3 years. Except if denied PDI benefits.	Yes, for 2 years. Except for workers with severe disabilities.
Estimated SSDI Savings	The authors estimate $5 - $7 billion federal savings over 10 years, but the SSDI and PDI data are not comparable.	The author asserts significant potential savings, but does not provide an estimate.	The authors assert that savings would greatly improve Social Security's financial health and could allow for a lower payroll tax rate or an increase in the longevity of the Disability Insurance Trust Fund, but do not provide an estimate.

Source: GAO analysis of proposals. | GAO-18-248.

Note: The term PDI in this table refers to employer-sponsored long-term disability insurance.

Many Unknowns Make an Assessment of the Potential for SSDI Savings Uncertain

Differences in Covered Populations

Existing differences in the SSDI and PDI covered populations may play a role in determining the potential impacts of expanding PDI. As previously noted, SSDI covers almost all workers, whereas PDI coverage tended to be for those with higher wages and was more prevalent in certain industries. Based on our review of BLS data, in order to expand significantly, PDI would need to cover more lower-wage workers and other occupations and industries where it is currently less common, such as in retail and construction. However, as indicated in the Autor and Duggan proposal, expanding PDI to workers currently not covered could affect PDI premiums, based on the type of industry and wage levels. According to various stakeholder groups we interviewed, changes in PDI premiums would, in turn, have implications for the attractiveness of PDI to employers and employees under voluntary proposals.

The overlap in PDI with the SSDI beneficiary population also plays a role in determining any potential impact of expanding PDI. As previously noted, one industry survey reported that 72 percent of PDI beneficiaries of its member companies also received SSDI. One insurer told us that the longer PDI beneficiaries remain on PDI, the more likely they will also receive SSDI. In fact, for beneficiaries on PDI for 2 years, 58 percent also get SSDI benefits; and for beneficiaries on PDI for more than 5 years, more than 90 percent also receive SSDI.[58] Our review of these data suggests that for those receiving both SSDI and PDI benefits, it may be difficult to attribute return to work and other changes in circumstances, such as changes in health, to either PDI or SSDI. For example, it is possible that any differences in return-to-work outcomes for SSDI beneficiaries who receive PDI versus those who do not may have more to do with the specific characteristics and circumstances of the beneficiaries than as a result of having PDI coverage.[59]

---

[58] This increasing percentage of PDI beneficiaries also receiving SSDI may be attributable, in part, to the convergence of the SSDI and PDI disability definitions over time. Workers covered by PDI can be approved for benefits even if they are expected to recover from their disability within 12 months, whereas SSDI requires that a disability be expected to last at least 12 months to qualify for benefits. Also, PDI policies may provide coverage for up to 2 years if someone is not able to continue to work in their current occupation based on a disability, whereas someone cannot qualify for SSDI unless the individual is unable to work in any job in the national economy.

[59] Researchers have highlighted various factors that may affect individuals' return to work. Such factors include the motivation of the individual and his or her job satisfaction, as well as if there are potential obstacles to employment, such as individuals lacking transferable skills, having less than a high school education, living in poverty, or lacking reliable transportation.

Types and Timing of Return-to-Work Assistance Offered

To achieve SSDI cost savings, the three proposals assume that insurers will provide or reimburse employers for providing vocational rehabilitation, workplace accommodation, and return-to-work services, but the proposals provide few, if any details about how this would occur. For example, the two proposals that describe voluntary PDI enrollment do not explicitly require that such services be provided through PDI.[60] The Autor and Duggan proposal, which includes a mandate for enrollment, requires that PDI provide workplace accommodations consistent with the Americans with Disabilities Act (ADA) and vocational rehabilitation services. The proposal includes a list of vocational rehabilitation services that insurers could provide, but the authors acknowledge that in practice it is not always "clear-cut" when a "reasonable accommodation" under the ADA is required and what the accommodation should be.[61] As noted previously, we were unable to find public data on the extent to which PDI policies currently provide such services and insurance representatives and researchers we contacted that collect and report PDI data said that they do not collect such data from insurance companies. According to our review of PDI policy provisions that allow for rehabilitation and workplace accommodation services, the decision of what assistance will be provided through the PDI policy, if any, and the extent of such assistance the insurer provides or helps the employer provide, is at the discretion of the insurer.[62]

---

[60] Babbel and Meyer stated that their proposal assumes it is in the economic interests of the insurers and employers to provide such assistance and that affected individuals desire to go back to work.

[61] The Autor and Duggan proposal states that its proposed PDI coverage "would not extend" the Americans with Disabilities Act (ADA) employer "mandate," but that it would simply require that employers pay ADA compliance costs prospectively through the insurance policy rather than on a one-off basis. The authors indicate that a pilot project would inform what types of case management, vocational rehabilitation, and workplace accommodation supports are most effective in assisting workers with disabilities to remain in employment. In addition, the proposal, published in 2010, also expected that medical costs would be paid by health insurance, which at the time was expected to become available to more people as a result of the Patient Protection and Affordable Care Act.

[62] As noted previously, one policy we reviewed stated that benefits may end if an employee is capable of participating in a rehabilitation program recommended by the insurer but fails to participate. However, according to an insurance association representative we spoke with, PDI policies commonly include reasonable accommodation and rehabilitation services

It is also possible that insurers would make less of an investment in return-to-work services for PDI beneficiaries under the two time-limited proposals because the insurers are only responsible for 2 to 3 years of disability payments, compared to traditional PDI policies where the employer may have financial responsibility to make payments to beneficiaries until they reach retirement age, unless insurers can help them return to work.

Several stakeholders said that additional uncertainty exists with respect to effectiveness or attractiveness of PDI expansion proposals for populations currently not covered by PDI, such as low-wage workers and those with physically demanding jobs. BLS data show that PDI is currently less prevalent among these workers, and therefore less is known about the type and effectiveness of return-to-work services that would be offered to them under PDI expansion.[63] For example, researchers report that lower-wage workers may have jobs that offer limited opportunities to adjust work schedules—a flexibility that one research group said could assist workers in the case of disability. In addition, researchers stated that lower paying jobs tend to not offer sick leave and other key benefits, and the absence of such benefits may present another potential obstacle for successful rehabilitation and workplace accommodation efforts. According to various stakeholder groups we interviewed, employers in low-paying industries or who otherwise do not offer these benefits would have less of an incentive to offer PDI or other supports to help retain their workers compared to employers who compete for skilled employees that are also typically more

provisions, but insurers select very carefully for whom and when such services are appropriate.

[63] According to a Mathematica study, private insurers and others have developed proprietary tools and services to target the right services to the right workers at the right time and support progress monitoring and service adjustment. However, this study also notes that evidence from studies involving workers with PDI may not pertain to likely SSDI entrants, because PDI workers tend to have more human capital and work for larger employers. It further noted that only a minority of those individuals at risk of entering the SSDI rolls are likely to be helped by early intervention services. The study emphasized the importance—as well as difficulty—of targeting individuals that share three characteristics: limited access to evidence-based early intervention (EBEI), likely to exit the labor force and enter SSDI rolls without EBEI, and likely to stay in the labor force if given EBEI. Mathematica Center for Studying Disability Policy, *Targeting Early Intervention to Workers Who Need Help to Stay in the Labor Force* (Washington, D.C.: October 2015).

difficult to replace.[64] These factors—in combination with previously discussed unknowns related to the cost of PDI in non-traditional sectors—reflect complexity and uncertainty about the extent to which PDI may be expanded through a voluntary system.

The proposals assert that expanded PDI would provide financial support, accommodations, and rehabilitation services much sooner than SSDI. However, based on our review, it is not clear if this would happen for two of the proposals. As previously noted, the SSDI elimination period is 5 months, after which SSDI beneficiaries become eligible for return-to-work assistance through the TTW program and financial incentives, but lengthy SSA decision times may significantly delay when individuals receive return-to-work supports.[65] The Autor and Duggan mandatory proposal has PDI benefits commencing within 3 months of disability onset, which is sooner than SSDI, and therefore, depending on the circumstances, may allow for the provision of return-to-work services sooner than under SSDI. The Babbel and Meyer and Greszler voluntary proposals do not specify the length of elimination periods.[66] While the Babbel and Meyer and Greszler proposals indicate PDI will provide return-to-work services sooner than SSDI, it is unclear whether or how the timing of return-to-work services might evolve under the two voluntary proposals. Moreover, while data exist on SSDI initial and appeal decision times, we were unable to find current industry-wide data on the average decision period for PDI, or on the extent of appeals and how long on average these take to decide.[67]

---

[64] BLS data and an insurance company also indicated that the size of the employer's workforce affects the likelihood of an employer offering PDI. According to BLS, for employees that work for employers with less than 100 employees, 24 percent of employees are provided access to PDI, whereas for employees who work for employers with more than 500 employees, 54 percent of employees are provided access. This would suggest that efforts to expand PDI may also need to consider characteristics and needs of smaller employers as well.

[65] As noted previously, SSA took an average of 111 days to make initial decisions in fiscal year 2017 and, for claims that were appealed to an Administrative Law Judge, the decision time in fiscal year 2017 was an average of 605 days.

[66] Babbel and Meyer assumed that short-term disability benefits would bridge any time between a disabling incident and the commencement of long-term disability benefits.

[67] A thorough comparison of decision times should compare similar cases, including complexity and other characteristics of the claims. Also, although both SSDI- and PDIdenied claimants can appeal and can file lawsuits, the processes and standards of review can differ between SSDI and PDI.

Other Factors That Could Affect PDI Enrollment and SSDI Cost Savings

Based on our review of the PDI expansion proposals and interviews with stakeholder groups, we identified several additional factors that could affect the extent to which the PDI proposals could increase PDI coverage and result in SSDI cost savings, especially under the two voluntary proposals (Babbel and Meyer and Greszler). Such factors include the likelihood that efforts to encourage PDI enrollment might be successful, the effect of policy premiums and tax credits on employers' willingness to offer PDI policies, and whether expanded PDI might lead to more people also going on to SSDI.

Babbel and Meyer asserted that congressional action and federal outreach would clarify for employers that automatic enrollment with opt-out arrangements is legally permissible and thereby result in voluntary PDI expansion.[68] According to the authors, their approach was motivated by the success of similar automatic enrollment provisions in the Pension Protection Act of 2006 in raising the participation and savings rates in 401(k) defined contribution savings programs. However, since PDI automatic enrollment is already available, it is not clear how their proposal for congressional action and federal outreach would result in more employers adopting it and employees participating.[69] The Babbel and

---

[68] According to Babbel and Meyer, the confusion stems from state laws that require employers to have an employee's consent before automatically withholding contributions from wages. However, a 2008 Advisory Opinion from the Department of Labor (DOL) expressed DOL's view that such a state law was preempted by ERISA to the extent it was interpreted to limit, prohibit, or regulate deductions from wages for contributions to ERISAcovered plans. See DOL Advisory Opinion 2008-02A, Feb. 8, 2008. A 2012 ERISA Advisory Council report recommended that DOL issue guidance for plan sponsors and plan administrators on the permissibility of auto-enrollment for employee contributory PDI plans. Even though the Council stated that automatic enrollment processes are permitted under current law and regulatory guidance issued by DOL, the Council concluded that such knowledge is not widespread or widely understood. See, *2012 ERISA Advisory Council Report: Managing Disability Risks in an Environment of Individual Responsibility,* December 2012.

[69] An insurance association indicated that this might increase enrollment as was the case for 401(k) participation from automatic enrollment after the enactment of the Pension Protection Act of 2006, while we heard from an insurer discussion group that employees would opt out of PDI at a higher rate than they have with 401(k)s. Three employee advocacy groups said that the 401(k) experience is not comparable, since it is a savings plan, not a benefit expense, as is a disability insurance premium. Also, an employee

Meyer proposal is also based on requiring employees to pay part or all of the insurance premiums. According to employee advocacy groups, workers at the lowest end of the wage spectrum in particular may have little, if any, disposable income to pay for PDI, and also little incentive to participate when SSDI already replaces a relatively high proportion of their wages.[70] Further, in an employer discussion session we heard that employees willing to contribute in part or the entire premium may also have a greater risk of needing PDI benefits, and adverse selection could result in higher premiums, which in turn, fewer workers may be willing to pay.[71]

The Greszler proposal anticipates potential significant savings for SSDI assuming that employers who had not previously offered PDI to their employees would opt to offer PDI in exchange for a payroll tax credit. According to an employer association, in making this choice, employers would need to compare the financial benefit of a payroll tax credit with the cost of PDI premiums, among other things—which may evolve under the proposal, according to insurers in a discussion group we held. According to insurance industry representatives, the direction of possible premium changes under the Greszler proposal is unclear because the proposal reduces employers' financial responsibility to 2 to 3 years of potential disability benefit costs. This shorter benefit period could reduce premiums typical for longer term policies. However, since persons would not generally be able to receive SSDI benefits during this period under the

---

advocacy group said that auto-enrollment in 401(k) participation has not increased overall participation in retirement savings plans.

[70] However, some workers may not qualify for SSDI benefits, such as those who have not worked long enough. Also, workers with PDI may receive other services in addition to the PDI cash benefit.

[71] The State of Maine and other efforts may provide insight regarding the efficacy of voluntary PDI enrollment. The State of Maine passed a law effective January 1, 2017, that allows employers to automatically enroll employees in an employee-sponsored group disability income protection plan paid for at least in part by employee premiums that allows employees to opt-out of coverage. Employers can receive a $30 tax credit for each of 3 tax years for each employee newly enrolled in such a plan. See Me. Rev. Stat. tit. 24-A, § 2804-B and Me. Rev. Stat. tit. 36, § 5219-OO (2017). Also, the National Conference of Insurance Legislators adopted a model act in November 2016 for Employer-Sponsored Group Disability Income Protection for states to consider. The model act would provide employers a credit against their annual state income tax liability in an amount equal to 25 percent of the costs of establishing and administering a group disability plan for employees, for each of 3 years. Employers would also receive a state tax credit of $100 for each employee newly enrolled in a group disability income plan, of not more than $10,000 in any year.

proposal, there would be no offset of SSDI benefits against PDI benefits (as discussed earlier). According to an industry association and an insurer discussion group we held, the absence of the SSDI offset could increase premiums, possibly substantially.[72]

Another consideration raised by SSA officials is whether PDI expansion would increase SSDI applications and benefits paid, which would reduce potential SSDI savings from the proposals and could increase the cost of the SSDI program. Typical PDI policies may effectively require PDI beneficiaries to apply for SSDI, and PDI insurers may assist beneficiaries with SSDI applications.[73] Insurance association representatives told us that in addition to helping keep PDI premiums attractively low,[74] such practices benefit those who become eligible for SSDI benefits by providing health care benefits that they might not otherwise be able to access.[75] One insurance association further noted that by helping PDI beneficiaries complete SSDI applications, SSA may receive well-supported applications that are more efficient to process. On the other hand, researchers and SSA officials indicated that such PDI practices may result in some individuals applying for and receiving SSDI who would not have otherwise done so.

---

[72] In comparing the cost of SSDI and PDI, Greszler asserts that PDI would likely increase premiums by 111 percent, absent the SSDI offset that reduces the PDI benefit by the amount of the SSDI benefit for individuals receiving both benefits. According to Greszler, this premium increase was calculated for PDI providing permanent benefits and not benefits for 2 to 3 years as she proposes. ACLI has estimated that without a SSDI offset, premium costs may become so prohibitive that the employer and/or employee could not afford PDI coverage. ACLI has reported estimates of 40 percent to 100 percent increases in premiums if SSDI offsets were eliminated in group policies, with the increase depending on the demographics of the specific group. In two insurer discussion groups we heard that without the SSDI offset, PDI premiums would "skyrocket" and could be three times as high.

[73] While some PDI policies might not explicitly require someone who is receiving PDI to apply for SSDI, policies may allow the insurer to reduce the PDI benefit by the amount that the insurer estimates the individual could have received from SSDI if they did apply, thereby creating a potentially significant financial incentive for the PDI beneficiary to apply for SSDI.

[74] The proposals we reviewed, published from 2010 to 2016, cited PDI premiums ranging from around $250 to $400 per covered employee, per year.

[75] As noted previously, SSDI beneficiaries have access to Medicare after 2 years.

Cost Saving Estimates Are Unreliable or Unsupported

Each proposal states that expanding PDI would reduce SSDI costs. The proposals indicate that this would be achieved mainly through PDI early intervention after employees' onset of disabilities and a resulting reduction in the number of SSDI claimants or duration of SSDI beneficiaries' status. Only the Babbel and Meyer proposal developed an estimate of potential savings. In forecasting SSDI savings,

- *The Babbel and Meyer* proposal estimated cost savings by assuming that automatic enrollment would result in PDI coverage increasing from 33 percent to just over 50 percent of private sector employees. Comparing PDI disability termination rates from the Society of Actuaries[76] with SSDI termination rates, Babbel and Meyer estimated that PDI expansion would save the federal government an additional \$500 million to \$700 million per year, with a 10-year cumulative savings of \$5 billion to \$7 billion. They said that because they were unable to conduct a rigorous and comprehensive study of disability, recovery, and reemployment, their proposal "quantifies the benefits of group disability insurance indirectly, using publicly available data that are sparse, aggregated, and often difficult to interpret."[77]
- *The Greszler* proposal relied on the Babbel and Meyer analysis in concluding that there would be significant SSDI savings. According to Greszler, early intervention would keep individuals

[76] The Society of Actuaries (SOA) is an actuarial professional organization. SOA periodically analyzes and publishes data on group long term disability experience using claims data that it obtains from insurance companies.

[77] Babbel and Meyer, *Expanding Private Disability Insurance*. The authors noted the absence of studies comparing SSDI and PDI outcomes and the difficulty in conducting a rigorous evaluation of cost savings. Therefore, Babbel and Meyer developed their cost estimate by first estimating how many people would avoid SSDI because of PDI and then used the average annual SSDI worker benefit (\$13,757) to compute the savings. To determine SSDI avoidance due to PDI, Babbel and Meyer compared rates for "SSDI Aggregate Termination for Work" with "Group Disability Insured Recovery," (see table 2, Babbel and Meyer, *Expanding Private Disability Insurance)*. The Babbel and Meyer analysis of recovery rates has also been used as a basis for estimating savings to states from PDI, see Mark F. Meyer and David F. Babbel, Charles River Associates, *The Benefits of Private Disability Income Protection Coverage to State Budgets: Overview and Details for Four States* (July 2015).

on the job and reduce the number of potential SSDI beneficiaries. Further, Greszler assumes that the loss of tax revenue from the proposed payroll tax credit would be made up by lower SSDI expenditures incurred during the 2-3 years that employees are covered by PDI instead of SSDI.

However, the Greszler proposal did not quantify the magnitude of the tax credit or the overall savings to SSDI.[78]

- The Autor and Dugan proposal noted that SSDI expenditures would be lower because mandated PDI policies would pay the first 2 years of benefits, instead of SSDI. The authors also noted that, over the longer-term, 2-year mandated PDI for employees has the potential to pay for itself and generate SSDI savings if the proposed mandate succeeds in allowing 1 in 11 would-be SSDI beneficiaries to remain gainfully employed. However, Autor and Duggan's proposal did not include an explanation of how, or data or evidence supporting that, the proposed PDI mandate would achieve employment for 1 in 11 would-be SSDI beneficiaries.

Our analysis of the Babbel and Meyer proposal found that the available data used to develop the SSDI cost savings estimates due to PDI expansion were not comparable and therefore did not result in a reliable estimate of the financial impact of current or expanded PDI on SSDI. In their proposal, Babbel and Meyer estimated cost savings by comparing SSDI's and PDI's recovery rates. For SSDI, Babbel and Meyer used an SSDI work termination rate that includes the number of SSDI beneficiaries terminated during the year due to having earnings that exceeded the substantial gainful activity amount, divided by the total number of SSDI beneficiaries during the year. For PDI, Babbel and Meyer used a PDI recovery rate that

[78] When we spoke to the author, she told us that in aggregate, the tax credit should offset what the SSDI costs would have otherwise been during the period. She indicated that to achieve this for a 3-year period, the tax credit might reduce the SSDI share of the employer payroll tax by 0.35 percent, from 0.9 percent to 0.55 percent. However, she did not provide supporting data or evidence to us for these estimates.

includes the number of PDI benefit awards terminated during the year for multiple reasons, divided by the cumulative number of months all PDI benefits were received by PDI beneficiaries who received PDI benefits during the year.[79]

However, we found that the numerators and denominators used to compare SSDI and PDI recovery rates are not comparable. For example, the PDI numerator reflects a much broader definition of recovery than the SSDI numerator, which may contribute to overestimating PDI's relative recovery rate. Specifically, the SSDI numerator is limited to those terminated from SSDI for earnings exceeding SGA, whereas the PDI numerator includes terminations for reasons besides return to work, such as medical improvement (even if an individual did not return to work), failure to submit required documents to continue receiving benefits, changes in coverage from inability to perform own occupation to any occupation coverage, and other non-specified terminations. The denominator used in the comparison also differs. For SSDI, it is the number of people receiving SSDI benefits during the year. For PDI, it is the cumulative number of months of all PDI benefits that were received by PDI beneficiaries who received PDI benefits during the year. Because the denominators are different, we were unable to determine whether they contributed to an under- or overestimate of PDI's relative recovery rate. Regardless, we determined that the non-comparable rates in Babbel and Meyer's proposal affect the reliability of its cost savings estimate.[80] SSA's Office of the Chief Actuary also reviewed the proposal at our request and concluded that the SSDI and PDI termination rates shown in the proposal were comparable neither in concept nor in unit of analysis. Even with common units of analysis in SSDI and PDI termination rates, estimates of the

[79] The denominator only includes months of PDI benefits received during the period of the experience study for which the recovery rates are being computed. It does not include months of benefits received by PDI beneficiaries in prior years who continued to receive benefits during the period of the experience study.

[80] In the Babbel and Meyer estimate of SSDI cost savings, they used this comparison of SSDI and PDI recovery rates to estimate the number of individuals receiving PDI who they believe would have received SSDI had they not received PDI benefits. The authors applied their recovery rate analysis to data from an industry survey that reported the percentage of individuals receiving PDI but not SSDI, and data from yet another source, on annual PDI claims and terminations.

impact of PDI on SSDI would also need to consider the other differences that we described above, such as differences in covered populations.

Authors Suggested Proposals Be Pilot Tested

The authors of two proposals we spoke to suggested that any proposal to expand PDI should be pilot tested before being implemented nationwide due to the number and complexity of factors involved and their potential effect on SSDI. For example, in their proposal, Autor and Duggan noted that, given the inevitable challenges and uncertainties associated with rolling out a major program innovation, it would be desirable to phase in such a plan and to run pilot programs in a limited number of states.[81] They also suggested that pilot programs could be targeted, such as to larger firms. In discussing the Greszler proposal with the author, she told us that a pilot test of her proposal might help show if the program works better in some industries or occupations than others, as well as determine how employers respond to the tax incentive and if employees feel they are treated fairly by private insurers.[82]

Similarly, we have previously reported that changes affecting the SSDI program may raise particular implementation challenges, given the program's inherent complexity; any changes may require pilot testing to evaluate the potential effects or unintended consequences that the Congress, the administration, SSA, and the broader public will need to know to make an informed decision about whether to implement program changes nationwide.[83] SSA and DOL have funded and overseen pilot

---

[81] In discussing the Autor and Duggan proposal with the authors, they told us that their proposal assumed that people covered by PDI would also have access to health insurance. They said that without health insurance, PDI would be less effective under their proposal.

[82] For a similar proposal, by authors Jason Seligman and Jason Fichtner, they recommended that their proposal be piloted in a few select states. Unlike the other proposals we reviewed, Seligman and Fichtner propose that SSDI benefits be temporary and that SSDI provide partial disability awards, as well as giving employers an expanded role in providing disability insurance in exchange for tax incentives. See *SSDI Solutions: Ideas To Strengthen the Social Security Disability Insurance Program*, by Jim McCrery and Earl Pomeroy (Infinity Publishing, West Conshohocken, PA, March 2016), chapter 13. *Beyond All Or Nothing: Reforming Social Security Disability Insurance To Encourage Work and Wealth, Jason J. Fichtner and Jason S. Seligman*. We did not include this proposal in our review.

[83] GAO, *Social Security's Future: Answers to Key Questions*, GAO-16-75SP (Washington, D.C.: October 2015).

programs to test other proposals to help individuals with disabilities participate in the workforce.[84]

Missing Details Make Identifying the Implications of the Proposals for Stakeholders Uncertain

Employee advocacy groups,[85] employers, and insurance companies we spoke with raised various questions and concerns about the potential impacts of expanding PDI—implications that the proposals did not explicitly or fully address and therefore remain uncertain. The proposals also provided few details on any oversight role that would be needed by federal or state governments.

Potential Impacts on Employees

The proposals assert that employees could potentially benefit in the event of a disability from PDI cash benefits that may be higher than SSDI benefits; however this outcome is not certain. Based on our review of SSDI and PDI policies and interviews with employee and advocacy groups, whether or not workers would opt for PDI benefits under voluntary expansion would depend on the attractiveness of PDI relative to SSDI and other benefits. For example, an employee benefits survey and several stakeholder groups we spoke with suggested that employees tend to value other benefits, such as health insurance, more than disability insurance. According to employee groups, lower-wage workers, in particular, may opt-out of PDI under the Babbel and Meyer proposal in favor of paying for

---

[84] The Consolidated and Further Continuing Appropriations Act of 2015 appropriated funds to SSA to design, develop, and implement an early intervention demonstration to test innovative strategies aimed at helping people with disabilities remain in the workforce. SSA is currently conducting a Supported Employment Demonstration to provide employment and health support to recently denied applicants alleging mental impairments. It is also exploring a demonstration project on how to best support individuals with musculoskeletal disabilities early. DOL is in the process of implementing pilots to test return-to-work strategies for people with disabilities.

[85] We use the term “employee advocacy groups” to include disability advocacy groups, general employee advocacy groups, and unions.

other benefits, or forgo benefits entirely, especially if premiums are high. In addition, based on our review, PDI may not provide much additional benefit for lower-wage workers, and employee groups told us that, given a choice, lower-wage workers might choose not to participate in PDI since SSDI benefits replace a relatively high share of their wages.[86] Based on our review of SSDI and PDI policies, current PDI policies typically do not include dependent and spousal benefits offered by SSDI, and unlike SSDI have exclusions and pre-existing condition provisions, as well as have time limits on benefit payments for some conditions, which may result in workers finding SSDI more attractive than PDI. To the extent that employees see PDI benefits as less attractive than SSDI and their willingness to participate in PDI declines, cost savings to SSDI resulting from voluntary PDI proposals would likely be affected.

Two employee advocacy groups also expressed concern that all three proposals focus on employer-provided PDI, and two of three proposals do not explicitly address self-employed and part-time workers.[87] As we have previously noted, an increasing number of people are part of the contingent workforce, with limited access to employer-sponsored benefits.[88] Other individuals may have already left the workforce or otherwise be unemployed and thus have no connection to an employer.[89] Further, two employee advocacy groups explained that individuals who will eventually

---

[86] Any workers who were covered by PDI, but who had not yet earned enough work credits for SSDI, would not have their benefits reduced for SSDI under the three policies we reviewed and the Babbel and Meyer proposal.

[87] In an interview with Mr. Autor and Mr. Duggan they said that their proposed system could provide graduated benefits for part-time workers. Ms. Greszler also said that she would fully support PDI being available to part-time workers through their employers and also allowing self-employed workers to receive the same SSDI tax credits as businesses for purchasing their own qualified PDI policy.

[88] Contingent workers can include those that do not have standard work arrangements—permanent jobs with a traditional employer-employee relationship. Rather, they are in temporary, contract, or other forms of non-standard employment arrangements in which they may not receive employer-provided benefits. GAO, *Contingent Workforce: Size, Characteristics, Earnings, and Benefits*, GAO-15-168R (Washington, D.C.: April 20, 2015).

[89] The Autor and Duggan proposal would allow unemployed individuals to purchase disability coverage from insurers at no more than 110 percent of the rate paid by the now-unemployed individuals' previous employers. Individuals without PDI coverage that were insured for SSDI would be given access to PDI policies through a market financed by insurer surcharges.

be unable to work due to a disability initially experience symptoms that may cause them to work part-time or take a different position or job, which may affect their access to PDI through their current or new employer. On the other hand, the proposals allow for persons not covered under the proposals to apply for SSDI.[90]

Two employee advocacy groups also expressed concern that workers who are auto-enrolled under the Babbel and Meyer proposal may not make an informed choice about participating due to the complexity of disability contracts. One employee advocacy group was particularly concerned for low-wage workers who may be struggling financially and cannot afford disability insurance, but do not initially opt-out of coverage because of inertia, language barriers, or not understanding the product, including the tradeoffs involved in choosing to keep it or opt out.[91]

Employee advocacy groups told us that more needs to be done to get SSDI beneficiaries back to work, but noted a range of concerns about using PDI to do this. Their concerns included the following:

- Employers are moving away from providing other key employee benefits, such as health care benefits (which may be more important to workers than PDI and without which PDI would be less effective).
- Employers are moving away from full-time employment (which is usually a stipulation of PDI policies).

---

[90] Even for those covered by the proposals, under each of the proposals, applications for SSDI are still allowed. For example, the Autor and Duggan proposal allows employees with severe disabilities to apply for SSDI In addition, according to Greszler, under her proposal, employees whose PDI claims are denied could apply for SSDI.

[91] Three employee advocacy groups also pointed out that auto-enrollment for PDI would be less beneficial for the employee than auto-enrollment for retirement, because contributions to the latter belong to the employee. Nevertheless, we have previously reported concerns about low-earning households being able to save for retirement because they feel they cannot afford to make contributions without taking on additional debt or postponing important expenditures, such as preventive healthcare expenses. See GAO, *Retirement Security: Low Defined Contribution Savings May Pose Challenges,* GAO-16-408 *(Washington, D.C.: May 5, 2016).*

- Employers might discriminate in not hiring individuals at higher risk of disability under proposals that make employers responsible for the first few years of providing disability assistance.
- The transition from receiving PDI to qualifying and getting approved for SSDI under the proposals might delay receipt of SSDI.[92]
- Insurers might not actually provide rehabilitative and accommodation services.
- There would not be standardization of PDI eligibility determination, coverage, and appeal processes to ensure fair and equitable treatment of workers.

All employee advocacy groups we spoke to emphasized the need for consumer protections and strong oversight under the PDI proposals. One employee advocacy group said that there are too many problems, gaps, and concerns with the proposals to expand PDI, when SSDI already provides near universal coverage and is a system that is up and running. Moreover, the employee advocacy group said that SSA could identify the key reasons that PDI has had success in getting people back to work and incorporate those lessons into SSDI, because more effort needs to be spent improving SSDI and increasing its return-to-work efforts.

Potential Impact on Employers

Individual employers and employer associations we spoke to said that more details would be needed to determine how they might be impacted by the proposals.

- Regarding the Babel and Meyer proposal (which as previously discussed, cites the need for congressional action to address potential legal uncertainties regarding automatic enrollment) one employer association representative expressed concern about whether state garnishment laws would prohibit employers from

[92] This would apply to individuals receiving PDI for the 2-3 year periods under the Autor and Dugan and the Greszler proposals.

making automatic deductions for PDI premiums from employees' pay without their permission.[93]

- Regarding the Greszler proposal, employers and representatives of an employer association we spoke to indicated they would need to know more details, such as the exact amount of the tax credits and how insurance premiums might be affected.
- Regarding the Autor and Duggan proposal, representatives of the two employer associations stated that their members would oppose a mandate. One employer association said there are often additional requirements that come along with any mandates, even for actions that employers are already taking, such as offering PDI. The employer association also expressed concern that doing more than is required under any mandate generally exposes employers to liability, which could result in employers providing only the minimum benefits and assistance required by law. One employer said that mandated PDI could crowd out the amount of other benefits an employer is willing to provide, such as the amount of medical coverage that it offers to employees.

In addition, one employer association we spoke with was concerned about the potential administrative burdens associated with expanding PDI, particularly for small employers. They noted that administering any benefit requires financial resources to provide, monitor, and maintain the benefit, stating that once employers provide a benefit to employees, they are generally reluctant to take it away. Employers in one discussion group we held were also concerned that providing disability assistance through a PDI policy for 2 to 3 years under two of the proposals would require that they

---

[93] We have previously reported that although automatic enrollment for retirement savings had been addressed and clarified by IRS as permissible, there were still concerns among employers about state laws that prohibit withholding employee pay without employee consent, until that passage of the Pension Protection Act of 2006 (PPA). PPA provisions and subsequent regulations further facilitated the adoption of automatic enrollment by providing incentives to do so and by protecting plans from fiduciary and legal liability if certain conditions were met. See, GAO, *Retirement Savings: Automatic Enrollment Shows Promise for Some Workers, but Proposals to Broaden Retirement Savings for Other Workers Could Face Challenges,* GAO-10-31 (Washington D.C.: October 23, 2009).

retain employees and provide benefits even when employees are unable to continue work.[94] Employers in a discussion group and an employer association we spoke to also wanted to know how the PDI plans would be overseen at the state and federal levels under the proposals, and what additional requirements that would entail.

Potential Impact on Insurance Companies

Insurance companies and associations we spoke to generally supported efforts to expand PDI, but also expressed some concerns about related unknowns. In particular, insurers in one of our discussion groups and both insurance associations we spoke with supported the Babbel and Meyer proposal to encourage employers to automatically enroll employees, with an opt-out provision, which came out of a study funded by America's Health Insurance Plans (AHIP) and the American Council of Life Insurers (ACLI). One insurance association said that, relative to the other proposals that provide a tax credit or mandate coverage, the Babbel and Meyer proposal to expand PDI would not be a problem for insurers' capacity. Representatives from this insurance association suggested first taking initial steps proposed by Babbel and Meyer through encouraging automatic enrollment before considering a more major restructuring of PDI that would supplant SSDI for 2 to 3 years. On the other hand, two insurance associations expressed concerns about the potential for additional requirements that could result from implementing the Babbel and Meyer proposal, for example in relation to employee consent or the quality of coverage offered.

Insurance associations and insurers we spoke with also raised concerns about the other two proposals (Autor and Duggan, and Greszler), especially related to how they would fundamentally and unpredictably change the PDI market. On the one hand, one insurance association pointed out that these proposals would eliminate the SSDI offset from PDI payments for the 2 to 3 year period, which could lead insurance companies to significantly increase PDI premiums for such policies. On the other

---

[94] According to one insurance company, employers generally do not retain employees for more than 1 year when employees cannot work due to a disability.

hand, if the insurance company is only liable for 2-3 years of benefit payments and services, this could reduce insurers' costs.

In addition, in one insurer discussion group that we held, insurers said that if there was not an SSDI offset of PDI benefits during the 2 to 3 year period, the industry would be more aggressive about return to work efforts. However, in another insurer discussion group we heard that they would do less for return to work under such policies, because future savings to the insurance company are not as great under a 2 to 3 year policy as if the insurance company is liable for paying benefits until an individual reaches normal SSA retirement age, as with current policies. Finally, representatives from one insurance association said that the Greszler and Autor and Duggan proposed PDI expansions would create extreme capacity problems for insurers. Under the Autor and Duggan proposal nearly all employees would need to be covered.

One insurance association also noted its view that SSDI might benefit under the proposals to expand PDI. Specifically, the insurance association said that after someone goes through the PDI claim process, a subsequent claim for SSDI may be of higher quality, potentially reducing the administrative costs of a subsequent SSDI determination.[95]

Potential Impact on Federal and State Governments Oversight

The three proposals we reviewed did not specify the government's role in overseeing the expanded PDI market. Babbel and Meyer proposed a stronger federal role in encouraging automatic enrollment by passing a law to clarify its permissibility, but the proposal did not provide details on implementation and oversight.[96] Greszler proposed that participating employers provide benefits at least equivalent to SSDI benefits, but provided no other details on how compliance would be overseen. Neither the Autor and Duggan nor the Greszler proposals addressed whether

---

[95] The Greszler proposal specifically states that evidence and findings from the private determination potentially could be used in the public determination process.

[96] Babbel and Meyer said that there are minimal implementation requirements and costs for their proposal because it only requires the passage of legislation allowing for automatic enrollment. They said that the benefits of their proposal are independent of, and in addition to, other SSDI program specific proposals.

individuals denied PDI could apply for SSDI within the 2 to 3 year period covered by their proposals.[97]

Stakeholders we spoke to expressed divergent perspectives on whether federal and state governments would need to provide additional regulation, supervision, and/or oversight related to expanded PDI markets.[98] One insurance association said that insurance providers are already very well regulated by ERISA and by states, and a major insurer said that there already exists an array of federal and state laws governing employer-sponsored PDI coverage that establishes a robust regulatory framework for protecting participants. In contrast, representatives from all employee advocacy groups we spoke with cited problems identified with private insurance company practices and stressed the need for additional consumer protections and government oversight. We found instances of federal and state enforcement actions regarding disability insurance improper practices in the past potentially affecting hundreds of thousands of people over many years,[99] as well as more recent rulemaking by DOL that said that "disability cases dominate the ERISA litigation landscape." These actions suggest that expanding PDI or including new PDI requirements, in lieu of

---

97 Greszler told us that those individuals denied benefits through PDI could still apply to SSDI and because the PDI determination process usually takes less than 60 days, they would not be far behind in the SSDI process.

98 According to these stakeholders, areas where regulation, supervision, or oversight might apply include acceptable contracts and premium levels, and penalties for noncompliance.

99 For example, in 2004, the insurance regulators for all 50 states, the District of Columbia, and American Samoa and the U.S. Department of Labor entered into settlement agreements with three UnumProvident companies requiring them to change their claims practice and to reassess certain claims going back to 1997. The settlement indicated that it could include the re-assessment of approximately 200,000 claims. The multi-state examination and DOL investigation that lead to the settlement identified several areas of concern pertaining to insurer practices for handling claims, including excessive reliance on in-house medical staff to support the denial, termination, or reduction of benefits; unfair evaluation and interpretation of attending physician or independent medical examiner reports; failure to evaluate the totality of the claimant's medical condition including co-morbid conditions; an inappropriate burden placed on claimants to justify eligibility for benefits; and a failure to give weight to Social Security determinations of disability. The companies were required to pay a $15 million fine and comprehensively revise their operations. According to the subsequent 2008 report of the Multi-State Conduct Examination, an additional $676.2 million was paid by the companies to claimants immediately upon reassessment or was reserved for future payments.

SSDI, would likely involve some degree of additional federal and state oversight.[100]

Any costs associated with expanded state and federal roles would reduce potential cost savings from the proposals, although the extent to which this might affect the Disability Insurance Trust Fund is unclear. According to DOL officials, an expansion in the number of private disability benefit plans and an increase in the complexity in the legal requirements governing the design and operation of such plans would require DOL to provide proportionally more interpretive guidance, compliance assistance, and enforcement and oversight activities. Estimating the potential impact of the proposals on DOL's functions and capabilities would require more specific information on the statutory and regulatory changes envisioned by the proposals and the likely impact of those changes on the private disability plan marketplace. SSA officials said that whether or not SSA would experience an expanded role would depend on any changes in law regarding the proposals.

AGENCY COMMENTS

We provided a draft of this chapter for review and comment to SSA and DOL. Neither SSA nor DOL provided written comments, although

---

[100] In December 2016, DOL issued a final rule on claims procedures for plans providing disability benefits, explaining why it thought it was appropriate to re-examine the rules governing ERISA-covered disability benefit claims. "Even though fewer private-sector employees participate in disability plans than in group health and other types of plans, disability cases dominate the ERISA litigation landscape today. An empirical study of ERISA employee benefits litigation from 2006 to 2010 concluded that cases involving long-term disability claims accounted for 64.5 percent of benefits litigation, whereas lawsuits involving health care plans and pension plans accounted for only 14.4 percent and 9.3 percent respectively. Insurers and plans looking to contain disability costs may be motivated to aggressively dispute disability claims." Claims Procedure for Plans Providing Disability Benefits, 81 Fed. Reg. 92316 (Dec. 19, 2016). On November 29, 2017, DOL published a final rule delaying the applicability date of the 2016 final rule for 90 days, until April 1, 2018. Claims Procedure for Plans Providing Disability Benefits; 90-Day Delay of Applicability Date, 82 Fed. Reg. 56560 (Nov. 29, 2017).

both provided technical comments, which we incorporated as appropriate.

Elizabeth H. Curda
Director, Education, Workforce, and Income Security

In: Social Security Disability
Editor: Michael Dimitriadis
ISBN: 978-1-53615-747-5

Chapter 5

SOCIAL SECURITY DISABILITY: BETTER TIMELINESS METRICS NEEDED TO ASSESS TRANSFERS OF APPEALS WORK*

United States Government Accountability Office

ABBREVIATIONS

ALJ	administrative law judge
APT	average processing time
CARES	Compassionate and Response Service
CPMS	Case Processing and Management System
DART	Disability Adjudication Reporting Tool
DDS	Disability Determination Services
DI	Disability Insurance
DWM	Division of Workload Management
eBB	Electronic Bench Book

* This is an edited, reformatted and augmented version of United States Government Accountability Office, Report to Congressional Requesters, Publication No. GAO-18-501, dated July 2018.

FIT	Findings Integrated Template
NCAC	national case assistance center
NHC	national hearing center
OHO	Office of Hearings Operations
OIG	Office of the Inspector General
SGA	substantial gainful activity
SSA	Social Security Administration
SSI S	Supplemental Security Income.

WHY GAO DID THIS STUDY

Individuals who do not agree with an initial decision on a claim for Social Security disability benefits can ultimately appeal by requesting a hearing before an administrative law judge. At the end of fiscal year 2017, more than 1 million claimants who had appealed were awaiting a decision, and they waited, on average, 605 days. To help reduce processing times of appeals, SSA transfers cases from backlogged offices to those with greater capacity. GAO was asked to review SSA's efforts to redistribute its appeals work.

This chapter examines (1) trends in SSA's transfers and processing times of appealed cases over the past decade, (2) SSA's monitoring of efforts to meet processing time goals through case transfers, and (3) any challenges SSA faces in transferring cases between offices.

GAO analyzed SSA case processing data from fiscal years 2008-2017; reviewed SSA policies and operational guidance; observed SSA's systems for case transfers; and interviewed SSA officials at the agency's headquarters and offices in 3 of its 10 regions, selected for the large number of cases transferred and proximity to national centers established to process transferred cases.

What GAO Recommends

GAO recommends SSA (1) develop timeliness metrics that more accurately reflect offices' performance in light of case transfers, and (2) evaluate costs and benefits of changing system limitations that hinder users from correctly and efficiently identifying cases to transfer. SSA agreed with both recommendations.

What GAO Found

Over the past decade, the Social Security Administration (SSA) increasingly transferred appealed disability cases awaiting decisions from offices with backlogs to offices with more capacity as processing times lengthened. From fiscal years 2008 through 2017, the percentage of cases that were transferred increased from 14 to 43 percent. Although transfers are meant to improve timeliness of appeal decisions, average processing times grew and older pending cases increased over fiscal years 2012 through 2017. According to SSA officials, multiple factors, such as an increase in hearing requests after the 2007- 2009 recession, contributed to longer processing times.

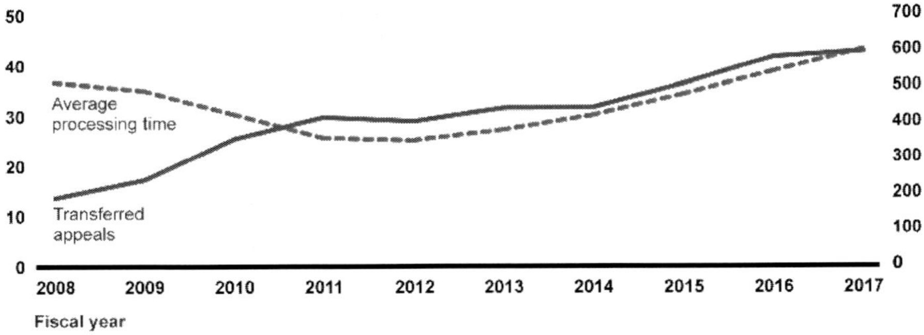

Source: GAO analysis of Social Security Administration. | GAO-18-501.

Percentage of Appeals Transferred to Redistribute Work and Average Processing Time of Appeals, Fiscal Years 2008-2017.

SSA monitors transfers of appealed cases to improve timeliness, but lacks measures to accurately assess how individual offices contribute to processing times. According to SSA officials, staff in both SSA headquarters and the offices that receive transfers check that older cases are being prioritized for transfer. SSA ranks offices on various dimensions including timeliness metrics. However, its metrics do not hold individual offices accountable for the time they were responsible for a case because the entire processing time is attributed to the office that finalizes the case. GAO work has shown that managers need appropriate measures to create incentives and accurate performance information to make decisions. Because of other priorities, SSA has not changed its performance metrics to give individual offices credit for the work performed, so it cannot assess how offices contribute to processing times.

SSA staff described and GAO observed challenges related to case transfers. For example, hearing office staff demonstrated difficulties they face in accurately and efficiently identifying cases to transfer because of software limitations. As a result, staff use a variety of time-consuming workarounds that could increase the chance of transferring cases that do not meet SSA's selection criteria. SSA's plans call for technology improvements that remove inefficiencies in its case processing systems and redirect staff from manual work. However, SSA does not intend to address these software limitations as it upgrades its case processing systems this year, thus contributing to ongoing impediments to staff productivity.

July 19, 2018

The Honorable Ron Johnson
Chairman

The Honorable Claire McCaskill
Ranking Member
Committee on Homeland Security and Governmental Affairs
United States Senate

The Honorable Sam Johnson Chairman
Subcommittee on Social Security
Committee on Ways and Means
House of Representatives

The Social Security Administration (SSA) manages two disability benefit programs—Disability Insurance (DI) and Supplemental Security Income (SSI)—that together provide about 16 million Americans with about $200 billion in benefits annually. Overall, according to SSA reports, more than 6 percent of the U.S. working-age population received disability benefits from one or both of these programs in recent years.[1]

A claimant who is dissatisfied with the initial decision on his or her application for disability benefits can ultimately appeal the decision at a hearing, where an administrative law judge (ALJ)[2] reviews the case and any new evidence submitted by the claimant. At the end of fiscal year 2017, SSA reported that more than 1 million claimants who had requested a hearing before an ALJ were awaiting a decision on disability benefits, and claimants waited, on average, 605 days. Across the country, there were wide variations in the number of pending cases and processing times, with some hearing offices taking over 750 days—more than 2 years—to issue an appeals decision. SSA is striving to achieve an average appeals processing time of 270 days by the end of fiscal year 2022. Transferring cases from backlogged offices to offices with greater capacity is one of several ongoing SSA efforts to reduce the number of pending cases and the average time claimants wait for a decision. In 2009, SSA's Office of the Inspector General (OIG) cited transferring cases between offices as a best practice for improving SSA's processing times of appeals.

You asked us to review SSA's efforts to manage the workload of appealed disability cases through transfers. This chapter examines (1)

---

[1] Social Security Administration, *Annual Statistical Report on the Social Security Disability Insurance Program, 2016*, Publication No. 13-11826 (Washington, D.C.: October 2017); and *Annual Statistical Report on the Social Security Disability Insurance Program, 2015*, Publication No. 13-11826 (Washington, D.C.: October 2016).

[2] For readability, we are using the term administrative law judge (ALJ) and judge interchangeably.

trends in SSA's transfers and processing times of appealed disability cases over the past decade, (2) SSA's monitoring of its efforts to meet processing time goals through case transfers, and (3) any challenges SSA faces in transferring cases between offices.

To examine trends in the number of cases transferred and processing times, we analyzed summary data from SSA's Case Processing Management System for fiscal years 2008 through 2017. We limited our analysis to cases transferred for workload redistribution.[3] We assessed the reliability of these data by conducting electronic data tests and interviewing knowledgeable officials about how the data were collected, and found the data to be sufficiently reliable for the purposes of this review. To assess SSA's monitoring of its efforts to meet processing time goals, we reviewed SSA policies and operational guidance about case transfers. In addition, within SSA's Office of Hearings Operations (OHO), we visited headquarters as well as three regional offices and six hearing offices. We selected the regional offices for processing a large number of transferred cases, being near an assistance center established to process transferred cases, or both. Within each selected region, we selected two hearing offices that, among other factors, sent or received a relatively large number of case transfers. We also visited assistance centers near the regional and hearing offices we visited to gain additional perspectives. To identify any challenges SSA faces in transferring cases between offices, we reviewed operational guidance such as OHO memorandums, observed how staff select cases to transfer and the steps they take and systems used to process transfers, and interviewed staff in the offices we visited. We evaluated the agency's oversight of transfers and related challenges against SSA planning documents, federal standards for internal control for defining objectives, and other performance management practices we have identified in our prior work. For further details on our scope and methodology, see appendix I.

We conducted this performance audit from May 2017 to July 2018 in accordance with generally accepted government auditing standards. Those

[3] SSA also transfers cases between offices for other reasons such as when claimants move. In this chapter, "case transfers" only refers to cases transferred for workload redistribution.

standards require that we plan and perform the audit to obtain sufficient, appropriate evidence to provide a reasonable basis for our findings and conclusions based on our audit objectives. We believe that the evidence obtained provides a reasonable basis for our findings and conclusions based on our audit objectives.

BACKGROUND

SSA provides benefits to individuals with disabilities through two main programs: DI and SSI. Under the Social Security Act, individuals are generally considered disabled if they are unable to engage in any substantial gainful activity due to a medically determinable physical or mental impairment that has lasted or is expected to last at least 1 year or is expected to result in death.[4]

Table 1. Overview of Disability Insurance and Supplemental Security Income Programs

	Disability Insurance (DI)	**Supplemental Security Income (SSI)**
Purpose	Provides benefits to persons who become unable to work because of disability and eligible family members.	Provides benefits for disabled, blind, or aged people who have low income and limited resources.
Prior work requirement	Requirement depends on age of claimant, but is generally 40 quarters of coverage.[a]	No prior work requirement.
Number of recipients (fiscal year 2017)	10.6 million	8.3 million
Benefits paid (fiscal year 2017)	$142.8 billion[b]	$57.2 billion[c]

Source: GAO analysis of relevant federal laws and Social Security Administration documents. | GAO-18-501.

[a] Generally, individuals need 40 work quarters (credits) to qualify, 20 of which must have been earned in the 10 years prior to becoming disabled. Individuals may earn up to four work credits per year, and the amount of earnings needed for credit is calculated using the national average wage index. In 2018, $1,320 is needed for each credit.

[b] This figure includes both persons with a disability and their family members who receive benefits.

[c] This figure includes federal benefits and state supplementary payments.

---

[4] 42 U.S.C. §§ 423(d), 1382c(a)(3).

See Table 1 for additional key features and requirements of the DI and SSI programs.

Disability Application and Appeals Process

Although DI and SSI have different purposes and target populations, the disability criteria for adults are the same for both programs. To be considered eligible for either program as an adult based on a disability, a person must have a medically determinable physical or mental impairment that (1) has lasted or is expected to last for at least a continuous period of 1 year or result in death, and (2) prevents them from engaging in any substantial gainful activity (SGA).[5]

To apply for benefits, a claimant must file an application online, by telephone, mail, or in person at a local Social Security office. Local office staff forward most new cases to the appropriate state Disability Determination Services (DDS) office for a medical determination.[6] DDS staff—generally a team comprised of disability examiners and medical consultants—review medical and other evidence provided by the claimant, obtain additional evidence as needed, and make the initial disability determination. In fiscal year 2017, SSA reported it received more than 2.4 million disability claims.

If the claimant is not satisfied with the initial determination, in most states he or she may request a reconsideration of the decision within the same DDS office.[7] If the claimant is dissatisfied with the reconsideration, he or she may request a hearing before a judge. In fiscal year 2017, SSA

---

[5] 42 U.S.C. §§ 423(d) and 1382c(a)(3)(A). SGA is work activity that involves significant physical or mental activities that is done for pay or profit, regardless of whether profit is realized. For 2018, SSA set SGA as monthly earnings above $1,970 for blind individuals and $1,180 for non-blind individuals.

[6] The work performed by DDSs is federally financed and carried out under SSA disability program laws, regulations, policies, and guidelines.

[7] In one of several initiatives to improve the disability determination process, SSA has eliminated the reconsideration step of the process in 10 states, allowing the claimant to appeal the initial decision directly to a judge. The 10 states are Alabama, Alaska, California (Los Angeles North and Los Angeles West Branches), Colorado, Louisiana, Michigan, Missouri, New Hampshire, New York, and Pennsylvania.

reported that claimants appealed approximately 620,000 decisions to the hearings level.

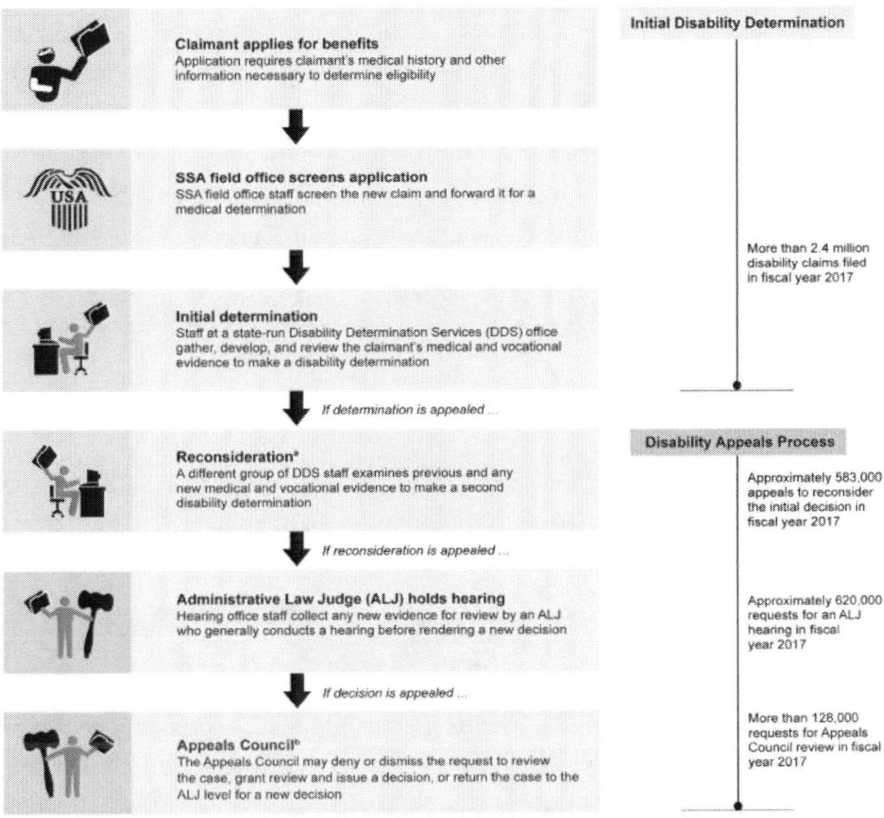

Source: GAO analysis of SSA information. | GAO-18-501.

[a]In 1999, SSA eliminated the reconsideration step in 10 states (Alabama, Alaska, Colorado, Louisiana, Michigan, Missouri, New Hampshire, New York, Pennsylvania, and in the Los Angeles area of California) as part of the Prototype Initiative. In these states, claimants who wish to appeal their initial DDS determination must appeal for review before an administrative law judge.

[b]If parties are not satisfied with the Appeals Council decision, they may pursue the matter further in federal district court.

Figure 1. Social Security Administration's (SSA) Disability Appeals Process.

In general, cases are randomly assigned to judges within the area each hearing office serves, in the order in which the requests for a hearing are received. The judge reviews the claimant's file, including any additional evidence the claimant submitted after the initial determination, and generally conducts a hearing. At the hearing, the judge may hear testimony from the claimant, medical experts on the claimant's medical condition, and vocational experts regarding the claimant's past work and ability to work in jobs currently available in significant numbers in the national economy. If the claimant is not satisfied with the judge's decision, he or she may request a review by SSA's Appeals Council, which is the final administrative appeal within SSA. Figure 1 provides an overview of SSA's disability appeals process.

SSA's Hearing Operations

SSA's hearing operations are conducted by judges and other staff across the country. More than 1,600 judges conduct hearings and make decisions on appealed cases. They are assisted by decision writers and other support staff who play key roles in one of three phases of the appeals decision process:

1. Case workup: During this phase, support staff prepare the claim file by conducting initial case screening and organizing evidence to be considered by a judge.
2. Judicial decision: During this phase, a judge evaluates the evidence and makes a decision on whether the claimant will be allowed disability benefits. In most cases, the judge holds a hearing at which the claimant provides testimony about his or her disability.
3. Decision writing: The final phase of the process involves a decision writer who drafts a judge's decision according to the judge's instructions after the judicial decision phase. The judge is responsible for reviewing the decision before it is released, according to SSA.

Hearings operations staff are organized in 164 hearing offices and two satellite offices within 10 regions across the country.[8] These offices each have a geographic area of responsibility. In addition, SSA has assistance centers—known as national hearing centers (NHC) and national case assistance centers (NCAC)—that provide additional case processing capacity nationwide (see Figure 2). At SSA's headquarters, the Division of Workload Management (DWM) within the Office of Hearings Operations analyzes offices' workloads and oversees case transfers.

SSA transfers cases between offices in an effort to alleviate hearing offices' backlogs at each of the three stages of the appeals decision process. SSA uses technology such as electronic case files and video conferencing to process transferred cases and hold hearings across locations. There are three types of case transfers: (1) temporary transfers for workup, (2) permanent case transfers, and (3) temporary transfers for decision writing. Figure 3 describes each type of transfer and the associated types of offices that generally provide assistance.

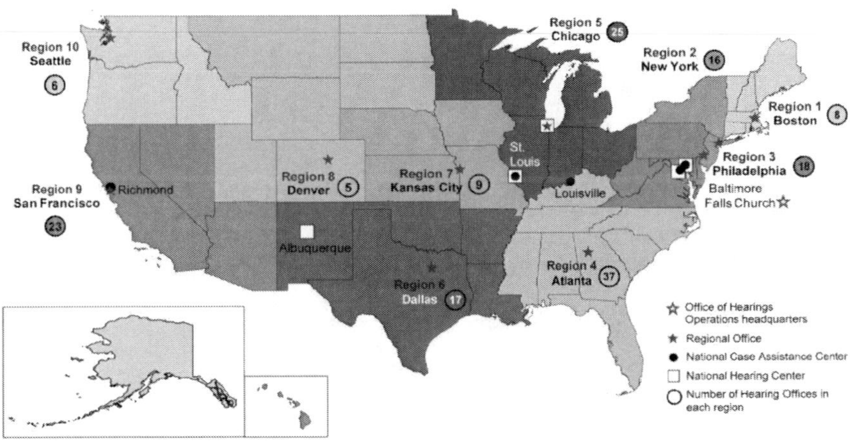

Sources: GAO analysis of SSA information; MapInfo (map). | GAO-18-501.

Figure 2. Map of Social Security Administration (SSA) Hearings Operations.

[8] Satellite offices provide support to their parent hearing offices.

Case Transfer Type	Description	Types of Assisting Office
Temporary transfer for workup	Staff in an assisting office collect evidence and prepare cases prior to a hearing before a judge from the originating office. The case is temporarily held by the assisting office before being transferred back to the originating office.	Another hearing office; National case assistance center
Permanent case transfer	A case is permanently transferred to a judge in another office to conduct a hearing to decide the case. A video hearing is generally involved because the judge and claimant are not in the same location. The claimant is typically in the originating office for the hearing. See fig. 4.	Another hearing office; National hearing center
Temporary transfer for decision writing	A decision writer in an assisting office drafts a decision after a judge in the originating office has held a hearing and prepared instructions. The case is temporarily transferred to the assisting office for the decision writing before being transferred back to the originating office for final review.	Another hearing office; National case assistance center; National hearing center

Figure 3. Types of Case Transfers and Assisting Offices.

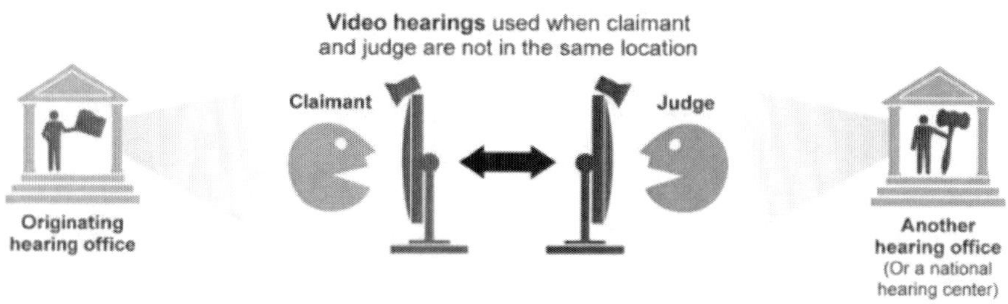

Source: GAO analysis of Social Security Administration. | GAO-18-501.

Figure 4. Sample Video Hearing Setup.

Cases may be transferred to another hearing office or to an assistance center such as an NHC, which primarily processes permanent transfers, or an NCAC, which primarily processes temporary transfers, according to SSA officials. Permanent transfers typically result in a video hearing because the claimant and judge are usually not in the same location as depicted in Figure 4.

Performance Management

SSA measures timeliness of appeals case processing in a number of ways. For example, it measures average processing time (APT), which is the average number of calendar days from hearing request to disposition for all dispositions—cases decided or dismissed—in a reporting period. In fiscal year 2017, SSA reported it met its APT goal of 605 days at the national level. Its APT goal remains at 605 days for fiscal year 2018 and then drops to 535 days for fiscal year 2019.

SSA also measures the average wait time for a hearing and monitors the number of pending cases. Pending cases are appeals that have not yet had a disposition, and include cases at different stages of the appeals process. SSA has a goal to reduce the number of pending "aged cases" which it currently defines as those cases that were at least 430 days old when the fiscal year began. SSA's aged cases goal is to decide 97 percent of those cases by the end of the fiscal year. SSA reported that it almost met this goal in fiscal year 2017, having decided 96 percent of aged cases.

Case Transfers Have Increased over the Past Decade, but Processing Times Have Continued to Grow in Recent Years

SSA's Use of Case Transfers to Redistribute Work Increased from Fiscal Years 2008-2017

SSA has increasingly transferred appealed disability cases to redistribute work from offices with backlogs to offices with more capacity. From fiscal years 2008 through 2017, the percentage of dispositions—

decided or dismissed cases—that had been transferred increased from 14 to 43 percent or from approximately 79,000 to more than 290,000 cases (see Figure 5). Most of these cases were transferred just once for workload redistribution, but over the years a growing percentage were transferred multiple times—from about 2 percent in fiscal year 2008 to over 10 percent in fiscal year 2017. For example, according to SSA officials, a case may be transferred once as a permanent transfer to an assisting hearing office, and then that office temporarily transfers it to an NCAC for decision writing.

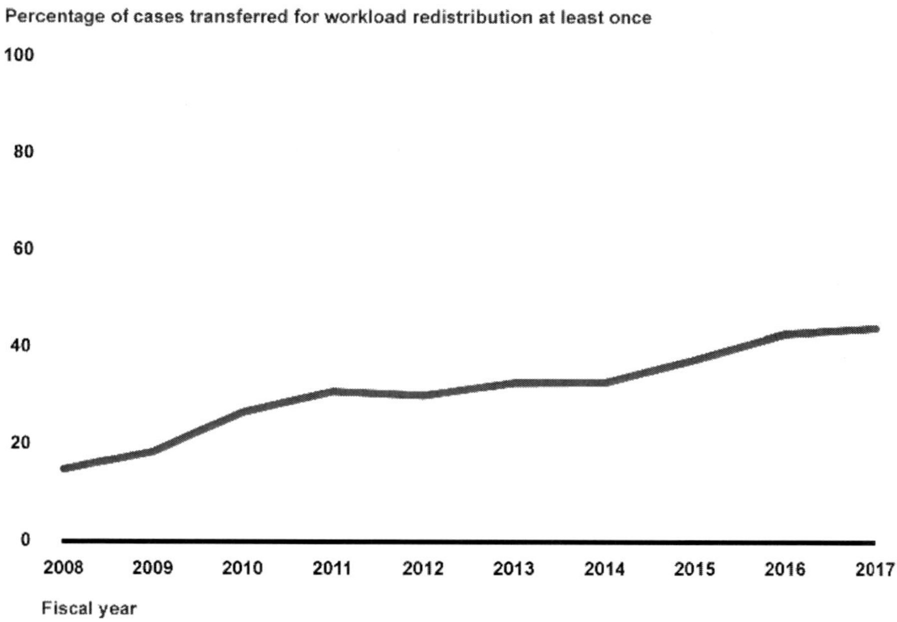

Source: GAO analysis of Social Security Administration. | GAO-18-501.

Figure 5. Percentage of Disability Appeals Cases Transferred to Redistribute Work at Least Once, Fiscal Years 2008-2017.

The number of appeals case transfers for workload redistribution quadrupled over the last decade.

From fiscal years 2008 through 2017, the number of transfers increased from about 100,000 to nearly 450,000 (see Figure 6).

Growth occurred across all three types of transfers: permanent transfers, temporary transfers for workup, and temporary transfers for decision writing (see Figure 7). Nearly all hearing offices sent or received a case transfer in recent years. Permanent transfers comprised nearly half of the roughly 3 million appeals case transfers in fiscal years 2008 through 2017.

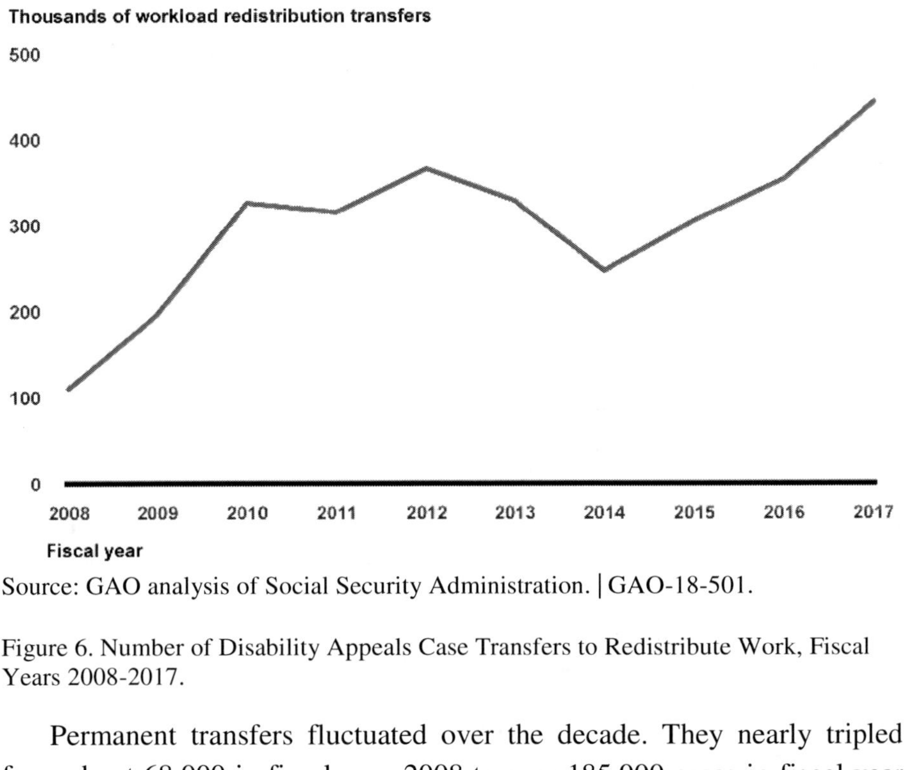

Source: GAO analysis of Social Security Administration. | GAO-18-501.

Figure 6. Number of Disability Appeals Case Transfers to Redistribute Work, Fiscal Years 2008-2017.

Permanent transfers fluctuated over the decade. They nearly tripled from about 68,000 in fiscal year 2008 to over 185,000 cases in fiscal year 2017, peaking during this time in fiscal year 2010. Growth in permanent transfers from fiscal years 2008 to 2010 coincided with the opening of SSA's five NHCs, which ultimately received about a third of all permanent transfers over the decade. However, growth in permanent transfers was not consistent year to year. From fiscal years 2010 through 2015, permanent transfers declined.

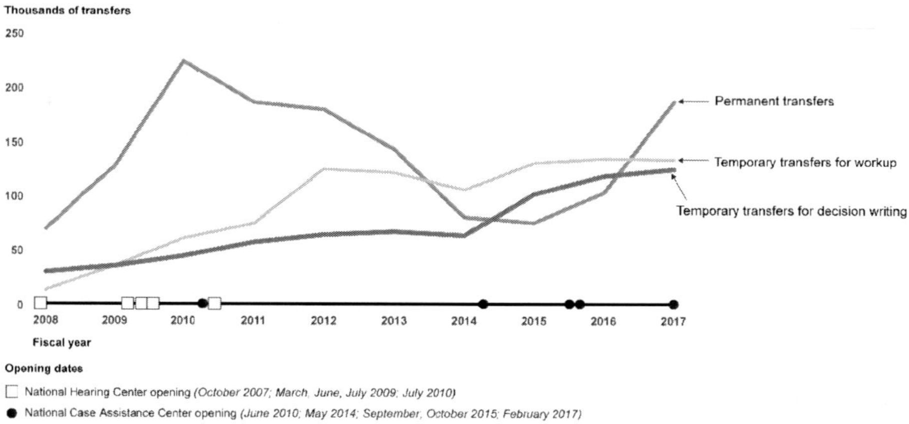

Source: GAO analysis of Social Security Administration. | GAO-18-501.

Figure 7. Number of Disability Appeals Case Transfers by Type, and Timeline of Assistance Center Openings, Fiscal Years 2008-2017.

According to SSA officials, this decline and subsequent increase occurred partly because of corresponding changes in the number of informal remands which are a subset of permanent transfers.[9]

Temporary transfers for workup and decision writing increased from fiscal years 2008 through 2017 as SSA opened five NCACs during that time. Temporary transfers for workup—case file and evidence preparation prior to a hearing—comprised about a third of all transfers and increased more than tenfold (from about 12,000 to over 130,000 cases). Temporary transfers for decision writing comprised about a fourth of all transfers and quadrupled over the decade (from about 30,000 to over 120,000 cases). SSA opened four NCACs over fiscal years 2014 through 2017, which allowed the agency to process more temporary transfers for decision writing. NCACs received about a fifth of all temporary transfers for decision writing over the decade.[10]

---

[9] Informal remands—which count as workload redistribution transfers—are cases transferred to a DDS office for reconsideration after being permanently transferred to an SSA office, such as an NCAC, which serves as a holding area for the case as it is reconsidered. SSA uses informal remands when it perceives cases may be granted benefits without a hearing on the basis of, for example, new information, and that the DDSs have relatively more capacity.

[10] Each NCAC does decision writing; two NCACs also provide assistance with workup.

Average Processing Times Increased in Recent Years

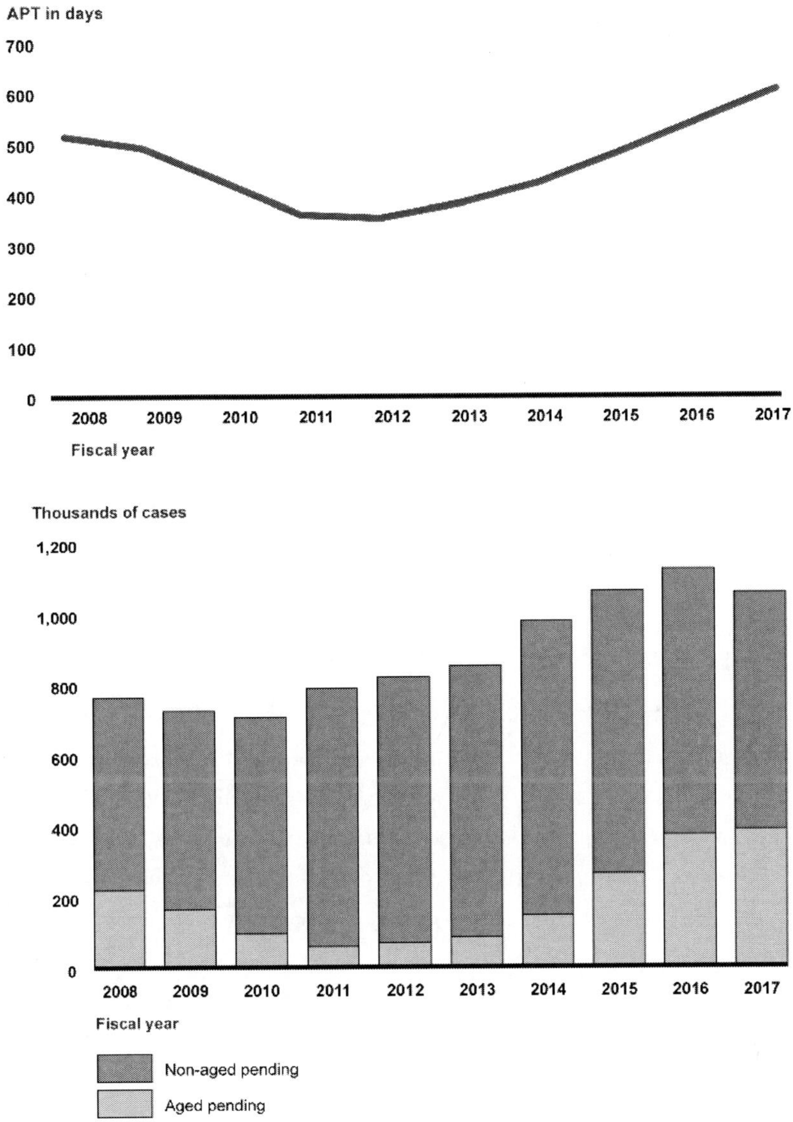

Source: GAO analysis of Social Security Administration. | GAO-18-501.

Note: Pending case counts are as of the end of the fiscal year.

Figure 8. Average Processing Time (APT) and Number of Pending Disability Appeals Cases, Fiscal Years 2008-2017.

Although SSA made an effort to improve timeliness through appeals case transfers, average processing times (APT) and pending caseloads grew in recent years. According to SSA, various factors such as changes in the number of hearing requests contributed to these trends.

APT—the average number of calendar days between the hearing request and the case disposition date in a reporting period—decreased by about 30 percent over fiscal years 2008 through 2012 (see Figure 8). However, APT increased by approximately 70 percent from fiscal years 2012 through 2017, peaking at 605 days—or about a year and eight months— in fiscal year 2017. Pending caseloads followed a similar pattern to APT. Specifically, pending caseloads declined through fiscal year 2010 and then grew through fiscal year 2016 to over 1.1 million cases. However, the number of pending cases declined by six percent in fiscal year 2017 to just over 1 million cases, which SSA attributed in part to declines in hearing requests and growth in the number of judges. Aged cases— cases pending 430 or more days at the beginning of the fiscal year[11] — declined about 75 percent through fiscal year 2011 to about 57,000 cases but then grew through fiscal year 2017 to 385,000 cases, or about 35 percent of all pending cases.

Various factors contributed to increases in processing times and pending caseloads for disability appeals cases over fiscal years 2008 through 2017. According to SSA officials and the agency's Office of Inspector General (OIG), these factors include changes in the number of hearing requests, hearing operations staffing levels, and judges' workloads.

Hearing Requests

An increase in disability applications starting around 2007 led to a subsequent increase in appeals hearing requests, which contributed to a larger case backlog. According to SSA, the 2007-2009 recession contributed to an increase in disability applications, which then led to an increase in hearing requests until 2011. As the economy recovered, the

[11] SSA's definition of an aged case has varied over time. In fiscal year 2017, the agency defined an aged case as a case pending 430 or more days at the beginning of the fiscal year. We used this definition in our analysis for consistency.

number of hearing requests declined from about 860,000 in fiscal year 2011 to about 620,000 in fiscal year 2017(see Figure 9). However, according to SSA officials, APT continued to rise because it takes time for cases to work through the appeals process as well as other factors such as staffing and changes affecting judges' workloads.

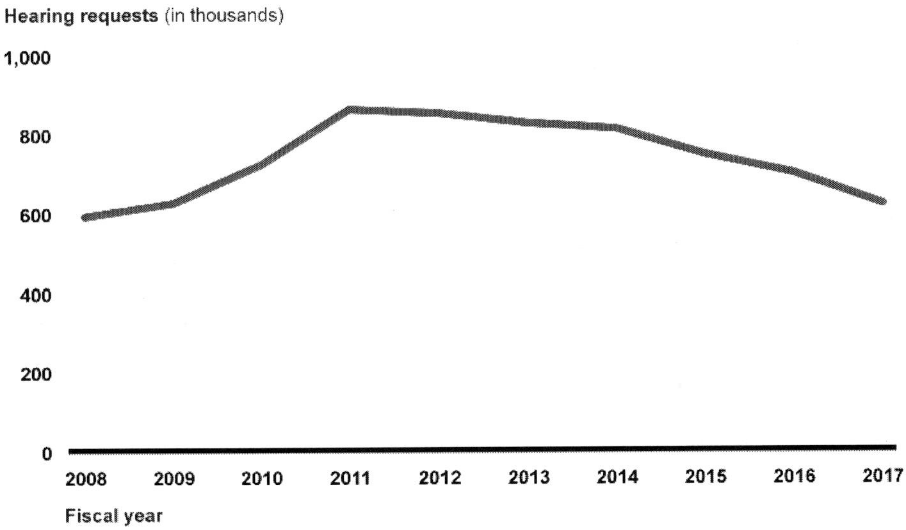

Source: GAO analysis of Social Security Administration. | GAO-18-501.

Figure 9. Disability Appeals Hearing Requests, Fiscal Years 2008-2017.

Staffing Levels

Staffing levels among judges, decision writers, and other support staff grew over the decade yet declined in recent years as average processing times increased (see Figure 10). In fiscal years 2008 through 2017, the number of judges grew by almost 40 percent (1,187 to 1,641), the number of decision writers grew by about 60 percent (1,763 to 2,830), and the number of support staff grew by nearly 20 percent (3,395 to 4,030).

However, most of this growth occurred during fiscal years 2008 to 2012. In the last 5 years, staffing growth slowed to 6 percent for judges and 3 percent for decision writers, and declined 11 percent for other support staff.

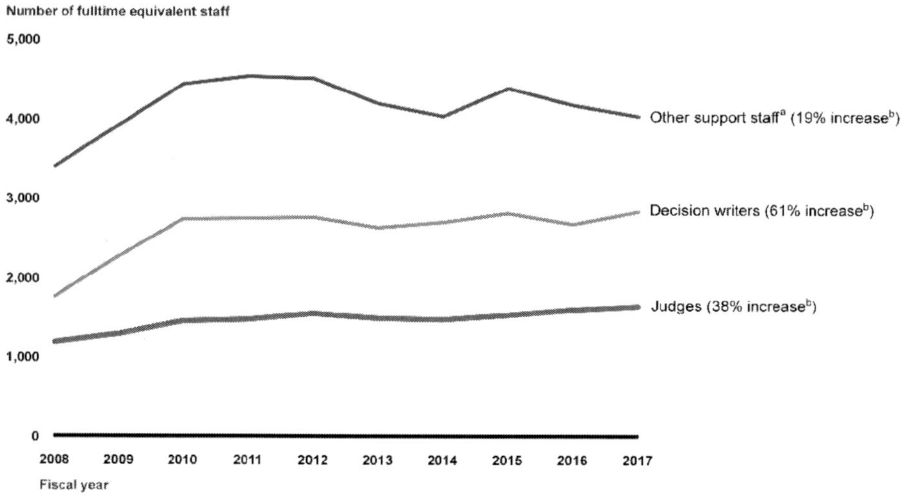

Source: GAO analysis of Social Security Administration. | GAO-18-501.

[a] Other support staff include intake assistants and case technicians who collect evidence and prepare cases prior to hearings among other tasks.

[b] The change is from fiscal year 2008 to fiscal year 2017.

Figure 10. Staffing for Disability Appeals Hearings by Function, Fiscal Years 2008-2017.

While there were overall increases in staffing levels over the study period, APT increased. According to SSA officials, hiring more staff does not immediately result in reduced APTs for several reasons. First, hearing office staff are not interchangeable across functions. This can create bottlenecks at particular stages in the appeals process. For example, an increase in support staff to prepare cases for hearings is helpful for APT only to the extent that there are enough judges to promptly hear those cases. In addition, the effect of a staffing increase is not immediately reflected in APT because it takes time for new staff to reach full productivity, and the ramp-up time varies by function, according to SSA officials. For example, officials said that new judges face a learning curve in their first year, such that they are not expected to match the productivity of experienced judges during that time.

Beyond staffing levels, creating a balance of decision writers and other support staff to judges is essential to maintaining judge productivity, according to an OIG report.[12] SSA struggled to maintain this balance, agency officials said, because of not being able to hire enough qualified judges. The Office of Personnel Management maintains a register of qualified judges from which SSA and other agencies hire; however, according to SSA officials, SSA does not consider all of these judges to be qualified for the SSA AUJ role. As a consequence, in some years SSA was unable to hire its planned number of judges. For example, in fiscal year 2013 SSA hired 30 judges when it planned to hire around 200, according to SSA officials. In addition, according to SSA's plan to address its appeals backlog, hiring freezes the agency implemented hindered its ability to maintain desired staffing levels by function during the study period. SSA hired 264 judges in fiscal year 2016, but due to its own hiring freeze was unable to hire the 500 to 600 decision writers needed to keep up with the writing backlog, according to SSA officials. As a result, they said the number of cases waiting to be written increased from about 35,000 to 75,000 in a year.

As a result of variations in the timing of hiring for judges and for support staff, the ratio of support staff including decision writers per judge also varied across hearing offices over fiscal years 2008 through 2017. In June 2017, SSA was close to meeting its nationwide staffing ratio goal of 4.2 support staff including decision writers per judge.[13] In the same year, staffing ratios in hearing offices ranged from 2.2 in Toledo, Ohio (the lowest) to 7.5 in the Orange, California office (the highest). In addition, as SSA hired more judges and the number of support staff decreased in fiscal years 2011 through 2017, the percentage of hearing offices with a staffing ratio less than 4.2 increased from 13 percent to 68 percent. According to SSA officials, the agency may mitigate some of the delays caused by the variation in staffing ratios across hearing offices by transferring cases from offices with a backlog to offices with staff available to assist.

[12] Social Security Administration, Office of the Inspector General, *Factors Related to Decreased Administrative Law Judge Productivity* (A-12-18-50289), Sept. 11, 2017.

[13] SSA had a ratio of 3.91 support staff per judge in June 2017.

Judges' Workloads

Regulatory changes and an increase in the rate of judges denying appeals may have negatively affected judges' processing times. SSA officials and the OIG cited regulatory changes that could be lengthening processing times for appeals cases. For example, a regulatory change that became effective in 2015 generally requires claimants to inform the agency about or submit all evidence known to them that relates to whether or not they are disabled or blind.[14] This change may create lengthier files for judges to review and thus require more time to decide cases. In addition, SSA officials said that a regulation that took effect in 2017 requiring more time for notifying claimants of hearing dates slowed processing times as hearing offices adjusted to it.[15] Furthermore, judges have increasingly denied benefits in recent years, with overall allowance rates dropping from 75 percent in fiscal year 1994 to a 23-year low of 54 percent in fiscal year 2015. Increases in denied appeals affect processing times, according to an OIG report, because relative to allowances, denials typically take longer to process as judges spend more time hearing and documenting the case to ensure it can withstand a subsequent appeal.[16]

SSA Monitors Case Transfers but Lacks Measures to Assess How Individual Offices Contribute to Processing Times

To help achieve timeliness goals for processing appeals, the Division of Workload Management (DWM) is responsible for monitoring workloads and adjusting transfer plans throughout the year. The Office of Hearings Operations' regional offices and DWM help decide how many cases to transfer and where to transfer them. Each region is generally expected to balance its offices' workloads within the region and to transfer

---

[14] Submission of Evidence in Disability Claims, 80 Fed. Reg. 14,828 (March 20, 2015).

[15] See Ensuring Program Uniformity at the Hearing and Appeals Council Levels of the Administrative Review Process, 81 Fed. Reg. 90,987 (December 16, 2016).

[16] SSA, OIG, A-12-18-50289.

cases to offices outside the region if it cannot meet its goals on its own. To do so, each regional office is responsible for considering the workloads and capacities of the hearing offices in its region. DWM is to determine which regions and national resources, such as NHCs and NCACs, can help process cases and how much assistance they can provide.

Working collaboratively with the regional offices, DWM analyzes offices' workloads and staff productivity to refine transfer plans if need be, according to SSA officials. To inform any adjustments, DWM holds a separate monthly call with each region to discuss the status of its aged cases and conducts quarterly reassessments of the regions' needs for assistance. In addition, the Deputy Commissioner of the Office of Hearings Operations holds a biweekly call with officials from any region that is not on track to meet its aged case goal to consider additional transfers.

In addition to monitoring the number and types of case transfers, according to agency officials, SSA monitors whether hearing offices are following set criteria when selecting individual cases to transfer.[17] Given that the age of the case is a key criterion, SSA checks whether eligible older cases are transferred in two ways, according to agency officials. First, DWM periodically reviews the ages of transferred cases and generates reports that flag transferred cases with relatively recent hearing request dates. Second, offices receiving transfers also check to make sure that transferred cases have generally older hearing request dates and meet other criteria. If cases that have been transferred do not meet the criteria, staff from the receiving office will alert the originating office and swap cases received for cases that do meet the criteria. Four of the 10 hearing offices or assistance centers we visited reported receiving cases that should not have been transferred, but officials said that this problem occurs rarely. For example, one hearing office we visited received 50 cases for decision

[17] SSA has established criteria for selecting cases to transfer. For example, cases selected for any transfer should have fully electronic files. Other selection criteria vary by transfer type. For permanent transfers, for example, the claimant should not have opted out of having a hearing by video. In addition, cases must be at the appropriate stage in the case process for the type of assistance to be provided. For example, temporary transfers for decision writing are selected among cases that have had a hearing and the judge has provided written instructions, whereas permanent case transfers are selected among cases whose file has been prepared for a hearing but not yet assigned to a judge.

writing that staff thought were selected because the cases were among the most challenging to process, and not because they were the oldest cases. The hearing office staff raised the issue with the regional office, which stepped in and had a more balanced set of cases transferred.

Although SSA monitors appeals case transfers in these ways, it does not meaningfully measure the timeliness of case processing by individual hearing offices involved in case transfers. SSA generates reports that rank hearing offices based on various dimensions of performance. These include timeliness, which includes APT.[18] However, for transferred cases, these metrics do not hold individual offices accountable for the time they held a case because the entire processing time is attributed to the office that finalized the case, regardless of whether the case was held by another office for months before being transferred.

The lack of office-specific timeliness measures for transferred cases has several consequences. Because the timeliness measures for transferred cases do not reflect individual office contributions, the metrics do not provide effective incentives for offices involved in transfers to improve their own timeliness. Our prior work has shown that performance measures, when well-designed, can create powerful incentives to influence behavior.[19] SSA's current APT does not create these incentives for offices that process transfers. In fact, the metrics as currently formulated may have a demoralizing effect for offices that receive many transfers because receiving aged cases will likely increase the office's APT. As a result, the current office-level rankings based on APT may not be meaningful or fair for these offices because they could receive a lower ranking as a result of taking transfers. The rankings may induce some offices to transfer out their most time-consuming cases. However, as previously noted, such transfers occur rarely and are corrected when identified, according to hearing office officials.

---

[18] In December 2017, we recommended that SSA develop a more balanced set of publicly reported performance measures, to include accuracy and consistency, as well as timeliness, of judges' disability decisions. SSA concurred but has not yet done so. GAO, *Social Security Disability: Additional Measures and Evaluation Needed to Enhance Accuracy and Consistency of Hearings Decisions*, GAO-18-37 (Washington, D.C.: Dec. 7, 2017).

[19] GAO, *Executive Guide: Effectively Implementing the Government Performance and Results Act*, GAO/GGD-96-118 (Washington, D.C.: June 1996).

Because APTs do not accurately reflect the individual contributions of offices, SSA managers in offices that receive high numbers of transfers reported that they sometimes downplay the office-level APT. For example, officials at one hearing office said that they may publicize a good APT ranking internally to help boost morale, but do not worry about a poor ranking because APT does not fairly reflect individual offices' performances in light of permanent transfers. Officials from another office that receives high numbers of transfers said that, to boost morale, they do not highlight APT but rather focus on the fact that their office is doing so well it is able to assist other offices by taking transferred cases.

Another consequence of the current APT measure is that SSA does not have an accurate metric to assess how individual offices contribute to processing times. Our prior work has shown that federal managers should use accurate performance information in decision making to improve results.[20] Further, standards for internal control call for program managers to define objectives in measurable terms so that performance toward achieving those objectives can be assessed.[21] According to SSA officials in headquarters, the agency does not use APT to rank or otherwise assess individual offices' timeliness. Instead, they focus on overall APT at the agency level. They also said APTs should not be used to measure the performance of NHCs and NCACs, which have workloads entirely comprised of transferred cases. SSA uses other measures of productivity, such as number of cases decided, to evaluate these offices, the officials said. Nonetheless, reducing wait times for decisions on appeals is a performance goal for SSA, and APT is a key measure aligned with this goal. Not assessing how individual offices contribute to processing times could make it difficult for regional and headquarters managers to identify problems and inform decision making about how to improve the timeliness of processing appeals.

---

[20] GAO, *Managing for Results: Executive Branch Should More Fully Implement the GPRA Modernization Act to Address Pressing Governance Challenges*, GAO-13-518 (Washington, D.C.: June 26, 2013), and GAO, *Managing for Results: Enhancing Agency Use of Performance Information for Management Decision Making*, GAO-05-927 (Washington, D.C.: Sept. 9, 2005).

[21] GAO, *Standards for Internal Control in the Federal Government*, GAO-14-704G (Washington, D.C.: September 2014), Principle 6.04.

SSA officials said that they recognize the limitations of the current metrics for monitoring office-level timeliness. For example, the NHCs created their own internal measure of processing time, starting the clock when an NHC receives a transfer. In other words, this modified APT captures only the time the transferred case is at the NHC, which officials said was a more informative way of gauging its performance relative to other offices. SSA officials at the headquarters level also recognized the need to modify the measures and give credit for the work performed by individual offices. They said that they are considering ways to do this, but have not taken action due to other priorities. Without office-specific measures of timeliness for transferred appeals cases, SSA lacks critical information needed to assess the effectiveness of transfers in meeting timeliness goals intended to better serve disability claimants.

SSA Has Taken Steps to Address Challenges in Transferring Cases, but Some Remain

Through interviews with SSA staff, observation of staff practices, and review of agency guidance and policy documents, we identified three main challenges related to transferring appeals cases. Staff described steps they have taken to address these challenges. Interviewees emphasized challenges in: (1) providing clear instructions for decision writers, (2) software limitations for selecting cases to transfer, and (3) coordinating video hearings.

Improving the Quality of Judges' Instructions to Decision Writers

SSA staff we interviewed in all three regions we visited reported facing challenges in efficiently processing cases that have been transferred for decision writing because some judges do not provide legible or adequate instructions, which can then require follow-up communication that slows down the process. When cases are heard and written in the same hearing office, decision writers can gain familiarity with the communication styles and preferences of the judges with whom they repeatedly work. This includes understanding how to interpret certain instructions that are not spelled out or written clearly. In contrast, staff who write decisions for transferred cases must rely on the instructions' legibility and completeness in order to write policy-compliant decisions within the expected timeframe. While staff working remotely are able to contact judges directly to obtain further instructions, they said this step slows down the writing process.

There is no standard format that judges must adhere to when providing instructions to decision writers, but judges are supposed to provide complete and clear instructions and avoid handwriting them, according to SSA's hearings operations manual.[22] Some judges use templates SSA has designed to assist them with providing a complete set of instructions in a typed, electronic format, while other judges write their instructions, which then have to be scanned into the case processing system. For example, in one hearing office we visited, 11 of 14 judges typed their instructions and the other 3 wrote instructions by hand. In another office we visited 1 of the office's 7 judges wrote instructions by hand.

Instructions can be problematic for decision writers when judges do not provide sufficiently clear information. In one case assistance center we visited, officials estimated that about 30 to 40 percent of instructions they receive require follow-up work because they contain contradictory, incomplete, or illegible information. For example, decision writers cited a judge's instructions that supported contradictory conclusions about whether the claimant was disabled. As another example, decision writers sometimes receive 20 pages of instructions, which in effect are just the judge's case notes and not actual instructions on how to document the hearing decision. In such instances, decision writers have to do additional work to understand the circumstances of the case. Specifically, they may

[22] The hearings operations manual lists specific information that judges will generally include as applicable.

have to thoroughly review the judge's notes as well as listen to the audio recording of the hearing, and examine the case evidence file, all of which adds time to processing the case. Figure 11 illustrates how difficult it can be to read handwritten instructions. Three of the six hearing offices we spoke with have taken steps to mitigate this problem by not transferring cases from judges who handwrite their instructions.

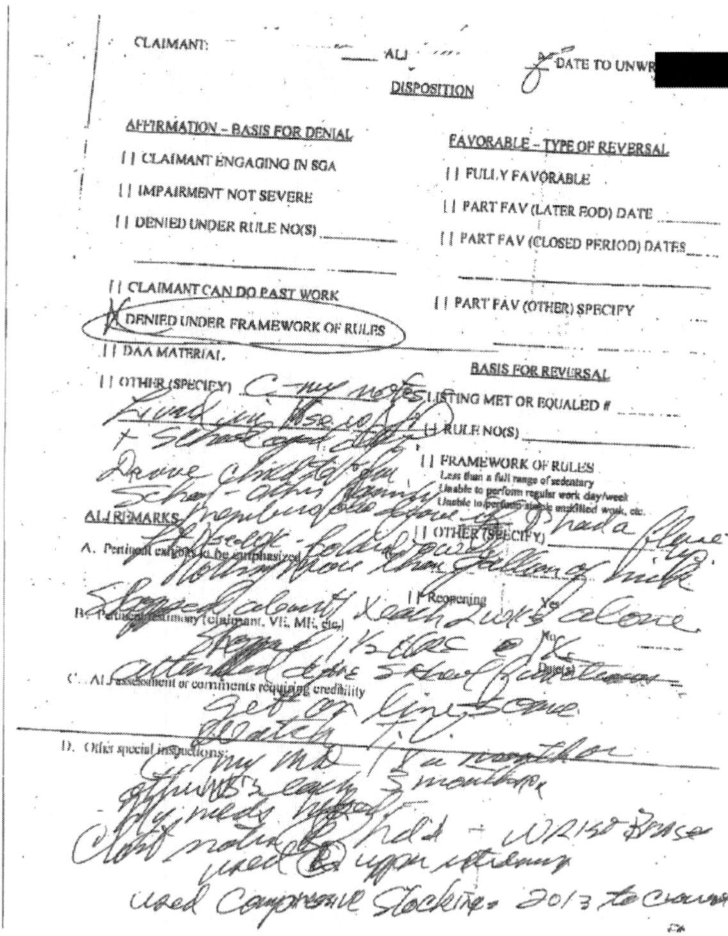
CLAIMANT: ALJ DATE TO UNWR [redacted]

DISPOSITION

AFFIRMATION – BASIS FOR DENIAL

[ ] CLAIMANT ENGAGING IN SGA
[ ] IMPAIRMENT NOT SEVERE
[ ] DENIED UNDER RULE NO(S) ______
[ ] CLAIMANT CAN DO PAST WORK
[X] DENIED UNDER FRAMEWORK OF RULES
[ ] DAA MATERIAL
[ ] OTHER (SPECIFY)

FAVORABLE – TYPE OF REVERSAL

[ ] FULLY FAVORABLE
[ ] PART FAV (LATER EOD) DATE ______
[ ] PART FAV (CLOSED PERIOD) DATES ______
[ ] PART FAV (OTHER) SPECIFY

BASIS FOR REVERSAL

[ ] LISTING MET OR EQUALED # ______
[ ] RULE NO(S) ______
[ ] FRAMEWORK OF RULES
Less than a full range of sedentary
Unable to perform regular work day/week
Unable to perform simple unskilled work, etc.
[ ] OTHER (SPECIFY)

ALJ REMARKS

A. Pertinent exhibits to be emphasized
B. Pertinent testimony (claimant, VE, ME, etc.)
[ ] Reopening Yes No Date(s)
C. ALJ assessment or comments requiring credibility
D. Other special instructions:

Source: Social Security Administration. | GAO-18-501.

Figure 11. Excerpt from an Administrative Law Judge's Instructions of a Disability Case Transferred for Decision Writing.

To improve the quality and consistency of judge's instructions to decision writers, SSA has issued additional guidance, conducted training, and created tools. For example, in July 2013, SSA issued a memorandum clarifying expectations for the instructions that judges provide to decision writers. This memorandum emphasized judges' responsibility to provide complete, clear, and policy-compliant instructions and provided tips for doing so. In June 2016, SSA issued another memorandum to emphasize the essential elements judges need to include in instructions to decision writers. Further, in addition to judges' initial training period, judges receive quarterly continuing education training which include topics such as decision-writing expectations and clarity. In addition, to help judges prepare complete and typed instructions, SSA developed two electronic templates: the Electronic Bench Book (eBB) and the Findings Integrated Template (FIT). However, some judges have found these tools cumbersome to use given their design.[23] GAO reported in December 2017 that about one-third of judges used eBB in fiscal year 2016,[24] and officials in one NCAC we visited said that about one-quarter of judges use FIT. In response to some judges' concerns about using these tools, SSA recently developed a web-based tool that judges may use instead and is developing an internal marketing plan to encourage its use.

Using Available Software to Select Cases for Transfer

Hearing office staff reported and we observed challenges they face in efficiently and accurately identifying cases for permanent transfer because of current software limitations. Although staff have developed workarounds to overcome these limitations, the extra steps are inefficient and the potential to incorrectly select cases remains.

---

[23] A 2016 SSA OIG report identified three concerns with eBB based on interviews with judges and other staff: the training for eBB was insufficient, the design of eBB was not easy for users, and using eBB could increase case processing times. Social Security Administration, Office of the Inspector General, *Electronic Bench Book* (A-01-12-11217), Jun. 21, 2016.

[24] GAO-18-37.

We observed three main case processing system limitations in the three hearing offices we visited where SSA staff demonstrated how they process large batches of cases for permanent transfer to another office. First, staff cannot use the case processing system's search function to locate all appropriate cases to transfer. Because some cases may be categorized with a temporary status code—for instance when awaiting information from a claimant representative—searches by status do not always show all the cases that are available for transfer. Second, the case processing system restricts each search query to a 6-month time period to avoid slowing it down. As a result, staff cannot retrieve the universe of potential transfer cases at once for large transfer batches. Instead, to overcome this limitation, staff in four of the six hearing offices we visited employed several time-consuming strategies. In one office, for example, staff first created a report that lists all the cases that meet the selection criteria and used this chapter to identify the oldest cases and then retrieved the cases one at a time. Third, the case processing system restricts the transfers of batches of cases to a maximum of 100 cases at a time. As a result, staff have to repeat the transfer process several times because DWM often has hearing offices permanently transfer several hundred cases at a time. For example, one hearing office we visited reported that it typically transfers batches of between 500 and 1,200 cases. According to SSA officials, the batch transfer limit of 100 cases was designed to minimize the possibility of computer crashes which could lead to system-wide errors.

These system limitations impede productivity for the staff selecting cases to transfer and also can create the potential for error and misuse. Specifically, the constraints on searching for appropriate cases to transfer make it challenging for the sending office to identify the oldest cases—a key selection criterion as the agency works to meet its goal of reducing the backlog of aged cases. In addition, because these limitations cause staff to use manual workarounds, using the case processing system's search functions to retrieve cases might either omit cases that should be transferred or inadvertently include cases that should not be transferred. Officials we spoke with in five offices reported the potential for misuse of the system given its current limitations. For example, it would be possible to use the current system to select cases to transfer that might not strictly meet the criteria, but might be cases that are considered more difficult to process. One office we visited reported receiving cases that staff felt were deliberately selected for transfer because they were all handwritten by a judge or were a specific category of case that is more challenging to process than other categories. After identifying these cases as improperly transferred, staff were able to send them back to the originating office.

According to agency officials, SSA does not plan to address the software challenges associated with batch transfers, even though SSA's plan to improve its hearings and appeals process calls for modernizing its case processing system. Specifically, SSA's plan calls for information technology improvements that help to remove inefficiencies in the agency's case processing systems, drive policy compliance and consistency across offices, and redirect staff away from manual work.[25] SSA is planning to update its case processing system over the next 3 years including a release in September 2018 but does not plan to address the software-related challenges in accurately and efficiently selecting batches of cases to transfer because of concerns about system-wide computer processing capacity. However, SSA has not evaluated the costs versus benefits of potential software changes to help staff transfer cases in batches. Doing so would help SSA better understand any tradeoffs between maintaining the status quo of manual work—which is contrary to SSA's stated goal of redirecting staff away from manual work as part of its plan to improve its hearings and appeals process—and any impact on its system's capacity.

Coordinating Video Hearings

Coordinating video hearings for permanently transferred cases can be challenging according to SSA officials, but SSA has taken steps to improve coordination. Without effective coordination and communication between

[25] Social Security Administration, 2017 Updated Compassionate and Responsive Service (CARES) and Anomaly Plan.

offices, hearings may be delayed, according to SSA hearing office staff. Several offices we visited identified challenges with coordination of logistics and practices to mitigate them. For example, one hearing office we visited that received permanent transfers sometimes lacked a point of contact in the originating office to escort the claimant and help troubleshoot any logistical issues which necessitated some rescheduled hearings. Hearing office officials said that, to address this issue, it is important to have a point of contact in each office involved in the transfer to facilitate coordination. To further prevent such miscommunication, officials at one NHC we visited reported that they hold a video conference meeting when they start assisting a new hearing office. The NHC provides a protocol to the hearing office that describes what the NHC needs to successfully run a video hearing, including points of contact, logistics, and claimant escorts.

To set expectations about coordination for permanently transferred cases and to disseminate promising practices that some offices had adopted, SSA issued guidance to hearing office managers in June 2017. Among other things, the memo instructs offices to identify points of contact in each office, list the available hearing rooms in the originating office, and establish which office is responsible for providing an escort for the claimant on the hearing day. Hearing office staff we interviewed described taking similar actions to coordinate hearings for permanently transferred cases.

CONCLUSION

As SSA faces a backlog of over 1 million disability appeals waiting to be decided, it has undertaken numerous efforts to reduce processing times at the hearings level. Transferring cases across offices has increasingly become a key component of those efforts. Transfers provide the agency an opportunity to smooth its workloads and mitigate staffing constraints at the hearings level and potentially provide claimants with more timely decisions.

However, as a substantial and growing percentage of cases are transferred between offices, SSA has not adapted its metrics and electronic systems to take the transfer process into account. Its current performance metrics do not enable adequate oversight of individual offices' contributions. Although timeliness is just one dimension of hearing office performance, as it continues to monitor transfers, SSA would benefit from developing and using metrics that hold originating and assisting offices accountable for the time that they held cases. Without such metrics, SSA cannot accurately measure offices' performance and therefore may not be able to incentivize offices to process cases in a timely way. In addition, without metrics that reflect the time that individual offices held cases, SSA does not have key inputs for quantifying how case transfer efforts affect timeliness.

As SSA updates its case processing and management information system, SSA has the opportunity to consider addressing system limitations that create inefficiencies and vulnerabilities when staff transfer batches of cases. Without evaluating the costs and benefits of incorporating related software changes, SSA may be missing an opportunity to fully understand potential ways to improve its processing of appeals.

RECOMMENDATIONS FOR EXECUTIVE ACTION

We are making the following two recommendations to the Social Security Administration:

The Deputy Commissioner for Hearings Operations should develop a timeliness metric or set of metrics that more accurately reflect offices' performance in light of case transfers. For example, SSA could develop additional APT metrics for cases that are permanently transferred that reflect the time the originating and assisting offices held cases. (Recommendation 1).

The Deputy Commissioner for Hearings Operations should evaluate the costs versus the benefits of changing system limitations that hinder users' ability to correctly and efficiently identify and transfer batches of cases. (Recommendation 2)

AGENCY COMMENTS AND OUR EVALUATION

We provided a draft of this chapter to SSA for review and comment, and its written comments are reproduced as appendix II in this chapter. SSA agreed with our recommendations and emphasized its recent progress in reducing pending caseloads. The agency also provided technical comments, which we incorporated into the report as appropriate. SSA described how it plans to address our recommendations as follows.

- Regarding our recommendation to develop a timeliness metric or set of metrics of offices' performance in light of case transfers, SSA agreed and stated that it will refine existing metrics to more accurately reflect timeliness of cases before and after being transferred. Furthermore, SSA stated that it may develop additional reporting tools to better measure the contributions of individual offices that receive transferred cases.
- Regarding our recommendation to evaluate the costs versus the benefits of changing system limitations that hinder users' ability to correctly and efficiently identify and transfer batches of cases, SSA agreed and stated that it is developing a new case processing system that will replace its Case Processing and Management System. SSA expects the new system will eliminate the limitations that we cited.

As agreed with your office, unless you publicly announce the contents of this chapter earlier, we plan no further distribution until 30 days from the report date. At that time, we will send copies to the appropriate congressional committees and the Commissioner of Social Security.

Elizabeth H. Curda
Director, Education, Workforce, and Income Security Issues

APPENDIX I: OBJECTIVES, SCOPE, AND METHODOLOGY

The objectives of this chapter were to examine (1) trends in the Social Security Administration's (SSA) case transfers and processing times of appealed disability cases over the past decade, (2) SSA's monitoring of its efforts to meet processing time goals through case transfers, and (3) any challenges SSA faces in transferring cases between offices. We limited the scope of our analysis to cases transferred for workload redistribution.[26]

To inform all objectives, we reviewed relevant SSA documents and interviewed officials in SSA's Office of Hearings Operations (OHO). Specifically, we reviewed SSA planning documents, operational guidance about case transfers, SSA Office of the Inspector General reports, and relevant federal laws and regulations. For example, to help identify any challenges SSA faces in transferring cases between offices, we reviewed operational guidance such as OHO memorandums. To gather additional evidence about how SSA monitors case transfers in the context of its goals to reduce processing times and any challenges it faces in transferring cases, we visited and interviewed staff from OHO headquarters and four assistance centers established to process transferred cases.[27] We also interviewed OHO officials and staff in three regional offices and six hearing offices about the criteria for transferring cases for workload assistance, how they ensure that transferred cases satisfy selection criteria, and any challenges they face in transferring cases. We also observed how they select cases to transfer and the steps they take and systems used to process case transfers. See below for which specific locations we visited and how we selected them.

---

[26] SSA also transfers cases between offices for other reasons such as when claimants move. In this chapter, "case transfers" only refers to cases transferred for workload redistribution.

[27] The four assistance centers were a national hearing center; two national case assistance centers; and a regional case assistance center.

We evaluated the agency's oversight of transfers and related challenges against SSA planning documents to improve its hearings and appeals process, federal standards for internal control for defining objectives, and other performance management practices we have identified in our prior work.

Analysis of Case Processing and Staffing Data

To examine trends in case transfers and processing times of appeal disability cases, we analyzed nationwide, summary-level data from SSA's Case Processing and Management System (CPMS) and related Disability Adjudication Reporting Tool (DART) reports for fiscal years 2008 through 2017. We used CPMS data to analyze trends in hearing requests, pending caseloads, and average processing times. We used data from DART E15 reports to analyze trends in the number and type of case transfers and the offices involved (i.e., sending and receiving). We separately and collectively analyzed three types of case transfers: (1) permanent transfers, (2) temporary transfers for workup, and (3) temporary transfers for decision writing. We assessed the reliability of these data by conducting electronic data tests and interviewing knowledgeable officials about how the data were collected, and found the data to be sufficiently reliable for the purposes of this review.

To contextualize case processing trends, we analyzed staffing data from SSA's Payroll Operational Data Store system. Specifically, we analyzed the number of administrative law judges, decision writers, and other support staff OHO-wide and by hearing office in each fiscal year from 2008 through 2017. In addition, we examined how hearing offices' ratios of decision writers and other support staff per administrative law judge varied over time and nationwide. We excluded satellite offices and other OHO offices such as regional offices from this analysis because they are not designed to function like hearing offices. We also used the staffing data by office and year to determine the number of hearing offices by fiscal year because some offices did not exist (i.e., have staff) in certain years we analyzed. We assessed the reliability of SSA's staffing data by comparing them to published data from a different source, reviewing the agency's responses to questions about the data and their reliability, and reviewing related reports, and found the staffing data to be sufficiently reliable for the purposes of this review.

Site Visit Selection

To identify which of OHO's 10 regions to visit, we considered those with a relatively large number of cases transferred for workload redistribution, regional offices near OHO headquarters or a national or regional assistance center established to process transferred cases, or both. We used data from fiscal year 2016 because it was the most recent complete year when we made our selections. We chose regions with a relatively high number of transfers so that we could observe a reasonable workload of transfers. On the basis of these factors as detailed in Table 1, we chose to visit OHO's Philadelphia (#3), Atlanta (#4), and San Francisco (#9) regions.

We selected two hearing offices in each of the three regions we visited— in Region 3, we visited the Baltimore, Maryland and Philadelphia, Pennsylvania hearing offices; in Region 4, we visited the Atlanta Downtown and Covington offices in Georgia; and in Region 9, we visited the San Francisco and Stockton offices in California—on the basis of various factors. We selected relatively high-sending and high-receiving offices so that we could obtain perspectives from offices that commonly engage in workload assistance. Our selection also captured a mix of types of case transfers because the processes for permanent and temporary transfers differ. Two of the six hearing offices (Baltimore and Atlanta Downtown) sent a higher than average number of cases among all hearing offices in their respective regions. Three of the six hearing offices (Covington, San Francisco, and Stockton) received a higher than average number of cases among all hearing offices in their respective regions.

Table 2. Office of Hearings Operations (OHO) Region Selection Factors

Region	Percent of all transfers sent in fiscal year 2016	Percent of all transfers received in fiscal year 2016	Near[a] a National Hearing Center[b]	Near[a] a National Case Assistance Center[c]	Near[a] a Regional Case Assistance Center[d]	Near[a] OHO headquarters
1 – Boston	3	3	—	—	—	No
2 – New York	11	4	—	—	Queens, New York	No
3 – Philadelphia	10	4	Baltimore, Maryland Falls Church, Virginia	Baltimore, Maryland Falls Church, Virginia	Philadelphia, Pennsylvania Falls Church, Virginia	Yes
4 – Atlanta	26	14	—	—	—	No
5 – Chicago	12	10	Chicago, Illinois	—	—	No
6 – Dallas	11	8	—	—	—	No
7 – Kansas City	3	4	—	—	—	No
8 – Denver	4	1	—	—	—	No
9 – San Francisco	13	10	—	Richmond, California	Stockton, California	No
10 – Seattle	6	3	—	—	—	No

Source: GAO analysis of Social Security Administration information. | GAO-18-501.

a = within a 3 hour drive of a regional office or OHO headquarters in Falls Church, VA.

[b] National Hearing Centers are located in Albuquerque, NM; Baltimore, MD; Chicago, IL; Falls Church, VA; and St. Louis, MO.

[c] National Case Assistance Centers are located in Baltimore, MD; Falls Church, VA; Louisville, KY; Richmond, CA; and St. Louis, MO.

[d] Regional Case Assistance Centers are located in Falls Church, VA; Louisville, KY; Phoenix, AZ; Philadelphia, PA; St. Louis, MO; San Bernardino, CA; Stockton, CA; and Queens, NY.

We also considered the hearing offices' average processing time (APT) rank among all hearing offices to obtain different perspectives on performance management. For example, of the 164 hearing offices in fiscal year 2016, the APT of the Atlanta Downtown hearing office ranked 155th (the lowest we visited) and that of the Stockton office ranked 77th (the highest we visited). Finally, we selected hearing offices that were located within a 3-hour drive from their regional office.

To gain additional perspectives, we conducted interviews at four assistance centers selected because they were near the regional offices we visited or OHO headquarters. The four assistance centers were a national hearing center in Falls Church, Virginia; a national case assistance center in each of Richmond, California and Baltimore, Maryland; and a regional case assistance center in Stockton, California.

APPENDIX II: COMMENTS FROM THE SOCIAL SECURITY ADMINISTRATION

SOCIAL SECURITY
Office of the Commissioner

June 20, 2018

Ms. Elizabeth Curda
Director, Education, Workforce, and Income Security Issues
United States Government Accountability Office
441 G Street, NW
Washington, DC 20548

Dear Ms. Curda:

Thank you for the opportunity to review the draft report, "Social Security Disability: Better Timeliness Metrics Needed to Assess Transfers of Appeals Work" (GAO-18-501). Please see our enclosed comments.

If you have any questions, please contact me at (410) 965-9704. Your staff may contact Trae Sommer, Acting Director of the Audit Liaison Staff, at (410) 965-9102.

Sincerely,

Stephanie Hall

Stephanie Hall
Acting Deputy Chief of Staff

COMMENTS ON THE GOVERNMENT ACCOUNTABILITY OFFICE DRAFT REPORT, "SOCIAL SECURITY DISABILITY: BETTER TIMELINESS METRICS NEEDED TO ASSESS TRANSFERS OF APPEALS WORK" (GAO-18-501)

GENERAL COMMENTS

Our updated 2017 Compassionate And REsponsive Service (CARES) plan outlines a comprehensive and multi-layered approach to address the number of hearings pending and long wait times through increased decisional capacity, business process efficiencies, and Information Technology (IT) innovations and investments. At the end of fiscal year (FY) 2017, approximately 1,056,000 people were waiting for a decision on their hearing requests. With continued support from Congress, in the form of special funding in FYs 2017 and 2018 for the hearings operation, we reduced the number of pending cases in each of the last 17 months, and as of May 2018, the number of people awaiting a hearing is under 950,000. In addition, declining receipts and increased productivity have positioned us well in FY 2018, and we are on track to end FY 2018 with about 900,000 cases pending a hearing decision, a 15 percent decrease from FY 2017.

Essential to our efforts is our ability to balance workloads by transferring cases from heavily impacted hearing offices to hearing offices with the capacity to assist. We are maximizing the use of our National Hearings Centers (NHC) and National Case Assistance Centers (NCAC) — national resources designed to assist hearing offices prepare and adjudicate cases. We prioritize our oldest pending hearings with case transfers to NHCs, which hold video hearings and issue decisions. In addition, we implement case transfers to NCACs and regional case assistance centers to provide case preparation and decision writing assistance. Our workload redistribution ensures that we efficiently use our resources to adjudicate the oldest cases first, while also being responsive to unanticipated emergencies such as natural disasters. We continue to bolster centralized case assistance capacity by adding resources to provide greater assistance to hearing offices throughout the country.

Additionally, we have made significant progress on our priority goal of improving customer service in the hearings process by prioritizing the cases of those individuals who have waited the longest for a hearing decision, and we are on track to exceed our goal of deciding 97 percent of our oldest cases by the end of the fiscal year. We expect the reduction in hearings pending and the aggressive approach we have taken in the last 12 months towards our aged case goal will result in reduced wait times in FY 2019 and beyond.

We are also focused on key IT initiatives to support improved business processes in the hearings operation. In our future IT modernization efforts, we are replacing the aging hearings and appeals case processing systems with an end-to-end modern disability case processing system that will allow us to incorporate functionality to improve business processes and achieve efficiencies, such as those recommended by this audit.

Recommendation 1

The Deputy Commissioner for Hearings Operations should develop a timeliness metric or set of metrics that more accurately reflect offices' performance in light of case transfers. For example,

SSA could develop additional APT metrics for cases that are permanently transferred that reflect the time the originating and assisting offices held cases.

Response

We agree. We will explore refining existing metrics and reporting mechanisms to more accurately reflect timeliness of cases before and after they were transferred and, if necessary, develop additional reporting tools to better measure individual office contributions and ensure that an office's overall performance is accurately reflected when it receives transferred work.

Recommendation 2

The Deputy Commissioner for Hearing Operations should evaluate the costs versus the benefits of changing system limitations that hinder users' ability to correctly and efficiently identify and transfer batches of cases.

Response

We agree. Our legacy Case Processing Management System (CPMS) was initially designed to support a paper-based hearing process, and we recognize it is no longer sufficient to support our current business needs. In 2017, we started developing a comprehensive plan to modernize our case processing systems, which was integrated into our IT modernization efforts to develop a modern and cohesive end-to-end disability claims processing infrastructure that supports the full life-cycle of a disability claim. The new system will include hearings and appeals case processing functionality and will replace CPMS. We are prioritizing key features, including broad case transfer functionality, to support a national workload model, and we expect to eliminate the limitations cited in this report.

In: Social Security Disability
Editor: Michael Dimitriadis
ISBN: 978-1-53615-747-5

Chapter 6

SSA Disability Programs: Better Metrics and Evaluation Needed to Inform Decision-Making*

Elizabeth Curda

Chairman Johnson, Ranking Member Larson, and Members of the Subcommittee:

I am pleased to be here today to discuss the Social Security Administration's (SSA) efforts to manage its disability workloads. SSA provides cash benefits to Americans with disabilities who are unable to work through two main programs: Disability Insurance (DI) and Supplemental Security Income (SSI). Collectively, in fiscal year 2017, payments from these programs were about $200 billion to about 16 million individuals. SSA has faced long-standing challenges processing related workloads and has struggled to decide who is eligible for these

---

* This is an edited, reformatted and augmented version of United States Government Accountability Office, Testimony Before the Subcommittee on Social Security, Committee on Ways and Means, House of Representatives, Publication No. GAO-18-677T, dated July 25, 2018.

benefits in a timely way. Partly because of these challenges, we included "Improving and Modernizing Federal Disability Programs" on our High-Risk List of agencies and programs that are most in need of transformation or are vulnerable to fraud, waste, abuse, and mismanagement.[1]

In recent years, SSA's challenges processing disability workloads are particularly evident when individuals appeal initial decisions on their claims and request a hearing before an administrative law judge (ALJ). At the end of fiscal year 2017, SSA reported that more than 1 million claimants who had appealed their decision to an ALJ were awaiting a decision on disability benefits, and they waited, on average, 605 days (or nearly 20 months). SSA's workloads overall may remain a challenge as 80 million members of the baby boom generation pass through their most disability-prone years and enter retirement.

We have issued several reports describing SSA's challenges with managing its disability workloads, efforts to reduce claims processing times, and lack of systematic evaluation to determine the efficacy of those efforts. We highlighted many of these issues in our testimony to this committee in March of this year.[2] We noted the need for a sustained focus on the part of SSA leadership to approach these challenges strategically and follow through with rigorous plans to improve its disability programs. Today, we build on this body of work with the release of a new report on SSA's efforts to manage its appeals workload by transferring cases from hearing offices with backlogs to offices with more capacity.[3]

In summary, we found that SSA has increasingly transferred cases between offices to help manage its appeals workloads. At the same time, we found that SSA does not have an accurate metric to assess how

---

[1] GAO, *High-Risk Series: Progress on Many High-Risk Areas, While Substantial Efforts Needed on Others*, GAO-17-317 (Washington, D.C.: Feb. 15, 2017). We first designated improving and modernizing federal disability programs as high risk in 2003. In making and updating this designation, we considered actions of SSA and Department of Veterans Affairs as well as the Office of Management and Budget's efforts to create unified strategies and goals for federal programs that support employment for people with disabilities.

[2] GAO, *Social Security Administration: Continuing Leadership Focus Needed to Modernize How SSA Does Business*, GAO-18-432T (Washington, D.C.: March 7, 2018).

[3] GAO, *Social Security Disability: Better Timeliness Metrics Needed to Assess Transfers of Appeals Work*, GAO-18-501 (Washington, D.C.: July 19, 2018).

individual offices contribute to processing times, which could hinder the agency's ability to identify and address problems. My testimony today will cover these new findings and the long-standing issues that surround them. Specifically, I will touch on three areas: (1) SSA's challenges managing disability workloads, especially at the appeals level, (2) the extent to which SSA has metrics to assess its efforts to reduce processing times, and (3) limitations in SSA's case processing systems that hinder its efforts to reduce backlogs. In our report being released today, we made recommendations in these areas, which SSA agreed to implement.

In developing this testimony, we primarily relied on the report that we are releasing today. We also included information from several recent GAO reports that are cited throughout this statement and which each include detailed information on the objectives, scope and methodology of our reviews. The work on which this statement is based was conducted in accordance with generally accepted government auditing standards. More details on our objectives, scope and methodology can be found in the issued report.

BACKGROUND

SSA provides financial assistance to eligible individuals with disabilities through two major benefit programs:

- Disability Insurance (DI)—provides benefits to eligible workers who have qualifying disabilities, and their eligible family members; and
- Supplemental Security Income (SSI)—provides benefits for individuals with limited income and resources who are aged, blind, or have qualifying disabilities.

To apply for disability benefits through DI or SSI, an individual must file an application at a local SSA office. Local office staff forward most new claims to a state Disability Determination Services (DDS) office for a review of medical eligibility and an initial determination.[4] Individuals who do not agree with the initial determination can ultimately appeal by requesting a hearing before an administrative law judge (ALJ).

SSA's hearing operations are conducted by ALJs and other staff across the country. Hearing operations staff are organized in 164 hearing offices, with each office having a geographic area of responsibility. However, SSA can transfer appeals cases between offices in an effort to alleviate office backlogs. Staff use technology such as electronic case files and video conferencing to process transferred cases and hold hearings across locations.

SSA Faces Challenges Managing Disability Workloads, Especially at the Appeals Level

As we have noted in our High-Risk Series,[5] SSA has faced longstanding challenges managing its disability workloads, but has made some progress in recent years. For example, as highlighted in our 2017 High-Risk update, SSA has taken steps toward reducing its backlog of initial disability claims.[6] Specifically, SSA reduced the number of pending claims each fiscal year since 2010—from about 842,000 in fiscal year 2010 to about 523,000 in fiscal year 2017. Nonetheless, the 2017 update emphasized the need for SSA to address the growing backlog at the appeals level.

The report released today examines processing times and pending caseloads at the appeals level over the past decade and finds that both have grown in recent years. Specifically, average processing time (APT)—the average number of calendar days between a hearing request and case

[4] Although SSA is responsible for the programs, initial determinations of disability are generally made by state agencies.

[5] In 1990, we began a program to report on government operations that we identified as "high risk." Since then, generally coinciding with the start of each new Congress, we have reported on progress to address high-risk areas and updated the High-Risk List.

[6] GAO-17-317.

disposition for all dispositions during the period being analyzed—decreased by about 30 percent over fiscal years 2008 through 2012, but climbed by approximately 70 percent from fiscal years 2012 through 2017. APT peaked at 605 days, or about a year and eight months, in fiscal year 2017.

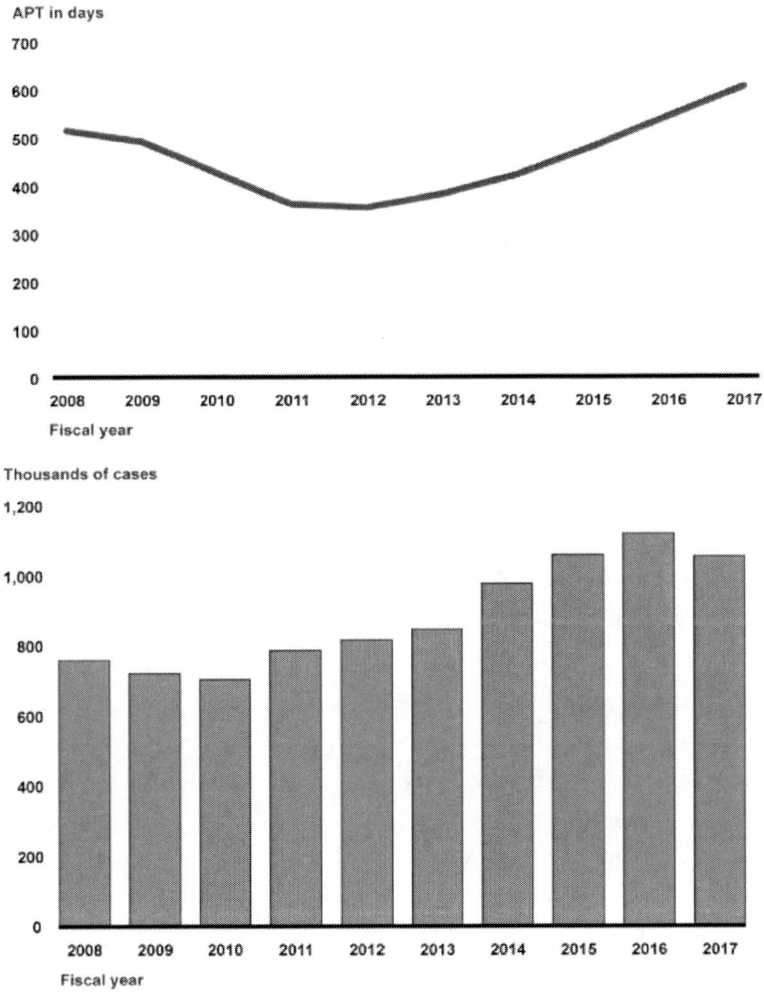

Source: GAO analysis of Social Security Administration data. | GAO-18-677T.
Note: Pending case counts are as of the end of the fiscal year.

Figure 1. Average Processing Time (APT) and Number of Pending Disability Appeals Cases, Fiscal Years 2008-2017.

Pending caseloads followed a similar pattern.[7] Specifically, pending caseloads declined through fiscal year 2010 and then grew through fiscal year 2016 to over 1.1 million cases. However, the number of pending cases declined by six percent in fiscal year 2017, to just over 1 million cases. (See Figure 1).

According to SSA officials and the agency's Office of Inspector General (OIG), factors contributing to rising processing times and numbers of pending cases include increases in the number of hearing requests after the 2007-2009 recession, recent declines in hearing operations staffing levels and imbalances in the ratio of support staff to judges, and regulatory changes that have affected judges' workloads.[8] For example, SSA officials highlighted a regulatory change which generally requires all claimants to submit all evidence known to them that relates to their disabling condition, resulting in potentially lengthier files for judges to review.

SSA Has Taken Steps to Reduce Processing Times, but Lacks Metrics to Assess its Efforts

In our recent work, we found that SSA has taken several steps to improve its processing of disability claims and appeals, but lacks metrics to determine the effect of some of these efforts. In the report we are releasing today, we examine one example. Specifically, one of SSA's key efforts to reduce processing times at the appeals level involves transferring appealed disability cases from offices with backlogs to offices with more capacity, but SSA lacks meaningful timeliness measures to assess its efforts. From fiscal years 2008 through 2017, the percentage of dispositions—decided or dismissed cases—that had been transferred increased from 14 to 43 percent, or from approximately 79,000 to more than 290,000 cases (see Figure 2).

---

[7] Pending cases are appeals that have not yet had a disposition, and include cases at different stages of the appeals process.

[8] Social Security Administration, Office of the Inspector General, *Factors Related to Decreased Administrative Law Judge Productivity* (A-12-18-50289), Sept. 11, 2017.

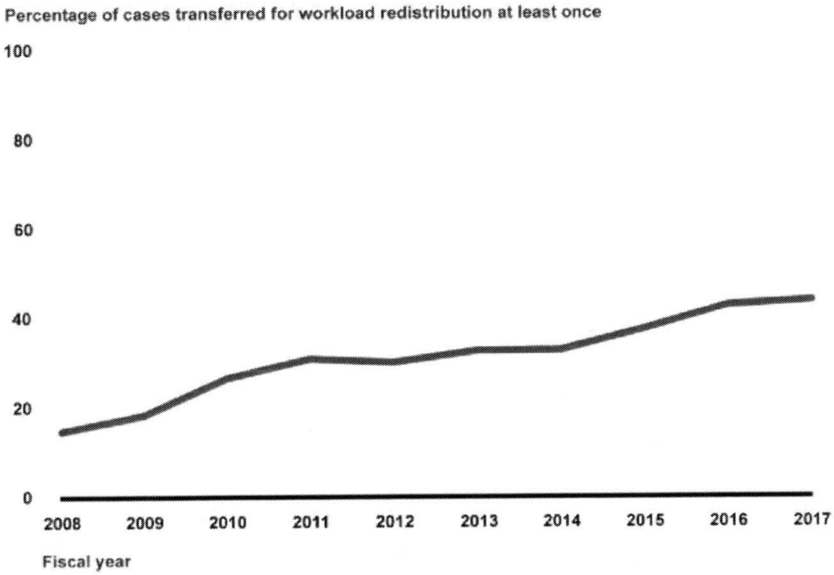

Source: GAO analysis of Social Security Administration data. | GAO-18-677T.

Figure 2. Percentage of Disability Appeals Cases Transferred to Redistribute Work at Least Once, Fiscal Years 2008-2017.

Despite the rising use of transfers over the past decade, SSA cannot assess the effectiveness of these efforts due to weaknesses in its timeliness metrics on APT. In particular, SSA lacks office-specific timeliness measures for transferred cases. Instead, SSA's current APT metric attributes the entire processing time for a case to the office that finishes it, regardless of the time the case was held by another office before being transferred. Without an office-specific measure of timeliness for transferred appeals cases, SSA does not have an accurate metric to assess how individual offices contribute to processing times—information critical to assessing the effectiveness of transferring cases in meeting timeliness goals. Given the growing use of case transfers, in the report we are releasing today, we are recommending that SSA develop a timeliness metric or set of metrics that more accurately reflect offices' performance in light of case transfers, and SSA agreed.

We have also highlighted the need for SSA to evaluate other efforts designed to reduce the backlog or improve program integrity at the appeals level. For example, our 2017 report on consistency in disability decision making at the appeals level found that SSA had adopted five types of quality assurance reviews of hearings decisions, several of which have similar goals and may look at similar claims, but SSA had not evaluated the efficiency or effectiveness of these reviews.[9] In the same report, we found that SSA lacked publicly reported metrics on the accuracy and consistency of hearings-level decisions. SSA agreed with our recommendations to evaluate its quality assurance reviews and publicly report metrics and stated that it would be addressing them as part of a comprehensive assessment and refinement of its oversight roles and processes.

SSA's Office of Inspector General (OIG) has also called on SSA to evaluate several efforts related to reducing processing times and improving the quality of decisions at the appeals level. For example, it recommended that SSA evaluate an electronic application it developed for documenting and making decisions at the appeals level to determine whether it should be continued.[10] The OIG concluded that by evaluating the effectiveness of its efforts, SSA could better ensure that it is using its resources for maximum benefit toward improving the timeliness and quality of its disability decisions.

SSA has recently taken important steps toward improving its evaluation and metrics that could enhance its ability to respond to these recommendations and others. Specifically, in October 2017 SSA created a deputy commissioner-level Office of Analytics, Review and Oversight with five offices—including the Office of Quality Review and Office of Analytics and Improvements—whose functions were previously spread among multiple divisions of SSA. In announcing this reorganization, SSA's acting commissioner stated that it will foster data analysis of SSA's programs and enhance oversight of the disability adjudication system. However, the specific effects of this change remain to be seen. In response to our recommendation in today's report related to timeliness metrics, SSA

---

[9] GAO, *Social Security Disability: Additional Measures and Evaluation Needed to Enhance Accuracy and Consistency of Hearings Decisions*, GAO-18-37 (Washington, D.C.: Dec. 7, 2017).

[10] SSA OIG, *Electronic Bench Book*, A-01-12-11217, (Baltimore, Md.: June 21, 2016).

stated that it will refine existing metrics to more accurately reflect timeliness of cases before and after being transferred. Furthermore, SSA stated that it may develop additional reporting tools to better measure the contributions of individual offices that receive transferred cases.

LIMITATIONS IN SSA'S CASE PROCESSING SYSTEMS HINDER EFFORTS TO REDUCE BACKLOGS

While SSA has made strides in modernizing its information technology (IT) systems to address growing workload demands, it continues to face challenges with these modernization efforts in dealing with backlogs.[11] Our report being released today found that SSA staff faced challenges related to case processing software. Specifically, hearing office staff reported and we observed difficulties in efficiently and accurately identifying appeals cases to transfer because of software limitations. For example, the current case processing system restricts search queries to a 6-month time period to avoid slowing down the system. As a result, staff cannot retrieve the universe of potential transfer cases at one time to facilitate transferring large batches of cases. Such limitations impeded productivity for the staff selecting cases to transfer and also created the potential for error and misuse. We recommended in today's report that SSA evaluate the costs versus benefits of changing system limitations that hinder users' ability to correctly and efficiently identify and transfer batches of cases. SSA agreed and stated that it is developing a new case processing system that will eliminate the limitations we identified.

Chairman Johnson, Ranking Member Larson, and Members of the Subcommittee, this concludes my prepared statement. I would be happy to answer any questions that you may have at this time.

---

[11] GAO, *Social Security Administration: Effective Planning and Management Practices Are Key to Overcoming IT Modernization Challenges*, GAO-16-815T (Washington, D.C.: July 14, 2016).

INDEX

A

B

E

F

G

H

I

J

L

M

N

O

P

R

S

T

U

V

W